th

Reclaiming the Feminist Vision

Consciousness-Raising and Small Group Practice

Janet L. Freedman

McFarland & Company, Inc., Publishers

Jefferson, North Carolina

LIBRARY OF CONGRESS CATALOGUING-IN-PUBLICATION DATA

Freedman, Janet L.
    Reclaiming the feminist vision : consciousness-raising and small
group practice / Janet L. Freedman.
        p.   cm.
    Includes bibliographical references and index.

    ISBN 978-0-7864-7212-3 (softcover : acid free paper) ∞
    ISBN 978-1-4766-1494-6 (ebook)

    1. Feminism.   2. Group relations training.   3. Women—Political
activity.   I. Title.
    HQ1150.F74 2014
    320.082—dc23   2014011794

BRITISH LIBRARY CATALOGUING DATA ARE AVAILABLE

On the cover: a group of women © iStock/Thinkstock

Printed in the United States of America

McFarland & Company, Inc., Publishers
    Box 611, Jefferson, North Carolina 28640
        www.mcfarlandpub.com

For my grandchildren,
Samuel, Hannah, Sarah, Lillian, and Sofia

Be who you are—and may you be blessed in all that you are.

Table of Contents

Preface

What would happen if one woman told the truth about her life?
The world would split open. —Muriel /Rukeyser[1]

— · — · —

Consciousness-Raising: A Whole New World

We told each other about our lives and reshaped the world.

Across time and cultures women have exchanged stories while working or sharing leisure time. In this country, yesteryear's quilting bees and sewing circles have been continued in today's knitting and book clubs. The gatherings of women in the late 1960s and early 1970s drew upon the ease and comfort that most women feel in groups, but had a deeper purpose. They utilized a technique called consciousness-raising (CR), defined by Catharine A. MacKinnon as "the process through which the contemporary radical feminist analysis of the situation of women has been shaped and shared."[2] Susan Griffin recalls that through consciousness-raising "a whole new world [became] visible to me, a world that I had inhabited every day without really seeing it."[3] CR brought women together in small groups not only to share experiences and offer support but also to analyze the ways in which personal conditions, roles, and attitudes have been influenced by political and social structures. The analysis led women to take concerted action against discrimination and misogyny in a movement for women's liberation.

This book traces the origins, principles, and enormous impact of consciousness-raising; it also reveals how the process migrated to other settings—often without using the term *consciousness-raising*—and calls for the renewal of CR to help women and their allies regain their voices and their power in shaping social movement history.

1

"The dismantling of consciousness-raising groups all but erased the notion that one had to learn about feminism and make an informed choice about embracing feminist politics to become a feminist advocate," wrote bell hooks in *Feminism Is for Everybody*.[4] hooks urged that there be "so many little feminist primers, easy to read pamphlets and books telling us all about feminism, that this book would be just another passionate voice speaking out on behalf of feminist politics." My book is a response to hooks' call.

I have embraced bell hooks' definition of feminism—"the struggle to end sexist oppression. Its aim is not to benefit solely any specific group of women, any particular race or class of women. It does not privilege women over men. It has the power to transform in a meaningful way all our lives."[5] In addition, "Feminism as a movement to end sexist oppression directs our attention to systems of domination and the inter-relatedness of sex, race, and class oppression."[6]

I've likewise adopted hooks' suggestion to say "I advocate feminism" rather than declare "I am a feminist." This invites an extended conversation about what that advocacy implies rather than a response to preconceived notions of feminism.

I also have drawn upon many other feminist theorists and practitioners. Some are referenced in these pages; others are unnamed but have contributed to the enormous body of feminist work that has informed and inspired me over more than five decades of learning about and advocating for "the second sex." The journey began with Simone de Beauvoir's book by that title.[7] As with other "revolutionary" moments, I can remember just where I was as I turned the pages and began turning my life in a new direction in the mid–1960s. But feminism aims for what Marilyn Frye calls the continual "unfurling of new vision,"[8] so I garner fresh sources and insights each day.

In one of my more recent reads, *How to Be a Woman*, Caitlin Moran calls for some old-fashioned consciousness-raising, telling "what it's *actually* like—rather than what we *pretend* it's like," and also doing "a bit of analysis-y, argument-y, 'this needs to change-y' stuff. You know. Feminism."[9]

Here are a few examples of CR applications that indicate the old-fashioned is alive, well, and effective. Sarah Byrnes in *On the Issues* (October 20, 2011) reports on "Resilience Circles: Consciousness-Raising Groups for Tough Economic Times," which are bringing people together to share experiences and respond personally and politically to times of economic crisis. Small groups led to the creation of Domestic Workers United, whose mission is "to organize for power, respect, fair labor standards, and to build a movement for social change."[10] Although Sheryl Sandberg doesn't use the term *consciousness-raising* to describe her "Lean In" circles spawned from the book of the same title,[11] many reviewers do. For example, from the *New York Daily News* blog: "Sandberg's social action plan outlined on leanin.org calls for women to create consciousness-raising groups called 'Lean-In' Circles."[12] And from *New York Magazine*: "Call it Lean In, call it consciousness-raising, call it whatever you want. When was the last time anybody talked this much about a woman's place in the world, *period?*"[13]

So let's call it consciousness-raising.

Reclaiming a Conversation: Description/Purpose/Background

Consciousness-raising and feminism are what this book is about. It is one woman's scrapbook of experiences in the small groups that brought about the big changes of the women's liberation movement—filled with successes and shortcomings, political and spiritual highs and lows, deep friendships, meaningful work, great joy and celebration, and frustrations and failures. To borrow Moran's way of speaking, it's a bit memoir-y, polemic-y, wishful-thinking-y and very feminist-y.

It started over twenty-five years ago when I wrote a short article for *Sojourner*, a Boston feminist newspaper, titled "Consciousness-Raising Revisited," in which I urged that small consciousness-raising groups be revived. I posited that the waning of CR groups had diminished the feminist critique of relationships and institutions, and limited the creation of alternatives based on always-evolving insights and values.[14] Raising children; sharing an intimate partnership; being a daughter, sister and friend; and making a living and a life intervened between that piece and this book.

During that period I took my own advice and participated in a number of small groups that drew upon the CR model and connected me to wonderful women who deepened my capacity for caring friendship and meaningful work. When I became affiliated with the Brandeis University Women's Studies Research Center in 2009, I began to reevaluate and expand on that long-ago article, and the result is this book.

My original intention was to base the book on interviews with women who had participated in consciousness-raising and related groups. I developed a questionnaire and decided to test it on several women with whom I had participated in CR groups in the early 1970s. When I discovered that their memories differed even to the point of recalling who was in the group, I determined that this process would not be fruitful! I did use comments from these and other conversations to supplement the many texts that capture the essence of the CR experience, including *Feminist Memoir Project: Voices from Women's*

Liberation,[15] edited by Rachel B. DuPlessis and Ann Snitow, and Anita Shreve's *Women Together, Women Alone: The Legacy of the Consciousness-Raising Movement*.[16] I also drew upon discussions of consciousness-raising in some of the classic histories of the women's liberation movement of the 1960s and 1970s.[17]

Once I moved from an interview-based format, my touchstone was a much-loved book by Bettina Aptheker, *Tapestries of Life*,[18] which I had used for several years as one of the texts in a class I taught in feminist theory. In writing that book Aptheker explicitly turned away from traditional research methods, drawing instead on her own experience and her respectful reading, listening, and viewing of women's creative productions and everyday work. Aptheker acknowledges that no single theoretical lens can encompass all women's cultures and does not intend to advance a new theory of women's oppression. Her book offers an approach to understanding women's consciousness of social reality, which, regardless of race, class, geographical location or religion, is shaped by the sexual division of labor and the institutionalized subordination of women to men. Her goal, like mine, is to use that consciousness to emancipate not only women but all people.

The intention of this book is not to look back either nostalgically or dismissively, but to use the past to set a context for the present. Finding ways to impart a legacy without romanticizing earlier practices, and acknowledging painful mistakes without negating what was positive, presents a poignant dilemma. I've tried to walk that narrow line in sharing my own experiences and citing the examples of others. The experiences recounted in this book reveal that consciousness-raising and small-group approaches have continued to keep the women's liberation movement alive through hard times, including the current period marked by the ironic juxtaposition of a persistent backlash from the right and a turn from narratives of hope and progress on the left.

I am optimistic about the possibilities of revived—and ongoing—CR practice. My enthusiasm for renewing the technique of meeting in small, face-to-face consciousness-raising groups is tempered by the awareness of repeated patterns that have resulted in the ebbing of the feminist movement.

One barrier is the sometimes willing usurpation of feminist theoretical insights and effective practices by other intellectual frameworks and movements; another is the mainstreaming of once radical impulses and organizations. Yet another is the failure to bring both flawed and successful insights and practices of earlier generations into current thinking and planning. Consciousness-raising begins with one's own experience and I believe strongly in the importance of acknowledging the past and bringing it into the present. These concerns are raised in the pages to come, not to discourage but to remind.

"A good conversation is neither a fight nor a contest. Circular in form, cooperative in manner, and constructive in intent, it is an interchange of ideas by those who see themselves, not as adversaries, but as human beings come together to talk and listen and learn from one another."[19]

I take it as a compliment that people frequently comment that I write the way I talk, but I know it is both a strength and a weakness. Being a librarian also has produced great plusses and some minuses. Practicing that profession provokes an interest in everything. Whether planning library services, developing a course or participating in a discussion, my thinking takes detours and blue highways in a search to discover more information and consider how issues and ideas fit into a larger picture. The reader of this book will not find a linear argument for consciousness-raising but rather an excursion through paths I've taken that have been illuminated by the CR technique and participation in small groups. The examples offered in the chapters outlined below are intended to engender a conversation about the renewal of consciousness-raising as a widely practiced technique that can preserve the past gains of the women's liberation movement and meet new challenges.

Chapter Outlines

The first chapter of this book provides background information on the origins and principles of consciousness-raising, the principal force in the resurgence of feminism in the late 1960s and early 1970s. Coupling personal experience in the women's liberation movement with interpretive studies of second-wave feminism, chapter I follows the trajectory of the small CR groups from the height of their influence to their waning and suggests reasons for their decline. With the past as prologue, readers are inspired to adapt the suggestions and guidelines in this and subsequent chapters to form their own small groups appropriate to the needs of women and girls today.

"Right Livelihood: Working as a Feminist," chapter II, stresses that a women's liberation movement must move beyond breaking the glass ceiling to addressing the economic needs of women workers worldwide. Betty Friedan's *Feminist Mystique* identified "the problem that has no name" among college-educated women who felt bored and unfulfilled by the routines of suburban life and wanted to use their academic degrees in the workplace. These women led the fight for legislation to provide women with equal opportunities in education and employment, and dramatic gains have been made in fields such as law, medicine, and business. Yet class, disability, race, ethnicity, and age have combined with gender to limit the ability of most women to be economically self-sufficient. Small groups can play a role in determining collective action to move us toward that goal, and be an effective setting to explore ways in which we can bring feminist values and vision into our work. The chapter suggests ways that small work groups within a job field or across occupations can explore feminist models of leadership, consider how work can promote social change, and begin to resolve the complexities of balancing paid work, family roles and community activism.

Chapter III, "Only Connect: Technology, Consciousness-Raising, and Feminist Activism" reveals how the common practices of face-to-face CR have migrated to blogs, chat rooms, discussion groups, tweets, and other electronic media exchanges. As Tracy L.M. Kennedy writes in "The Personal Is Political: Feminist Blogging and Virtual Consciousness-Raising," "The ubiquity of the Internet has located feminist advocacy and consciousness-raising within the virtual world."[20] This chapter assesses some of these sites to illuminate the potential of the Internet to replicate the CR process of moving from personal problems to shared experience, to the awareness that action is needed to change social and political institutions that support sexism. Yet "technotopian" promises may obscure the fact that the Internet can both liberate its participants and reinforce oppressive power relations. While social networks have proven to be effective in mobilizing activists across the globe, it is less clear how successful they are in moving from immediate responses to committed, long-term action. The chapter concludes with some possible responses to these challenges.

Chapter IV, "I and We: Consciousness-Raising, Mutual Aid and Participatory Democracy," maintains that having a sense of membership, hearing and being heard, practicing reciprocity, and learning skills of effective participation are essential for consciousness-raising and to the maintenance of democracy. The approaches to organizing that were rooted in the CR processes of the late 1960s and early 1970s have often been subsumed in a "larger" political framework or taken over by traditional organizations. Rape crisis projects, battered women's programs, welfare rights groups, and women's health care centers often moved to a "top-down" model staffed by professionals serving "clients." This chapter urges that leadership be assumed by group members rather than controlled by experts. The experiences, insights, and approaches to activism of those closest to particular conditions or situations can transform people and programs. This is demonstrated by neighborhood-based political organizing and mutual aid efforts, such as breast cancer awareness campaigns, that go beyond self-help to address the root causes of the epidemic. The chapter will conclude with some questions that might spark a CR group discussion on how to remove barriers to full and meaningful participation in the political processes that shape civil society.

Chapter V, "Consciousness-Raising in the Classroom and Beyond," focuses on women's studies classrooms and programs. In the first women's studies classes, students and faculty engaged in the consciousness-raising process together, discovering how every discipline could be reshaped when women are the subject of inquiry and raise and answer their own questions. Intersectional CR approaches—which pay attention to racial, class, national and other histories—are being used in women's studies classrooms today. "Small group pedagogy" can move from the classroom to multicultural centers, residence halls, and other campus settings. The CR approach also can be applied to many community settings where diverse perspectives and voices can be affirmed, skills and information exchanged, and other components of effective community organizing realized.

"Spirited Women," Chapter VI, provides examples of how women have organized, often initially in small groups, to bring a feminist perspective to traditional religious organizations and/or to create new spiritual practices. The chapter includes my own experience in a monthly gathering of Jewish women, and also in a group of a dozen women from many faith traditions and spiritual practices that met for over twenty years. Additional models are presented, from Catholic and Muslim to New Age and witchcraft, along with suggestions on ways in which women can build interfaith understanding and social action work using a CR approach. In the "spirit" of CR, questions will also be raised, including whether there is a point at which feminism and spiritual practices are in conflict and whether more reframing and re-visioning are needed.

The final chapter, "Consciousness-Raising Through the Lifespan," urges that the consciousness-raising process be applied to challenges throughout women's lives. Commercial messages continue to reinforce stereotypes and influence even preschoolers to focus on appearance. Sharing personal narratives about body image, dating, academic aspirations, and jealousy can lead to self- and community-affirming alternatives to competitive individualism. CR groups also support the struggles of mothers and caretakers juggling economic needs and the desire to build a positive, nurturing family life, which can be eased by collective responses. The small group can inspire older women to refuse to accept culturally induced ageism that disproportionately affects women both economically and socially. As with other chapters, examples and guidelines are offered on how to move from personal support to critical analysis leading to meaningful political action.

Acknowledgments and Appreciations

People often ask me how I can maintain involvement in so many small groups. The answer I hope this book will affirm is that I could not manage without them, and I hope that others also will benefit from creating intentional small communities.

I am grateful to all the members of my consciousness-raising groups, with whom I experienced the change and growth that inspired me to want to write about the transformative process of CR.

A women and work group that the members call the "ReCollective" has met since 1984 and is the source of the deep support, friendship, and insights described in the chapter on "right livelihood." My work as a librarian was nurtured by a Boston-area Women in Libraries group that was foundational to the national Women Library Workers, another gratifying involvement. Colleagues in a group that started with an American Council on Education program for women in academic administration gave me valuable counsel when I served as a dean and they continue to provide camaraderie. Two long-term communities also helped to shape the experiences I share in the chapter on spirited women. A group of Jewish women from southeastern Massachusetts gathered monthly to celebrate Rosh Chodesh, a holiday in the Jewish calendar that honors each new moon; another "spirituality" group that included women from several faith traditions and practices met for over twenty years—long enough that we began to call ourselves the Council of Crones.

I want to acknowledge the pleasures of participation in several book groups, the longest of which grew from a connection to the New Bedford Women's Center. We combine the literary with the personal, political, and culinary, and we continue to gather, with one member participating from the opposite coast.

Deep appreciation and admiration are extended to my colleagues at the Brandeis University Women's Studies Research Center (WSRC). This uniquely wonderful community is described in the conclusion of this book. I am especially indebted to the members of the social issues study group, who have provided particular insight and support for this project, and to the ritual studies and spirituality discussion groups, which have contributed to both my intellectual growth and my acceptance of the ineffable. I also want to express my respect for colleagues on the Forum Committee and the Gender and International Development Initiatives Committee with whom I've worked and learned so much.

I am grateful for the warm and mutually supportive friendships I have made with Brandeis students. Susannah Feinstein, my student-scholar partner, and I have spent many hours discussing the subjects touched upon in this book. Susannah has been helpful in so many ways, especially with the chapter on consciousness-raising on the Internet. Hailey McGee, another campus activist and former president of the Brandeis Feminist Majority Leadership Alliance (FMLA), has worked with me in applying the CR approach to intergenerational conversations and mentorships that have formed between the FMLA and the WSRC. Through my affiliation with the Hadassah Brandeis Institute, which shares space with the Women's Studies Research Center, I have enjoyed the support of three summer interns, Elana Weiner, Sydney Sadur, and the insightful and patient Ilannah Donaghue, who reviewed the manuscript just before I sent it to the publisher.

The following people kindly read one or more chapters and provided very helpful comments and advice: Rosalind Barnett, Helen Berger, Erica Bronstein, Andrea Dotollo, Linda Ferreira, Deborah Freedman, Beth Freedman Girioni, Samuel Freedman Girioni, Donna Huse, Hilda Kahne, Peter London, Frinde Maher, Naomi Myrvaagnes, Phoebe Schnitzer and Beverlee Sclar.

I have shared many deep friendships with women, mostly within and sometimes outside the groups honored in this book. Helaine Hazlett has been my "mostly" companion from my youth until today. The joy, passion and compassion I bring to all I do is inspired by Beverlee Sclar. Vincenza Petrilli was with me at the beginning of my feminist journey; she has traveled far but remains close by. Holidays and everydays shared with Magali Carrera and her dear family, including our godchildren, enrich all our lives. I am blessed with the care I have received and tried always to return to Peggy Bacon, Evy Baum, Bettina Borders, Erica Bronstein, Kathy Condon, Deborah Ehrens, Harriet Gottesman, Marilyn Halter, Donna Huse, Julianne Kelly, Sandee Krupp, Leslie Lipkind, Marion London, Joan Ouellette of blessed memory, Juli Parker, Phyllis Holman Weisbard, the late Celeste West (who will always have, as she would put it, "a garden room in my heart"), and Laurie Roberge Yang. Thoughts of the many long walks and good talks with these dear and wonderful people fill me with gratitude.

I was fortunate to have devoted parents, Irving and Frances Cook Saltz, to whom I can never pay tribute enough. My brother Bob and sister-in-law Lynne Saltz continue their tradition of support and generous love.

My beloved Andrew proves each day the truth of hooks' belief that "feminism is for everybody." He is my soul mate. As a wonderful partner, parent and "papa" Andy is the model of kindness and decency that defines manliness in our family. I also am inspired daily by my dear daughters, who have continued to unfurl the banner of feminism in their own special ways. Deborah's gift of a women's symbol she helped Andy carve when she was 9 or 10 remains on my desk. Beth and her three college roommates loved to recite—en masse and loudly—the Judy Grahn quote I have framed in my kitchen where I regularly bake bread: "The common woman is as common as a common loaf of bread—and will rise."[21] And now I am the proud grandmother of another generation that I hope will benefit from and contribute to continued feminist activism, and to whom I dedicate this work.[22]

I

Consciousness-Raising:
The Mother Lode

I stood in the middle of my own experience, turning and turning. In every direction I saw a roomful of women, also turning and turning.... That is a moment of joy, when a sufficiently large number of people are galvanized by a social explanation of how their lives have taken shape and are gathered together in the same place at the same time, speaking the same language, making the same analysis, meeting again and again ... for the pleasure of elaborating the insight and repeating the analysis.

— · — · —

That's how Vivian Gornick described her experience of the women's liberation movement of the late 1960s and early 1970s.[1]

Then and now identification with the women's movement could come in many ways—reading a life-changing book, hearing a speaker tell a truth you hadn't known before, becoming a member of an organization, joining a protest.

But participation in a small consciousness-raising group was the entry point for many second-wave feminists. What occurred in consciousness-raising groups was not just the sharing of the "aha" moments when women become aware of how sexism affects their lives, but also a new way of being and seeing and learning.

Catharine A. MacKinnon defines consciousness-raising as "the process through which the contemporary radical feminist analysis of the situation of women has been shaped and shared" and notes that "the characteristic structure, ethic, process and approach to social change which mark such groups ... are integral to many of the substantive contributions of feminist theory."[2]

The CR group provided a dedicated space where roomfuls of women met each other and exchanged stories of growing up female, dating, schooling, sexuality, marriage, work and so much more. Each woman's story was her own, but there were also many commonalities that led to an understanding of how personal conditions, roles, and attitudes were shaped by political and social structures. And from this understanding grew an agenda for change and an array of activist projects.

Loretta Ross, national coordinator of SisterSong Women of Color Reproductive Justice Collective, illuminates the process:

> We may have more formally called it 'consciousness-raising' but in essence we were telling each other stories to reclaim ourselves and our humanity. We created a feminist culture with these stories, not through narratives of logic and structure, but by creating verbal snapshots of the lived experiences of women. We didn't have to all tell the same story in order to resonate with each other. Each story was unique but the act of telling our stories created strong bonds among diverse women who worked together to change our realities. We could imagine a world in which women lived in freedom from violence and we set about building rape crisis centers and domestic violence shelters not only to help women who had been violated, but also to project a vision of what a world without violence could look like for women.[3]

The Origins of CR

In *Freedom for Women: Forging the Women's Liberation Movement, 1953–1970*, Carol Giardina revisits the roots of second-wave feminism and corrects many misconceptions of the period that have overemphasized the influences of white, middle-class women.[4] Betty Friedan's *The Feminist Mystique*[5] certainly resonated with college-educated housewives. Yet claims, such as this one from the *New York Times* obituary of Friedan, that "it ignited the contemporary women's movement in 1963 and as a result permanently transformed the social fabric of the United States and countries around the world"[6] simplify and misrepresent a far more complex history.

Giardina demonstrates that black women were key in forming the feminist movement of the 1960s. She cites the strong influences of the civil rights movement, first-wave feminism in the late nineteenth and early twentieth centuries, and old and new left political involvements in creating the conditions for a revitalized women's movement. Friedan herself had learned much from the progressive grassroots political work in which she had been involved, but her famous book was based on interviews with graduates of Smith and Radcliffe who voiced dissatisfaction with the routines of suburban life and the lack of opportunities to utilize their academic training. Its mainstream success obscured other influences and agendas.

While not denying the sexism of men involved in the black liberation movement and the New Left, Giardina notes that there were positive aspects for women who were participants in these movements. They experienced the power of community, learned valuable skills as organizers and gained self-respect through their work for social justice. Having recognized their potential for making a difference, they were ready to take on roles that made a women's movement possible. Consciousness-raising was influenced by the "testifying" used to build unity among civil rights workers and by the approaches socialists used to develop the class consciousness of workers under capitalism. Dissatisfied with the male leaders who demeaned their contributions and refused to take their insights seriously, the initiators of the early women's groups adapted the CR techniques to reveal the common oppression that women experienced in a patriarchal society in which male authority was usually unquestioned.

Loretta Ross took her consciousness-raising experience to work at the first rape crisis center in the United States founded in 1972 in Washington, DC. When she was interviewed by the "Voices of Feminism" project at Smith College, she accepted the request of archivists to assist them in gathering more oral histories of women of color. Now fifty pioneering feminists of color have told their stories in their own words, continuing to correct a distorted history of feminist and social movement history.

Guiding the Process

In the spring 2010 edition of *On the Issues,* Carol Hanisch recalls a comment made by Anne Forer at a meeting of New York Radical Women in 1968—that women needed to "raise our consciousness" about common behaviors that grew from trying to be attractive to men, such as playing dumb, wearing uncomfortable shoes and clothing, and dieting.[7] Her remark led to Kathie Sarachild's Program for Feminist Consciousness-Raising, which was presented at the first National Women's Liberation Conference near Chicago in the fall of that year.[8] According to Sarachild, "The decision to emphasize our own feelings and experiences as women and to test all generalizations and reading we did by our own experience was actually the scientific method of research. We were in effect repeating the 17th century challenge of science to scholasticism: 'study nature, not books,' and put all theories to the test of living practice and action. It was also a method of radical organizing tested by other revolutions. We were applying to women and to ourselves as women's liberation organizers the practice a number of us had learned as organizers in the civil rights movement in the South in the early 1960's."[9]

Given what occurred thereafter, it is hard to believe that the guidelines received a lukewarm reception at the conference. Within a short time they were circulated widely and the small groups that sparked the women's liberation movement were being formed throughout the United States and beyond. The New York Radical Women also produced articles, including Pat Mainardi's "The Politics of Housework,"[10] Anne Koedt's "Myth of the Vaginal Orgasm,"[11] and Hanisch's own piece, "The Personal Is the Political,"[12] all of which participants in my own CR group read with enthusiasm and concurrence. Soon Pamela Allen's *Free Space,* a variation on Sarachild's program, appeared in California.[13] Eventually, the National Organization for Women, which initially had rejected CR, published its suggestions for conducting groups.[14] In an era before electronic communications, guidelines were copied, amended, edited and, in various cut-and-pasted forms, traveled from one emergent group to another. Consciousness-raising spread faster than the proverbial wildfire and the result was as transformational.

Consciousness-raising employed specific steps to proceed from sharing to analysis to action. The technique begins with a revelation of WHAT IS occurring in a woman's life, and goes on to probe the context and history of the issue or event. Group members go on to explore WHY the situations and conditions have come to be, a question that involves examining not only personal dilemmas and struggles but also patterns that evolve from individual stories that point to common concerns. Participation in a CR group was, and is, a gateway that can lead women to explore WHAT should change and HOW, working together, these changes can be implemented.

The power of the experience makes it easy for me to bring forth images of the living rooms of the several houses where members of my CR group held our meetings. Leslie's was filled with plants, Pat's with cats, Mary Jane's with the smells of baked goods (including her lemon bars, which were a particular favorite), and mine with pajama-clad toddlers peeking around the door frame. And I can recall the faces in our circle, and the range of emotions that accompanied discussions, and the discoveries that changed our personal lives and political choices.

Most CR groups were composed of six to ten women and structured (or unstructured!) to allow for maximum participation, learning and growth. Many groups made efforts to include women of different ages, backgrounds and experiences. Leadership of the sessions was rotated among the participants and techniques were utilized to ensure that no one or two people dominated the discussion. For example, tokens might be distributed and forfeited each time one spoke so that the more talkative members would have to yield to the more reticent. Women were discouraged from speaking a second time until each person had an opportunity to address the subject at hand. Although the goal was to have everyone speak, we learned that the choice to "pass," usually because the individual wasn't ready to discuss a topic, should be respected.

The depth of sharing evolved over time, but the CR approach made it easy to participate. The learning was based on exchanging personal experiences in a protective, supportive setting where participants could become aware of their roles as women, discover the common nature of problems, and develop self-respect and autonomy. Unlike classroom environments and work settings, telling our stories required no special expertise or preparation.

While some groups determined the topic of discussion by polling interests at the time of the meeting, most chose subjects in advance, selecting issues on which women were likely to have plenty of thoughts and feelings, such as mothers and daughters, friendship and sex. The first meetings were likely to be exchanges of autobiographies, prompted by questions such as these: Where did you grow up? Did you have siblings? Were you treated differently from boys in your family or at school? What activities, sports, games, or lessons occupied you? What television shows and films did you watch and how did they shape your view of yourself, and of the roles of girls and women?

By the time we began sharing stories of menstruation, first awareness of sexuality, dating experiences and body images, our laughter often mingled with tears, and it was not long before "this is what happened to me" became "this is what happened to us."

MacKinnon summarizes it this way: "Although a woman's specific race or class or physiology may define her among women, simply being a woman has a meaning that decisively defines all women, socially, from their most intimate moments to their most anonymous relations. This social meaning which is unattached to any actual anatomical differences between the sexes ... pervades everyday routine to the point that it becomes a reflex, a habit."[15] By sharing our stories, the CR process created "a lived knowing of the social reality of being female."[16]

I attended meetings of several groups before making a commitment to one that lasted for about a year. All the participants had some connection to the public college where I was employed, a largely commuter campus of first-generation college attendees from white, working-class backgrounds, mostly Irish and Italian Catholics. We were faculty, students, and community women. Some of us had experience in the political movements that preceded or coexisted with the burgeoning feminist movement. From the start, our discussions considered how class, racial, religious, and ethnic identities, along with gender, shaped our lives.

After several sessions, our group, following recommendations in many of the guidelines, was closed to new participants, a practice that created more

intimate connections and obviated the need to repeat to newcomers information that had already been heard by others a number of times. Members were
expected to attend every meeting, maintain strict confidentiality and listen
without judgment.

Consciousness-Raising, Not Therapy

Attention to personal experience with a topic, rather than an intellectual
analysis or a reference to a book, film or friend, was emphasized frequently in
consciousness-raising. Yet, from the start, distinctions were made between CR
and therapy. What many women had referred to as their "neuroses" or "hang-
ups" were not trivialized, but reframed as social rather than personal issues.
While none of us were exempt from negative feelings about our bodies, we
came to realize that these were shaped by culture, rather than actual imper-
fections. Being too fat, thin, flat, buxom, flabby, hippy, and other physical
"flaws" had parallels in our behaviors as well. Most of us struggled with ambiva-
lent feelings about our social presentation—again, "too" passive or pushy, loud
or timid. We learned to see that the dissatisfactions were rooted in efforts to
meet impossible role expectations for female perfection.

Consciousness-Raising, Not (Yet) Action

The goal of consciousness-raising was to utilize personal experiences to
develop a political analysis leading to social change. But CR groups were
intended to be separate from meetings to strategize activist projects. Consciousness-raising was the gateway to activism. The groups were intended to
respond to "what is" and "why is." Organizing to explore "what should" and
"how should"—brainstorming on solutions and detailing action plans—was
to take place in other venues. Yet it was hard to separate these functions since
discussion often led to a "why don't we ..."

One of the "why don't we ..." ideas led some participants in our CR group
to initiate "open" groups at the campus women's center, following suggestions
made by Dorothy Tennov in a piece titled "*Open Rapping.*"[17] We called these
SHARE sessions. The gatherings created the welcoming environment and
inclusive practices that Tennov felt were basic to CR, but eventually validated
those who urged closed groups. Most women were reluctant, in ever-changing
gatherings, to do the sharing our program's title urged. Some of the women
who were introduced to the process at these gatherings decided to form CR
groups of their own and/or became involved in other projects the women's
center sponsored.

In preparing this book I asked many women to share their memories of CR, including members of a women and work group of which I've been a member since 1984. We've come to call ourselves the ReCollective, and you'll meet these women in subsequent chapters. Here are some of the characteristics of the CR process as summarized by Donna:

Democratic: Every life is considered. Each person receives her equal time with the group attention.

Listening: Learning the great art of listening, and discovering and using methods for eliciting the full voice of each participant.

Anti-hierarchical: Each person is treasured for her unique way of being and insights, and every effort is made to bring out each individual's contribution. There is no one group leader or expert who dominates projects and time. Expertise and professionalism can be valued, but do not grant the holder more power or group attention.

Feelings: Feelings and the body are not only o.k. to discuss but also celebrated in the CR process. The group makes a special place for awareness and light to shine upon issues that are unmentionable in other settings.

Transformative: Each woman tells her story to the group and identities and meanings for the story are explored. Experiences of helplessness, stereotyping, and self-negation are relived and retold from an empowered perspective. New political perspectives about social roles and how they function are discussed and can lead to concrete action steps.

From CR to Action

Involvement in a CR group made it impossible for me NOT to become an activist. Initially, the politics were local. I was working as a librarian at Salem State College (now University) at that time. Soon I was part of a campus group discussing how to organize a women's center on our campus, which we did in short order, and a day-care center, which proved more difficult but, eventually, also was created. I was among those who advocated for and taught the earliest women's studies courses at Salem. Neither I nor the other course developers had academic preparation in the field because there was not yet a discipline called "women's studies"—we were creating it. Several of us working at the college reached out to community women to organize the North Shore Women's School, which paired women with skills to share, from auto repair to community organizing to dream interpretation, with those who wanted to learn. The classes moved from the college to union halls, church basements and other settings. More coalitions were formed with community women around issues of health, anti-violence, parenting and other concerns.

My practice as a librarian was transformed by the women's movement. I joined with other feminists working in libraries to form an organization, Boston Area Women in Libraries (our enthusiasm kept us from realizing the unfortunate acronym, BAWIL, produced by our name choice, and we laughed that we had formed such a descriptive movement). Together we discovered the sexism that pervaded our "women's profession" and turned the tables on the image of the passive, timid librarian. Our group of eight or nine took the same CR process that had raised our own awareness to other librarians. At one annual conference of our state library association a packed gathering of women broke down into small groups in which individuals shared their viewpoints and experiences. They responded to questions on why they had chosen library work, what hierarchies existed within individual libraries and the field of librarianship (then an 80 percent female profession with most administrative positions occupied by males, a fact that seldom had been questioned before the feminist movement), whether participants experienced feelings of self-worth and agency in their work, whether changing economic conditions affected their approaches to work, the risks they would take to fight for the institutions they served as well as their own jobs (then, as now, libraries were in crisis) and whether organizing political action groups or unions could make a difference.

Eventually the Boston group had a national presence in Women Library Workers, an organization that welcomed clerical personnel as well as librarians with the degrees required for professional status. WLW published a quarterly journal with bibliographies, media reviews and superb ideas for women who used (or could be enticed to use) libraries, in addition to holding conferences and issuing a S.HA.R.E. Directory (that concept was a popular one in those days). The acronym came from *Sisters Have Resources Everywhere*, and the directory connected library workers across the country for the purpose of sharing ideas, expertise, information on jobs, and homes and apartments where they'd be welcome if they were traveling in the area (hospitality I offered and accepted).

All around me women moved from their CR groups to make changes in their personal lives, community involvements and work. One of my dearest friends and some of her colleagues created the first feminist counseling center in the Boston area, which was about changing one's personal and social circumstances rather than adjusting to them. It exists to this day. A feminist bookstore and restaurant occupied space in the same neighborhood and I spent many hours in both.

The Boston Women's Health Book Collective also originated in the area where I was living, so members of our women's community were among the first to acquire the newsprint copy of the first edition of *Our Bodies, Ourselves,* described by Linda Gordon in a 2008 article in *The Nation* as "the feminist left's most valuable contribution to the world."[18] Gordon writes that her comments are intended to appear hyperbolic, but she defends her statement, and I concur. I remember a presentation by several founders of the collective in which there was palpable excitement as we learned how the personal stories related in a CR setting had led to the extensive research that was then reported in clear, jargon-free language. The work exemplified and modeled how we laypersons could acquire and share explicit and empowering information on heterosexual and lesbian sexuality, pregnancy and childbirth, contraception, sterilization, abortion, masturbation, sexually transmitted diseases and so much more. That first pamphlet led to a book that, in many editions and adaptations, eventually sold four million copies worldwide.

Women had created a revolution, and it was rooted in the small group.

The Decline, But Not the Demise, of CR

How did such an extraordinary and empowering phenomenon end so abruptly? Vivian Gornick describes when her "moment of joy" ended: "One day I woke up to realize the excitement, the longing, the expectation of community was over."[19] Her experience was echoed by the women Anita Shreve interviewed for her book, *Women Together, Women Alone,*[20] published twenty years after the CR movement had begun to flourish. "I don't think we have each other anymore," one respondent commented, capturing the feelings of isolation that replaced a sense of collective identity.

Both the abrupt ending of community and the isolation that ensued have been overstated. In her study of the feminist community in Columbus, Ohio, Nancy Whittier acknowledges the ebbing of the second wave in the 1980s, when feminism was being redefined from within the women's movement and stridently attacked from outside by increasingly vocal conservatism. Yet she documents that, even as some organizations disappeared, others continued and new ones were formed, and "everyday resistance" in workplaces, and through friendship and social networks—those small groups again—kept the movement alive.[21]

The *Our Bodies, Ourselves* collective continued its work, producing books for adolescents and older women and fostering translation projects in many countries, all rooted in the sharing of personal experience. While this is one of the most dramatic examples, I and countless other women have continued to do activist work drawing on the model of the small group.

bell hooks was critical of those who used the insights of some women to speak in the name of all, but she remained committed to the process of using personal experience to gain political awareness.[22] And in the book titled *All the Women Are White, All the Blacks Are Men, But Some of Us Are Brave,* Tia Cross, Freada Klein, Barbara Smith and Beverly Smith presented a model for race consciousness based on the assumption that "as a person you simply cannot do political action without personal interaction."[23] Their guidelines were incorporated in classroom and community CR gatherings and continue to be used today.

Yet between the mid- and late 1970s the CR process that had proliferated in living rooms and YWCA meeting rooms dwindled. Some groups ended because of the changes and challenges that occur in women's lives—miscarriages, moves, marriages, separations, and new relationships. But my call for reviving CR requires an examination of other, and often troubling, reasons for the decline.

Sisterhood as Hyperbole

The excitement of discovering commonalities in the late 1960s and early 1970s led to a facile assumption of "sisterhood." In *Once a Feminist,* Michelene Wandor describes this well: "We were criticized for being all white and middle class: neither criticism was wholly true, but there was real truth behind the criticism. As sisters we were too similar, or in stressing sisterhood and our common oppression and strengths as women, we repressed and ignored differences that should have been recognized."[24]

Factions

My CR experience, the ever-growing literature I devoured, and participation with feminist activism led me to see and describe myself as a "radical feminist," dedicated to changing, rather than reforming, the institutions that supported sexism. It soon became apparent that radical feminists were divided into many factions: pro-woman feminists who believed that ending patriarchal domination would resolve all other oppressions, socialist feminists who conjoined a class and gender analysis, lesbian feminists who presented their commitment to women as the most powerful statement against patriarchy, and more. Within each group there were further differences and divisions.

At first I read about these conflicts; soon I was living them. The introductory CR groups that we organized in our new Salem State College Women's Center became populated by members of the Young Socialist Alliance, the youth wing of the Socialist Workers Party, who were less interested in women's consciousness-raising than in efforts to recruit party members. Rumors that the FBI was infiltrating groups made membership seem dangerous. I lamented that this kept some women from joining our activities, but laughed at the notion that we were targets of J. Edgar Hoover's agents. As a friend discovered in later years when she requested her file under the Freedom of Information Act, the rumors were based on reality.

Splits occurred within groups, including ours. One member chose separatism for a time, meeting and doing political work primarily with other lesbians. Members of other groups, and the feminist movement as a whole, became sharply divided over the issue of pornography. Some agreed with Robin Morgan that "pornography is the theory; rape is the practice"[25]; others felt such a position was a judgmental and limiting view of sexual expression. Of course, there were many other perspectives on this and other issues.

Different Views of the CR Process

The shift from sharing experience to taking action certainly was a major factor in the diminishment of CR groups, and wasn't that exactly what the originators of the process hoped would happen? Yes, consciousness-raising was intended to be the initial step toward practice, but tensions developed when some women began to criticize those who remained in groups rather than engaging in feminist activism. The approach urged by some CR founders was that the groups should last fewer than six months, after which women were to challenge sexism in specific projects. Dorothy Tennov felt that the open CR groups she advocated would allow people who had become involved in action to return from time to time to "replenish." Pamela Allen, too, saw the CR process as cyclical and recommended study groups, in which personal experience could be examined through various intellectual perspectives.

Whether the CR experience was short or long, open or closed, in retrospect, one thing is clear: the assumption that a raised consciousness would be a permanent condition was wrong, and this is the significant rationale in my call for a new era of consciousness-raising.

The Personal Remained the Personal

Most narratives of the period, including this one, cite the central role of the New York Radical Feminists, whose civil rights and leftist perspectives shaped consciousness-raising as a principal organizing strategy of second-wave feminism.[26] Yet there were other influences that were important, although less often mentioned. Encounter groups and sensitivity training, or "T" groups, with roots in the post–WWII theories of Kurt Lewin and others, were enormously popular in the years leading up to the political fervor of the 1960s. Most of these groups encouraged self-expression and self-disclosure for the purpose of improving interpersonal communication and organizational performance, rather than explicitly to create social change.[27] Some women who participated in CR groups focused on individual growth and did not become part of a movement for systemic social change. Yet most felt transformed by the experience of discovering how gender shaped relationships, and they often created changes close to home in their intimate relationships, ways of parenting, or choices of work and work styles.

From Organizing Tool to Cultural Cliché

The emphasis on personal solutions was reinforced by media presentations of the women's movement. In her interesting study, *Feminism and Its Fictions,* Lisa Hogeland contends that consciousness-raising lost its effectiveness as a tool for radical organizing when the concept pervaded mass culture.[28] The moment that women became aware of how sexism affected their everyday lives, the "click" that Jane O'Reilly described in a famous 1971 article in *Ms. Magazine,*[29] became the theme of numerous novels and, eventually, films. A few CR novels portrayed women who became engaged in political activism and some, especially and fittingly science fiction works, expanded the feminist vision. Hogeland contrasts these "hard" CR works with the plethora of "soft" CR focused on white, middle-class housewives who question men, marriage and the limitations of their sexual expression and, after a click or two, are, at novel's end, on the verge of unrevealed new possibilities for *themselves.* Many of the books Hogeland cites are well written and led to the recognition of women as major contributors to contemporary literary fiction. Yet the abundance of these novels reinforced the notion of feminism as a white, middle-class movement, focused on personal change rather than collective action.

In an *Esquire* piece in 1973, humorist Nora Ephron revealed that her group (which she joined, among other reasons, so she could write on the CR phenomenon) narrowed its focus to discussions of men and marriage and was more akin to an encounter group, with women freely giving advice and sometimes expressing anger toward other members. When the group disbanded for the summer, Ephron went into therapy. She acknowledged that other groups "give women a real and new sense of pride, they help them change in important ways, they have to do with feminism and politics and the movement.... Mine didn't. My group thought the process could be used for something for which it was never intended."[30]

CR as It Wasn't Intended

Ephron's article presaged many adaptations that confounded the original goals of the small consciousness-raising group. Despite admonitions from originators of the technique that CR was not therapy, consciousness-raising approaches were used as a model for therapy groups. Even when practitioners attempted to bring the radical potential of CR into their work, the political aspects of the process often were sacrificed to the personal.

Some women organized, not to struggle against sexist injustice, but to survive it. CR groups morphed into assertiveness training programs, as well as support and networking groups among business and professional women. Some of the latter even limited membership to women who earned salaries above a particular figure or supervised a certain number of people. Lacking the combination of personal sharing and political analysis that characterized CR groups, some networks mimicked settings in which men traded secrets and information with a select few with whom they had chosen to share power and privilege. This emphasis also obscured other discoveries revealed in CR groups, such as which experiences affect all women across workplaces—and what differences exist for minority women, lesbians, older women, clerical and service workers and others around whose struggles women could unite.

More About "Groups Behaving Badly"

Internal problems often caused groups to collapse. Jo Freeman, writing under the pseudonym Joreen, disclosed the "tyranny of structurelessness."[31] CR meetings were intended to serve as examples of feminist forms of organization, countering the hierarchical, authoritarian practices of the male-dominated forums experienced by many of the early CR advocates. But Joreen's article suggested that "structureless group" is an oxymoron. Informal leaders always emerge who, sometimes without being aware of their power, influence the tone, subject matter and interpersonal dynamics within groups. In an interview with one of the members of my Salem group, Joreen's article was recalled for how appropriately it described the gap between our best intentions and the sometimes difficult reality.

The guiding principles of authenticity and honesty also were not always present in practice. In several of the groups in which I participated, it took some time for the issue of lesbianism to finally "come out." Despite the intention not to impart dogma, subtle pressure to adopt a particular viewpoint or choice certainly was present. I remember the misery I felt when, a year after my divorce, I shared with my group the joy I felt about meeting a man I cared for very much. One member responded with derision: "I always knew you'd end up choosing a man." Looking back, I realize that I was not alone in feeling judged and rejected; I'm sure I had not celebrated her choices as fully as I might have. Disappointing exchanges like this occurred because of the unrealistic expectation of understanding that women thought other women would offer, and the hopes that others would move in the same direction in their lives.

Another critic was on target when she spoke of "self-destruction" in the women's movement. Anselma Dell'Olio charged that some women within the movement resented others' achievement and productivity. Rather than discuss differences openly, they purged the threatening women from the group, masking their animosities with movement rhetoric.[32]

Audre Lorde's remark that "you can't dismantle the master's house with the master's tools"[33] gives some perspective on those days. Purges and trashing had a long history in the male-dominated left and came into the women's movement, along with the many positive organizing strategies that women learned from involvement in those arenas. Too often, our analysis was aimed at "them," rather than at our own behaviors that needed to be owned and changed.

Backlash: From Without ... and Within

A growing and well-documented political conservatism created a backlash toward all progressive social change in the Reagan era, continuing to the present. But some of the harshest critics of second-wave feminism came from within the women's movement.

Here's an example from Rory Dicker in her 2008 *A History of U.S. Feminisms.* Commenting on Rebecca Walker's *To Be Real,* Dicker writes, "Walker's depiction of the second wave, like many that would follow, evokes an image of a repressive, puritanical, even dogmatic mother who would school her daughter into submission to her political beliefs. In some ways, this image resembles the stereotypical anti-sex feminist who taught women's studies classes in the 1980s and early 1990s."[34]

Ouch! Did I resemble those remarks? Repressive, puritanical, anti-sex? NO! Dogmatic? I may have to say yes. In the early 1970s I clung to a radical feminist perspective (and dress, too, adopting overalls and combat-type boots). I eventually realized that I was something of a caricature of myself, a person with as many and more privileges as challenges (and at 5'1" and a little more than 100 pounds, not much of a combatant, even with the boots I had purchased in the boys' department). I also acknowledged that echoing calls for revolutionary change connected me to some women, but also alienated those who supported changes within existing institutions that could improve women's lives in dramatic ways. I still believe we need to challenge the root causes of sexism, but I have become more accepting of the multiplicity of ways decent people can work to implement change.

Many works that look back on the second wave either valorize or demonize the "radical" and diminish the contributions of other feminists. In fact, early in the second wave, the lines between radical and liberal became quite diffused. Many self-identified radicals were members of liberal feminist organizations, and many so-called liberals took radical stands, as Stephanie Gilmore notes in her article on feminist activism in Memphis between 1971 and 1982. The NOW chapter there, which usually worked to advance women's rights through structured, legislative action, took to the streets in "radical" style to protest violence against women. Gilmore concludes that "it may be more appropriate to think about feminist activism—then and now—in terms of dynamism rather than static labels. While the terms liberal and radical are clearly important to feminists and scholars, they are not mutually exclusive in terms of feminist activism. Feminists have been and continue to be, simultaneously, liberal and radical."[35] Just as there is no unified notion of "woman," there is no single way to interpret the past, work in the present, or shape the future. The woman in my CR group who chose separatism for a period has since become a leading spokesperson for legislative action on behalf of gay marriage and is a role model for men and women, LGBTQ and straight, radical and liberal, working to implement change.

My experience in a CR group helped me to understand the paradoxes that were present in my personal and political choices. My anti-capitalist rhetoric became liberal reality when, with some ambivalence, I offered my support to colleagues at our college in filing a class-action suit against the Commonwealth of Massachusetts. We had learned that many women faculty at Salem State College and throughout the public college system, despite more advanced degrees and years of service, were paid far less than their male counterparts. No, this wasn't the greatest of injustices, but it was one that had been revealed in our midst. Although in my librarian classification I did not benefit personally from the suit, I was able to help amass the data and hire the legal team that, finally, won the suit and corrected the inequities that made a difference for the individuals, and their life partners and families, in their current salaries and, later, in their retirement incomes.

Were we "co-opted?" Did the lawsuit divert us from addressing other, more grievous problems? The contradictions involved in work for equality and social justice at that time (not to mention this one) are myriad. But continuing the process of consciousness-raising can provide a way to reflect on the never perfect choices.

As for Dicker's observations of the second wave, we were just as guilty of similarly stereotyping the women's rights movement of the nineteenth century, resulting in a notion of uniformity that belied the complexity of the individuals and organizations that were involved. Later in her book, Dicker acknowledges that "this collective disavowal of the second-wave relies more on impressionistic understandings ... than on solid engagement with the history of feminist movements."[36]

There is just as much diversity among this generation as there was in previous periods of activism. Yet some who were involved in earlier phases of the movement may fail to see, or trivialize, the many and varied dimensions of new thinking and work, and may not acknowledge how often the serious efforts of younger activists are being co-opted or manipulated by the media, just as they were in previous eras.

One of the most pervasive and undermining media myths is that we are now in a "postfeminist" era. As the years have passed many women have been lulled into a belief, despite hard data and the evidence of their own lives to the contrary, that the battles have been won. These women feel that continuing to raise issues of injustice under the banner of feminism is not just passé but also a bit embarrassing.

But postfeminism is not only a media manipulation. The term also resonates with theorists who have been influenced by postmodern thinking that denies the existence of *any* unifying theory, be it humanism, Marxism, or feminism. Recent analyses emphasize the primacy of language in shaping experience and the impossibility of capturing the ever-changing human subject or establishing fundamental truths about women or any group.

It is a tribute to younger and older feminists that many have engaged with new, and often arcane, philosophical frameworks and have advanced an intersectional feminism that embraces the multiple, and often conflicting, identities that coexist with gender. This generation of feminists refuses to be categorized and finds ways to live with, and even celebrate, contradictions in their search for authentic personal and political expression. Their perspective is not only multicultural but also global, and, rather than being a single mass movement, they seek strategic coalitions around common concerns in particular settings. They enthusiastically utilize new technologies and creatively challenge and adapt popular culture. Today's feminists work within and beyond the academy, and they are deeply concerned about the millions of girls and women who have no voice due to poverty, lack of education, and sexual and economic exploitation.

And Every Generation Has to Do It Again

The continuing difficulties that women face mean that a strong feminist movement is necessary. Even as we have come to understand that there is no unified "women's condition" or single solution, there is still the possibility of shaping collective responses to varied dilemmas. There has been renewed activism, locally, nationally and globally, and the CR process is again proving to be a powerful organizing tool, well suited to the challenges before us now.

For those who participated in CR groups, the approach is still "second nature." ReCollective member Donna says of our women and work group process, "The interesting point is that 40 years later, and after meeting for 30 years, WE KNOW HOW TO DO CR, without talking about it. We just start doing it through unstated, mutual agreement—the form of speaking, the turn taking, the listening, the catharsis, the feelings (laughter, tears), the story-telling, the affirmation and recognition, the goal setting, the action steps when the 'inward' perspective is directed outward toward social change."

Susan Griffin may be romanticizing, but, perhaps, only a little, when she concludes that the feminist organizing approach of small groups has influenced *all* groups.[37] Consciousness-raising groups went beyond the organizational development models of getting "input" to value deep listening and validated personal experience as an important way of knowing, often as meaningful as other data (or even more so).

Do It Yourself

With guidelines and assistance from a growing women's liberation movement, starting a group was not a daunting task in the 1970s. Readers of this book have certainly experienced the legacy of the process in, for just one example, the ubiquitous book groups that flourish today. But CR groups are intended to go beyond warm friendships and amiable discussions to a deeper examination of the impediments to social justice for women and all people, and to lead us to action to dismantle these barriers.

Why Meet?

To develop trusting, mutually supportive relationships; to gain self-confidence; to explore shared approaches to leadership; to determine if and how social and political structures influence personal experience; and to move from personal solutions to collective ways of problem-solving.

Where to Meet?

There are lots of organizations that will welcome small groups in their meeting spaces—religious institutions, community centers, libraries and more. Students can reserve a conference room in a dorm or the campus women's or multicultural center. But the living rooms or kitchens of members' homes and apartments are likely to create the most comfortable and intimate environments for sharing the stories of your lives, assuming that you can have a dedicated space to yourselves with no interruptions from roommates or children. It's a good idea to alternate among homes, with the host providing tea or coffee and a dessert. Some groups like to offer wine—that's up to you.

How Often?

Weekly meetings are best to keep the connection and conversation growing. The frequency depends on the ability of group members to attend the meetings. Once a schedule is determined, the obligation to be present should be honored.

Who Should Lead the Group?

If the group alternates meetings in private homes or apartments, the host may also serve as facilitator—the person charged with getting the conversation going. If it seems burdensome for the host to have this assignment as well as providing refreshments, the group may decide to have a volunteer for organizing the refreshments so the host is free from that chore. All this sharing of responsibilities makes it easy to gather.

How Many?

Six or eight is a good number; more than ten and there's a likelihood that not everyone will have a chance to speak as often as (s)he would like.

Who Should Attend?

This is a contested topic. Some may wish to form groups that include men, as some third-wave feminists suggest. Others may agree with Bridget Crawford, who urged a reinvigoration of women's CR groups in her 2008 blog: "Inclusive non-polarity has immediate emotional appeal. It allows us to live comfortably with our compromises. Our relationships with particular men—as boyfriends, husbands, lovers, friends, brothers, fathers, mentors and colleagues—coexist with our understanding that men as a group exert privilege over women as a group. But in the contemporary quest for an inclusive feminism, we have lost opportunities, outlets, groups, relationships in which we as women can share our experiences with other women."[38] Still others embrace both views, suggesting that men form their own groups and joint meetings take place occasionally.

Some groups may be limited to particular populations. LGBTQ individuals (or groups exploring one or more of those initials), young, old, people with disabilities, and others may benefit from meeting with those who share some common circumstances and challenges. Other groups may aim for diversity in race, age, gender, and class. And it may be that you'll participate in a number of groups as time passes and circumstances change. Whatever the case, today's feminist framework will ensure that disclosing a common "women's condition" will no longer be the group's sole purpose.

How to Start?

Sharing autobiographical information is an easy way to get to know one another. Information about one's earliest experiences can include concerns of race, gender and class backgrounds. After the first couple of meetings, the group may decide to choose a topic for the next session, giving members an opportunity to think about their experiences around the issue before meeting.

A good technique that helps the group focus is to have a brief "check-in," an opportunity to go around the room and have each person who wishes to do so share information they feel they need to "get off their chest" before the discussion on the selected topic starts. The technique serves several purposes: it provides a chance for members to separate from the often overwhelming routines of their lives to be fully present for the group, and it also gives space to share what may be a momentous event—a family illness, a miscarriage, a loss of job, or relationship breakup—that needs the attention and support of the group. A caveat: Keeping the check-in brief can be difficult.

How Long Should Each Meeting Last?

Groups that meet weekly probably should have a two-hour maximum limit, including check-in and wrap-up. A volunteer timekeeper can alert members when open discussion should end, allowing time for observations and analysis (are there common threads to our experiences that reveal reasons and causes for the situations we've described, that might reveal systemic sexism, classism, ageism, or racism that must be confronted?). Although earlier CR guidelines stressed that the small groups devoted to sharing and analyzing personal experience should not become action groups, too many rules can lead to a self-consciousness that limits the flow of conversation. Inevitably, there will be overlap in membership in a CR group and political and social change projects outside the group, but whether and how members move from discussion to action should be an individual, not group, decision.

How Long Should the Group Meet?

The group's purpose will decide this, but it's a good idea to take the pulse of the group from time to time.

How to Participate and Encourage Others

Supportive listening is the most important quality to bring to the group. Speaking to your own experience, rather than what you've read or heard about the subject; expressing feelings, rather than intellectualizing; and responding without judgment or advice are goals that aren't always easy to implement. A brief evaluation, or "check-out," at the end of each meeting can give members an opportunity to comment on what worked well and why, and what might improve participants' feelings of involvement and satisfaction with the process.

Topics

Although the answers may be different today, the questions on topics ranging from housework, relationships, racism, contraception, abortion, sexuality, and many others are still relevant. Here are a few, but you can see that they're easy to come up with:

What strengths do women have? What are the challenges of being a woman? How do you think things have changed from your grandmother's generation, or your mother's? How have they affected you?

Can you remember when you first became aware of gender? Of race? Of class? Of disabilities?

Are you happy with your body? If you could change anything about your appearance, what would it be? What messages have you received from your family, peers, or the media about your physical appearance? Do notions of physical beauty vary across racial and ethnic groups and ages? In what ways? Why?

How do you care for your body? Do you pay attention to what you eat and drink? Do you use products or medications aimed at improving health and beauty? To help with menstruation or menopause?

If you are in an intimate relationship, do you strive for mutuality? Do you think one partner has a stronger role in shaping the dynamic of the relationship? Does this shift and change? Do you care? Are you ever uncomfortable about your role in terms of economic contributions or sexual practices? Do you talk about it?

If you are involved in a heterosexual relationship, do you use contraception? If so, what method? How do you feel about the methods you have used? Do you use contraception or does your partner? Are you satisfied with this arrangement? Whatever your choice of sexual partner, do you consider protection against STDs? Why or why not? Have you ever had an abortion? Who was involved in the decision? What were your feelings afterward? Have they changed? Whether or not you chose or would choose an abortion, do you believe women should have this choice? What family, religious, and/or cultural messages are implicated in your views on this issue?

If you're living with someone, who does the housework? Is it a shared responsibility?

Other chapters will offer additional "starter" questions that can spark discussions on the topics covered therein.

II

Right Livelihood: Working as a Feminist

*The pitcher cries for water to carry
and a person for work that is real.*[1]

— ‧ — ‧ —

United for Social Change

They meet in church basements, living rooms and community centers. As with the consciousness-raising groups described in the first chapter, these women have come together to end isolation, share experiences, discover common issues, and take action.

Domestic Workers United was founded in New York City in 2000, and now it has 4,000 participants. The website describes an organization of Caribbean, Latina and African nannies, housekeepers and caregivers who seek power, respect and fair labor standards in their employment, and aim to build a movement to end exploitation and oppression for all: "We have a dream that one day all work will be valued equally."[2]

Their words reflect the title of this chapter. "Right livelihood" is a term from Buddhist tradition, but it is used in this book for work that provides self-worth, deep respect for others, and concern for the natural world.

The efforts of members of Domestic Workers United led to a Domestic Workers Bill of Rights, which became law in the state of New York in November 2010.[3] The legislation guarantees basic work standards, overtime pay, and three paid vacation days per year. The activism of the New York group has led to the creation of the National Domestic Workers Alliance, which has organized in 33 cities in the United States[4] and has stimulated an international response to the working conditions and frequent violence toward and abuse of domestic workers in every part of the globe, 83 percent of whom are female.[5] This is one powerful example of the ways in which sharing personal experiences in a small group can be a springboard to collective action for change.

Still a Distant Goal: Economic Self-Sufficiency for Women

Wherever they are and whatever their combinations of identities, women usually have faced unique or especially difficult work challenges. Much of women's work simply doesn't "count"; they receive no remuneration for many of the goods and services they provide. In addition to unpaid work in households and communities, a shocking number of women are enslaved—trafficked into sexual or domestic labor.[6]

Class divisions have been a major impediment to building a women's movement that could lead to social justice for all. Historically, a woman's status has been dependent on her relationship to a man, preferably an "important" man, rather than on her own economic, social and personal accomplishments, which, until very recently, were nearly impossible to achieve. Western notions of female liberation were rooted in that reality. Economic circumstances required British philosopher, writer and women's rights activist Mary Wollstonecraft to support herself from a young age, first as a "lady's companion," and later as a teacher. Yet her impassioned call for women's empowerment, *A Vindication of the Rights of Women* (1792),[7] which many consider the opening salvo for female liberation, was framed in an argument that education for women would provide husbands with more interesting partners who could raise their sons to be better citizens.

Nearly a century and a half passed before Virginia Woolf, in *A Room of One's Own* (1929)[8] and *Three Guineas* (1938),[9] presented her case for women to have the personal space to shape their own lives, and education equal to men's that could prepare them to earn independent incomes.

Like Woolf's writings, Betty Friedan's best-selling *The Feminist Mystique,* published in 1963,[10] spoke to women whose class and racial privilege could allow them to dream of such possibilities. The college-educated women who experienced what Friedan labeled "the problem that has no name" felt bored and unfulfilled by the routines of suburban life and wanted to use their academic degrees in the workplace.

Yet well before college-educated women began challenging the glass ceiling, women worked outside the home, as servants in other people's homes, on farms, in factories, and in service jobs. The vast majority of women workers still are clustered in "pink collar" jobs such as secretaries, wait staff, receptionists, retail clerks, or cosmetologists. Their pay is low, there are few career ladders, working conditions are difficult and few of these positions include benefits such as health care and vacation.

A number of organizations, including Friedan's National Organization for Women, promoted legislation to provide women with equal opportunities in education and employment that yielded dramatic gains in fields such as law, medicine and business. Motivated by economic necessity rather than restlessness, working-class women also sought to improve their job opportunities through equal employment legislation in the United States; yet class, disability, race, ethnicity, and age have combined with gender to limit the ability of the vast majority of women to be economically self-sufficient.

Most discussions of women and work continue to speak to the struggles of women in corporate and professional positions who seek equality with men from similar educational and class backgrounds. But the feminist movement needs to promote opportunities for "right livelihood" for all women.

What Does Consciousness-Raising Have to Do with It?

Personal histories are shaped by social and political structures. Consciousness-raising provides a way to take a deeper look at our experiences to reveal patterns of oppression and privilege that can lead to action for change. Although I didn't think of my own story as a tale of class privilege, through consciousness-raising, I came to understand that I benefited from just that. I grew up in a white working-class community where children freely exchanged ethnic slurs on the streets and playgrounds—*dago, polack, mick, kike*. We were equal-opportunity insulters of each other's heritage, but the prejudice behind the words was not coupled with the intention or ability to inflict pain. As the years passed, education and social opportunities separated many of my neighbors from people who could not escape through "whiteness." By the time I entered high school, my family had moved to a suburb where no one used derogatory language, even though racial, ethnic and other forms of discrimination were deeply entrenched.

Both of my immigrant grandmothers worked outside the home in menial jobs that were necessary to sustain their families, but their daughters' success was defined by the ability to choose NOT to work, to be provided for by male "breadwinners." My mother did not have to perform arduous, physical labor like her mother, and stopped working when she married. I received the college education my immigrant father and first-generation American mother had devoted so much of their lives to making possible, but it was assumed that my career also would be as wife and mother.

My mother often related a story about her teenage years. She had been asked to a school party by a boy she liked. One day before the event he walked her home and saw her mother working in the humble store that provided much of the family income. The next day he rescinded the invitation.

As a self-absorbed adolescent, I had assumed that my mother's story was told to commiserate with my own adolescent dating struggles. Through participation in a CR group, I began to understand how deeply shamed my mother had been by class. I then realized why my parents were not enthusiastic about my first serious love—a caring, hardworking boy who lived in the city next to our suburb. His father was a factory assembly worker who was frequently laid off, requiring his sons to work throughout high school. Only in retrospect did I see the irony of my choice. With an entire suburb of a "better" class of people to date, I chose a boy who might have lived next door in the neighborhood from which we'd fled.

The economic and social benefits of class mobility came with losses. My grandmothers' labors were not a source of pride or inspiration; their struggles were to move beyond, to forget. In fact, we heard very little about their lives, for our generation was encouraged not to learn their "foreign" languages.

My growing understanding of my own experiences helped me to see how various "isms" hurt others, even if their stories were very different from mine, and led me to a progressive political viewpoint and action based in feminist analysis. And it is why I remain convinced that consciousness-raising, the continual practice of revealing and analyzing our experience, is a vital tool for social change.

I still believe it is possible for women and their allies to work together to overcome sexist injustice. We can begin by ensuring that the diverse and interrelated experiences of race, gender, ethnicity, sexuality, disability, age, and more are addressed in all discussions of work. Those of us who have the privilege of whiteness, education, comparative affluence, and physical well-being can use these to dismantle a system that creates unearned advantages. We can come together to redefine notions of power and success and reshape workplaces to be participative, inclusive and socially responsible. (Peg McIntosh has put forth cogent ideas on ways to do this that will be discussed further in Chapter V.)

Recognizing and Challenging Power in the Workplace

My "right livelihood" journey began in the late 1960s, a period of social ferment when it seemed altogether possible, even likely, that the present social order would be replaced, and that poverty, racism, sexism and other forms of oppression could end. However, the activism of that era, as it often is now, was easily and regularly co-opted. My experience was benign, but typical of how easily radical impulses are absorbed into the service of those who have and maintain power. At a time when revolution was in the air, I was among many who saw our work lives as a contribution to radical change.

Early in my career as a librarian I had created a Library of Social Alternatives with the help of a progressive student who worked with me in the college library. As a member of the student senate, he proposed that a small portion of the required student activities fee be devoted to a student-determined collection of material on social and political change. We gathered journals, pamphlets and paperback books covering civil rights, liberation struggles in the United States and abroad, feminism, gay rights, anti-war activism, and political change movements, and we also hosted speakers and films on these topics. My "revolutionary" notions were deflated when I was asked by the college president to offer a tour of the collection to the trustees of the public college system, who heartily commended the creativity of the project. What we thought was a challenge to the power structure, the administration saw as a way to defuse and redirect some of the radical energy developing on the campus. Had our efforts been taken seriously, the response would have been very different.

Consciousness-raising can provide insight into the tenacity with which those in power hold on to power. The horrific, violent stifling of liberation movements around the globe, most recently in the Arab world, overwhelms the assaults on freedom within the United States. But the Patriot Act and other legislation intended to respond to terrorism has significantly limited our freedoms.

By exchanging experiences, members of a CR group can understand that legislative reforms often create the appearance of change while things remain largely the same. In this country gender, race, and other forms of discrimination are illegal, but sexism and racism continue. Through sharing and analyzing our ideas and experiences, feminists and their allies can be moved to become more tenacious watchdogs and ensure that the legislation that has been passed is implemented, even as we regroup to reaffirm more radical goals.

Telling our stories also can guard against the mythologizing of the past. Some look back on the 1960s and 1970s as a time of political purity and clear vision that is lacking today. Sharing our experiences can lead to a more honest view of that period which may reveal that ignorance and naiveté accompanied good intentions. While we young activists were quoting from Mao's Little Red Book, few of us were aware of the brutality that had occurred, and was continuing, including the egregious and murderous acts of Stalinism, the Chinese Cultural Revolution, Pol Pot and more. Learning from the abuses as well as the successes of previous actions can lead to discovering more promising ways to connect our work to social change.

Consciousness-raising can help us remain authentic. Feminism, like other major movements for social and political change, draws, and needs, allies from all segments of society. Men and women who have not experienced oppressive conditions can learn to respond with compassion and action on behalf of those who have. Changing women's working conditions will require many alliances, and much-needed changes will not occur unless women with privilege unite with, and advocate for, those who do not have the time, education, money, and platforms to highlight their plights.

In 1903, Marie and Bessie Van Vorst, reformers and authors of *The Woman Who Toils*,[11] went to Columbia, South Carolina, to work in a mill, the first of a number of jobs they took so they could experience firsthand the conditions of women workers. A century later, progressive journalist Barbara Ehrenreich did stints as a Wal-Mart retail clerk, a waitress, a nursing home aide and a housekeeper for a commercial maid service, all of which she described in *Nickel and Dimed: On (Not) Getting By in America*.[12] Placing themselves in others' shoes made these authors' advocacy more effective. But they had choices their erstwhile co-workers did not; they could leave those positions for better-paid work in far more pleasant environments and with greater autonomy. We can try to walk in the shoes of others whose conditions we want to change, but we can't really know what another's experience is like.

I may have roots in the immigrant and working class, but my education, class privileges and citizenship status separate me from that inheritance. When I first became politically active I knew university degreed people and was perhaps, at times, one of them, who mimicked the dress and language of blue-collar workers in an attempt at solidarity. But authenticity, working from where you currently are situated in a system that you wish to make just, is both respectful, and the only effective approach.

Steps to Right Livelihood

The National Domestic Workers Alliance and Jobs for Justice are calling for three thousand well-paying jobs for female caretakers. In July 2011 Secretary of Labor Hilda Solis and 700 supporters representing labor, health care, faith and advocacy organizations gathered in Washington, DC, to launch Caring Across Generations, a movement that expected to visit a dozen cities in the following months to support this campaign for quality care of the disabled and elderly, as well as the people who provide that care.[13]

Coalitions for progressive collective action often begin with a small number of people sharing their own experiences and addressing proximal conditions, but with the hope that these can lead to a larger movement for change. Many such initiatives are described in Paul Hawkens' *Blessed Unrest,*[14] which reveals that women's groups play a central role. Some of the topics that necessitate sharing, reflection and action in a CR work group include combining work with family, dealing with the still-pervasive issues of difference, competition between women, and finding work that has meaning.

Combining Work and Family

No woman can "do it all," despite the recurring model of the exceptional woman about which Adrienne Rich commented, "The exceptional women who have emerged from this (sexist) system are just that; the required exception used by every system to justify and maintain itself."[15] Sharing and analyzing experience with others can disabuse us of the notion of exceptionalism, and help us to find collective solutions to common problems.

The issue of combining work and family life remains a central dilemma for women. Whether or not they have children, a majority of women will be in a caretaking role at some point in their lives. Male contributions are still often referred to as "helping" with the housework and "babysitting" the children. The myriad organizing tasks remain a female role. Most women work out individual arrangements for child or elder care, usually depending on other women. Discussions in women and work groups can lead to action for public solutions to what are too often seen as individual challenges.

It seems it takes a war to give women equal access to the public sphere. Women ran the households and family farms during the Revolutionary and Civil Wars in the United States. Later, the skills of women workers were needed to produce the weapons to fight the Second World War and very quickly child-care centers were provided. The propaganda that made it a higher calling to work as opposed to staying at home with one's children was almost instantaneously reversed after the war, when stay-at-home mothering was deemed essential to a child's healthy development.

As current situations are shared and analyzed, participants in work groups may discover that solutions for double duty are sometimes double-edged swords. Using a CR approach and comparing experiences may reveal both the advantages and the flaws in some of these "solutions." Flex time should be a right, not a benefit, Joanna Weiss opined recently in the *Boston Globe.*[16] But how will part-time, flexible schedules affect women's careers over the span of their work lives? And what is the impact of such policies on women who need full-time, benefited employment? "Mommy tracks" may limit the chances or timeframe for a female corporate lawyer to become a partner, but the "mother's hours" touted by a posting in the local fast-food restaurant will keep a single mother and her family in poverty.

What "Difference" Does It Make?

CR offers a way to acknowledge that old scripts continue to be replayed. Just as in decades past, when women gather to talk about what happens at work, inevitably, someone will mention a meeting at which she offered a suggestion that was ignored until the very same idea was put forth by a man.

At first glance it seems that women, especially middle- and upper-class women, are succeeding, pursuing education at higher rates and equalling (and soon even surpassing) the numbers of males in some fields. For example, women now make up 56 percent of undergraduate accounting majors and represent 62 percent of accountants and auditors. But as of 2011, only 9 percent of women in this now female-dominated profession were chief financial officers.[17] As more women entered that previously male-dominated field, the requirements for leadership positions shifted to degrees in finance or MBA degrees, in which male students continue to predominate. In fact, whole fields have been "reorganized," with revised credentials that favor males and a large increase in administrative jobs with new titles and higher pay that are often filled by men. Paralleling accounting, in my own "women's profession" of librarianship, "chief information officers" (mostly male) are now at the top of the information services hierarchy, moving technologically savvy (and usually female) librarians down to middle management. The descriptor "librarian" is now shunned in favor of "information scientist," a term that isn't burdened with a female stereotype.

If you are seeking them, the statistics are available. But it is through experiencing and sharing the personal stories behind the data that continued sexism becomes real. Until then, many women, including the young college students with whom I interact regularly, believe that an earlier generation fought and won those struggles for equality and there is no longer a need for a feminist movement.

When we speak of our experiences, other contradictions become apparent.[18] Although feminist theory embraces a view that it is as likely that traits differ within individual men and women as much as between them, the dichotomy between "masculine" and "feminine" characteristics continues to underscore discussions about women in the workplace. Dozens of "how to" books suggesting that women suppress any characteristics resembling feminine stereotypes and "work like a man" continue to be published. Yet when men adopt "feminine" characteristics, such as intuition[19] or empathy,[20] these are celebrated and the men receive high praise for utilizing them in their work.

One example is an article in a professional publication of the American Institute for Certified Public Accountants that offers tips for those who want to get to the top of that field: be "multi-focused and social, participative, always soliciting ideas from others and want[ing] everyone to participate in gathering ideas and brainstorming ideas," instead of being "logical" and "uni-focused."[21] This advice is the very reverse of that offered to women.

Another example is *Better Together,* by Robert Putnam and Lewis Feld-stein,[22] an interesting book that responds to the growing lack of community connections in the United States and cites many hopeful instances of how institutions can grow through a relational model. I enjoyed reading it and looked for a reference to Jean Baker Miller, the principal shaper of relational cultural theory. In *Toward a New Psychology of Women,* Miller affirmed the fact that all human beings seek power, which she defined not as dominance, but as agency, the ability to make things happen. She advanced a model of healthy interpersonal and organizational relationships in which the focus is not on individualism, but on mutual empathy and empowerment for the well-being of all within families, homes, workplaces and communities.[23] But Miller is not mentioned in *Better Together* or cited in the bibliography, although her ideas permeate each page, especially the chapter on organizing women workers at Harvard University.[24] (Kim Rondeau, who headed the successful organizing campaign at Harvard, acknowledged Miller's influence when I spoke with her at a recent conference, "The New Majority? The Past, Present and Future of Women in the Workplace," at Radcliffe Institute for Advanced Study, Harvard University, on September 9, 2011.)

Miller's feminist analysis and recommendations transformed approaches to psychotherapy and organizational change. And it seems that Miller's theories have, at the very least, been incorporated without attribution by other writers and theorists. Why? Perhaps because she based her work not only on her train-ing as a medical doctor with a specialty in psychiatry but also on her own expe-riences as a woman and those of other women with whom she had shared insights. Miller herself described the phenomenon that maintains women's lack of recognition and subordination: "It would be difficult if we started from zero, but we do not. We start from a position in which others have power and do not hesitate to use it. Even if they do not consciously use it against women, all they have to do is remain in a position of dominance, keep doing what they are, and nothing will change."[25]

Women and men working for social justice can't keep doing what they have done; they need to alter their own behavior and advocate for social change, and CR is an important component in this process.

Competition and Conflict

According to numerous articles, men don't like to work for women and nei-ther do women. A *British Daily Mail* poll surveyed 3,000 employees; three quarters of the men and two thirds of the women said they preferred male bosses. Their reasons brought out all the old stereotypes: women are "bitches," "bimbos," "dragon ladies," "prisoners of their hormones," temperamental, "cliquey," worried about appearances, caught up in office politics, "loose cannons," and conniving, and they bring personal lives into the office and put other women down. "Because [we] women are very competitive with each other ... emotions and feelings get in the way," said one respondent, apparently speaking for us all.[26] The popular media of the postfeminist era reinforce these images of women as, to cite one example, "Desperate Housewives," who are clinging, manipulative and use sexual favors to maintain their precarious "power."

Consciousness-raising can help us claim our agency—the ability to make things happen for ourselves, other women and all people—without "feminine wiles" and other behaviors that are rooted in and sustain sexism. The CR groups that flourished in the "second wave" began to reverse one of the major blocks to women's power—the pitting of women against each other.

Wikipedia lists 36 pages of "women's occupational organizations," and these don't cover women's caucuses within coeducational organizations. These are settings where women can consciously give and receive support for personal and social change. Here's one example that changed my life: At a meeting of one such group, Massachusetts Women in Public Higher Education, I reconnected with a woman who was in my high school graduating class. Although we had shared some classes, Theo and I were not close friends. But when I called her to find out about the position of library director at the university where she was a professor of philosophy, she was warm and encouraging. I was invited for an interview and there was my former classmate smiling enthusiastically as I fielded questions in the open session for faculty. She even asked me to be her guest for dinner and we discovered how much we now had in common through our shared involvement in the women's movement. Over coffee, Theo, always known for her directness, said, "I'm so glad that the girl I disliked so much in high school has turned into such a wonderful woman." I know Theo's kindness, support and advocacy helped with my appointment to the position. I've told this story often because it is an amusing, but also very moving, example of a feminist's willingness to suspend judgment and support another woman—even one she didn't particularly like.

Along with celebrating the positive stories, CR offers the setting for continued efforts needed to challenge and question the roots of competition, conflict, and even animosity among women.

Meaningful Work

The words of Marge Piercy's poem that opened this chapter have it right: all people long for "work that is real." Barbara Garson's study of workers in low-wage routine jobs reveals that quest: "I expected to find resentment, and I found it. I expected to find boredom, and I found it. I expected to find sabotage, and I found it in clever forms I could never imagine. But the most dramatic thing I found was quite the opposite of noncooperation. People passionately want to work. That was true in industrial America and it's equally true in what's now heralded as the 'post-industrial society.'"[27]

The care and kindness that people bring to their work is captured beautifully in Stewart O'Nan's recent novel *Last Night at the Lobster*.[28] Like most workers, manager Manny DeLeon knows how to do his job well, and he cares more about his colleagues and customers than the company that owns the Red Lobster does about either. His staff returns that care when they brave a winter storm to come in to work the last shift at the restaurant located in a downscale mall that "corporate" has decided to close.

Consciousness-raising can offer a path for us to follow the fictional Manny's model in "real time," caring about both co-workers and the people who are the recipients of our labor. Garson's observations likewise show that small changes, like seeking input from workers (the people who know best) on ways they can improve their own jobs and the mission of the workplace, and providing workers with more opportunities for conversations with co-workers, can result in large transformations.

(Chapter IV will describe the shift from participatory organizations, including community women's centers, rape crisis and battered women's programs, and welfare rights groups, which involved women from diverse racial, ethnic and class backgrounds in defining ways to help themselves and others, to a "professional" model, and note ways in which these approaches are being/can be reinstituted.)

Work Groups: Collectives and ReCollectives

It helps to have the support of a small group of caring women with whom to explore ways of achieving right livelihood—work that can provide material sustenance for ourselves and our families, and also has personal worth and can contribute to the larger society. Coming together can yield sustaining friendships, joy and laughter, and insights to handle everyday challenges. These reasons alone merit gathering, but when combined with the analysis that is basic to consciousness-raising, we can create an activist agenda that can move us beyond commiseration to substantive change.

The makeup and longevity of women's work groups will be shaped by the reasons people have come together. I'll begin, in keeping with the CR approach, with my own experience and then briefly look at other models that can empower individuals and lead to organizational and social change.

My first work group involvement came shortly after I separated from my husband. Following a local women's conference that included a session on women and work, some participants decided to continue to meet. Divorce had moved several of us who had never intended to support ourselves, let alone a family, from a middle-class lifestyle to the category of "displaced homemaker"; others had decided that they wanted to combine work inside and outside the home.

I was among the few who had a postsecondary education that prepared me for work that could produce a modest income. Simmons College was founded to educate women for female-dominated fields, like nursing, K–12 teaching and social work, which were characterized by sociologist Amitai Etzioni as "semi-professions."[29] My family had urged this practical education for me, in the "goshafabid"—my mother's way of saying "God should forbid"—event that my breadwinner spouse experience an early death (divorce was not a consideration). From the array of "semis," I chose librarianship.

I recall vividly how women in that group expressed fears and hopes and supported each other in finding paid work, not always our "dream" job, but a giant step toward economic independence and the accompanying self-respect. At the same time that we were meeting to help one another with our particular struggles, many of us were also advocating for child-care centers, programs to aid adult students starting or returning to college, and other societal changes that could help many other women.

Discussions in that work group led me to the decision to enter a doctoral program when it became clear that I would need additional credentials to support myself and my daughters as a librarian. Exchanging energy, support, and insight with women who were involved in similar efforts to reshape their personal lives and the larger society gave meaning—indeed, made possible—those days packed with child care, a full-time job, part-time school, a new intimate relationship, friendships, and political activism. The realizations and caring discovered in that group continue to enrich my life today.

The ReCollective

Fortunately, when my work took me to the University of Massachusetts–Dartmouth, where I took a job as dean of library services and professor of education, I became part of another small work group that has been meeting for nearly twenty-five years, which we refer to as the ReCollective. Our definition of work includes not only our choice of paid jobs and the ways in which we do them but also the work of caring for family and making a difference in the community.

We now meet irregularly, sometimes because we haven't gathered for a while. But usually we set a date in response to one of the members calling or e-mailing with the now-familiar message: "I need the group." When that request comes, no matter how busy we are, we find the hours to be together—and those hours, regardless of the seriousness of the challenge that has prompted the request, are filled with good food, supportive listening, helpful conversation, and lots of laughter. Indeed, after more than a quarter century, members of our "work group" have begun to call it "the work and play group" to reflect both the important issues we discuss around our paid and unpaid labor and the ease, comfort, pleasure and fun of being together.

Although our geographical and class backgrounds are varied, we are all white, but our intimate partners, in-laws and grandchildren are Chinese, Balinese, Cape Verdean and Indian. We are all temporarily able-bodied, but not all our parents and progeny are. All of us are now in long-term relationships, but most members of our group have been through the painful challenges of divorce. We are all mothers and some of us have experienced the emotional and economic struggles of being single mothers.

Here's a bit more information about the individual women who make up the ReCollective.

Donna is a sociologist and university professor who retired early to pursue a new career as an artist. She was an inspiring teacher whose work focused on ways to challenge bureaucratic structures that stifle human creativity. She co-founded Spinner Publications, which captures, through oral histories and photography, the Yankee, French Canadian, Cape Verdean, Azorean, and mainland Portuguese immigrants whose labors as fishers, cranberry harvesters and textile workers shaped the economic and cultural life of southeastern Massachusetts.[30] Those who have been lucky enough to see the design and colors of her garden aren't surprised that she left the classrooms and students she loved to pursue art-making and has become a wonderful painter.

Before committing most of her working energy to painting, Sandee was a social worker and director of a community college program that prepared people to work in human services. She launched several community projects, including an alternative, free preschool for low-income children and a shelter/advocacy organization focusing on the needs of battered women. In addition to her beautiful paintings, she has created programs to engage women in the arts and developed other innovative community outreach projects that literally "draw" people together across differences in age, gender and other identities. "The support provided by the work group was central to my ability to name myself an artist. I've continued to grow through the collective intelligence, sensitivity, sense of humor and life wisdom of this group. Although we meet sporadically, the words, thoughts and caring I've absorbed from the group stay with me as an invaluable source of sustenance."

Marilyn, teacher and social activist, is a professor of history and American studies at Boston University. Her focus is on immigration. She authored a classic study of Cape Verdean immigration, *Between Race and Ethnicity*,[31] and is now collaborating with a colleague on a book about West African immigrants. An adventurer, during the school year Marilyn commutes to her classes from a boat docked in Boston Harbor. Marilyn's Cape Verdean *seder* (the ritual meal Jews celebrate at Passover) is just one example of how she links the various parts of her life to her work in the community.

Peg is the daughter of Quaker activists and she has continued her family's tradition, including her mother's commitment to feminism. A psychotherapist with a (too) full practice, Peg is also a writer and practitioner of meditation. She has done volunteer work in Thailand and, before the political coup, in Burma, sharing techniques for therapy with victims of trauma.

Kathy, a former acupuncturist, is now the owner of a retail clothing store that supports families in Bali, including her own sons, daughters-in-law and grandchildren. Kathy does "work that is real" in her appropriately named shop, Real Bodies, where customers won't buy anything that doesn't look and feel good to wear. She'll tell you, with warmth, humor and care, that an item is not right for you and then search through piles of shirts, dresses, and pants to find something you can wear for work or weeding or a wedding (and since her prices will not have emptied your pocketbook, you will have money left for a nice gift for the newlyweds). And, yes, she named her shop to celebrate "real bodies," the ones we have, not those of air-brushed, anorexic models and celebrities.

Bettina has worked as a women's center director and a lawyer, and she is now a Juvenile Court judge. She actively seeks alternatives to sentencing youthful offenders, including participation in an innovative program, Changing Lives Through Literature, which involves young men and women in small reading circles where they discuss ways in which their life experiences relate to those of characters in the novels they read. The program has reduced recidivism and opened new possibilities for participants. Bettina was also chair of the board of our local women's center, served on the YWCA Board of Directors, and founded the Women's Fund of Southeastern Massachusetts, dedicated to transforming the lives of women and girls in our area through "collaboration, diversity, bold leadership and social justice." Bettina had reaped the benefits of a supportive living arrangement after a divorce and, with the help of other women with children, was able to complete college and her professional training. When she established the regional women's foundation, her goal was to enable other women and girls to overcome obstacles to education and achieve economic independence.

When we began to meet, one of us had just passed the bar exam and was a fledgling lawyer, while another was trying to find a position—even as a low-paid, temporary "adjunct" faculty member. I had recently completed my doctoral program and begun adding classroom teaching to my role as university library director. We are all now in what Sara Lawrence-Lightfoot has labeled "the third chapter" in our lives,[32] and we can celebrate the accomplishments that came from those earlier challenges. What has created our deep bond is not only the knowledge of the struggles that brought us to our careers and relationships but also the commitment that isn't stated because it doesn't need to be—it just IS—to give back to the individuals, communities and movements that gave so much to us. Influenced by our earlier experiences in political and feminist movements, we (and for most of us, our children as well) see work as much more than a way to earn money.

Our group uses many techniques of CR. We begin each meeting with a check-in to catch each other up on what has happened since we last met. Even if we haven't been together for a while, we know what the issues were when we each left off and are eager for updates. Then the focus turns to the person who requested the meeting. Long ago the group helped me in my decision to leave my position heading the university library to move to full-time teaching; Bettina likewise turned to the group when she was considering whether to accept an offer to apply for an administrative job in the court system that would allow her to shape policy, but would keep her from her pioneering work with juvenile offenders and the unique relationships she had created in the region; and Peg sought the group to help her limit the number of clients she was seeing so she could have time for meditation, family, writing, and her projects abroad. At this time, Kathy is considering handing over her business to her children, which would mean that her daughters-in-law would move from Bali to New England. Over the years, we've also shared financial concerns about having enough funds for children's college tuitions, family crises, and, now, retirement. If the gathering has not been called to address a particular agenda, we'll combine our check-in with a request for some individual time, indicating how long we might need.

Then we listen. As in a CR group, advice is withheld, although we may ask the speaker for clarification. One member volunteers to take notes, so that we can give the speaker back the themes of her remarks. It is remarkable how "rehearing" our presentations of what initially seems to be an overwhelming challenge, even an impossibility, can lead to a doable agenda for change. The resolution, or, more often, short-term and intermediate steps that can lead to a resolution, is drawn from the person herself. Group members may ask questions like "What has made you feel better, more certain, less stressed in the past? Can you employ any of these strategies to this situation?" The person may set a deadline with the group's support to do/change something within a certain time. One or two members of the group might offer to call periodically to see if and how the decisions are being implemented.

The group offers a place to be real. We do not expect or offer comments like "It's OK ... don't worry about it" that we may have heard from others with whom we've discussed our dilemmas. We can be honest about our disappointments and rejections, our uncertainties about trying something new, and our concerns that we have made the wrong choice. We can also help each other to begin anew after mistaken choices and remind each other of what it was we said we wanted when we lose track of our goals. It is also a place to share contradictions. As a single mother with few resources, Bettina had never considered that she would become a judge. Now she acknowledges that the black robes and references to "her honor" are flattering and would be missed if she did not experience them.

When we say our good-byes, we are full, not only from the food and drink we always enjoy—a potluck feast, so no single person has the burden of doing it all—but also with the ideas, hope and encouragement we share. The examples and insights of our fellow members stay with us long after the meetings are over. Sandee commented recently that she often finds herself thinking, in a variation of the famous question, "What would Peg do?" or "How would Marilyn (or another member of the group) handle this?"

Other Groups

Many groups begin with a particular purpose and then move to another place. At a time when there were far fewer women and minorities in higher education administration, the American Council on Education sponsored a "National Identification Program," a terrible name for an excellent initiative to locate and support, through publications, workshops, conferences, and internships, women who might move into such positions. Several of us who had served together on the organization's state steering committee didn't want to stop meeting when our terms ended, so we decided to continue gathering. We have cheered each other on through career challenges and changes for over thirty years. The fact that we were from different institutions and occupied diverse positions in the academic hierarchy provided an opportunity to assess work issues from a variety of perspectives. Our conversations over dinner four or five times a year are far-ranging, covering all the things that make for right livelihood—not just jobs but also friends and family, social issues, books, films, music, travel, sports and our engagement in a variety of political, cultural and social organizations.

Forming a group within a work field is another formulation. Meeting with other library workers helped me find ways to bring commitment to social change to my everyday work. In the first chapter, I discussed the librarians' group that was brought together by Vocations for Social Change, as well as the feminist librarian meetings in the greater Boston area that led to a national organization. Once again, the initial purpose of meeting to improve our own working conditions and better serve the people who used our libraries led to much deeper personal connections. When the husband of one of the members of our Boston group left her with a young baby another member moved into her home to help with finances, child care, and friendship. I met my husband through a member who had asked if she could stay at my home for the weekend when she suddenly had to leave her housing arrangement. She lived with us for a couple of years and became a special "aunt" to my daughters.

Although the consciousness-raising model details a structure that moves from personal sharing to analysis to activism, these are not sequential steps. The origins of CR are in political activism and, in many instances, involvement in work for social change is the first step, and the more intimate connections with other women follow. That is true for some of the women activists in the southeastern Massachusetts Coalition Against Poverty. As one participant told me, "I was doing a research project on welfare reform for a class at BCC [Bristol Community College in Fall River, Massachusetts]. It was good timing. CAP [Coalition Against Poverty] had a speakout on welfare ... I immediately volunteered." She went on to tell me how she got to know people through working in teams with other women, many of them also single mothers. Another CAP activist said, "Until I met CAP, I wasn't educated on the issues. I just believed what the welfare people told me without knowing why. I didn't know I could fight for things. I thought I just had to accept." After sharing experiences with other women in the CR-like training program for organizers called "CAP 101," she started volunteering, going door-to-door to talk to people about housing issues, and eventually she went back to school. "I went to school to improve my work with CAP. I took speech so I could talk in public. I took sociology to learn about social issues.... By telling people my story I got them to open up."

How a Work Group Can Work for You and Others

Among my faded Xeroxed papers, I found the outline prepared for the workshop on women and work from which my first work group evolved: "Many women are finding the need for a support-discussion group on work issues, based on the model of the consciousness-raising group. Such groups serve as ways for women to share concrete tactics and information about employment, and as a place for each woman to articulate her own individual work needs and skills."

Following CR protocols with which we were familiar, we suggested that the groups be small, 5–10 women, and that there be weekly meetings for 6–8 weeks, after which the group could decide whether to continue. Like consciousness-raising groups, the work groups focused on the personal experiences, social values and political perspectives that we wished to bring to our work. The aim was to make all our work—what we did to earn money and the ways we used our energy within our families, relationships and communities—purposeful, even transformational. A lofty goal, perhaps naïve, but naming these aspirations made us mindful of the workplace and world we wanted to inhabit.

Here are some questions that your work group might want to consider.

Family Work Legacies

Has work been a source of satisfaction to you? Do you think work was satisfying to your mother? Aunts? Grandmothers? Who worked outside the home and why? Did they have other choices? What were their roles? Marital status? Family obligations? How did they influence you? What kinds of work did they do? What led them to their work? What were the conditions in their work settings? What sort of struggles have women in your family undergone to combine work outside the home and work within the home/family? What have you learned from these observations/experiences?

Gender, Race, Class, Disability, Ethnicity, Sexual Identity

Have gender, race, class, disability, ethnicity, sexual identity or other factors affected your choice of work, your assignments, career ladder? In what ways? How did you respond? How might you have responded?

If Money Were No Object

Why did you choose your job/occupation? What is the status of your field compared to other fields? What do you get from your work/why do you do it? Money? Self-esteem? Service to others? Habit? What don't you get from your work and how might you get it? What would you do if you did not have to worry about money? What would you really like to be doing? What do you care about? What would you like the effect of your work to be? Who would you like your work to touch? What kind of work would most satisfy your personal needs? Your political and social goals? Are these being met in the work you are doing now?

What We've Learned—And Might "Unlearn"

What good/not-so-good learning experiences have you had? Why were they good, or not? What role did you and others play? How would you have changed them? What do these experiences tell you about the work you want to do? What have you learned from formal education? From family and friends? From people you admire? From other experiences/settings? What do they tell you about the work you want to do? What skills/knowledge do you have now? How could these be useful to others? What do you want to learn? What intrigues you? What work experiences have you had? What has been good and bad about them and why? What have you learned from these experiences? Which of them would you want to repeat? Which aspects would you change and how? What role did you play in those situations?

Discovering and Being Role Models

Are there people whose work you have admired? What did you admire? What did they teach you? How can you make your own work life similar? Do you think it is important for women to break stereotyped job barriers? Do you know women who are working in nontraditional jobs (e.g., as tradeswomen)? Do you admire women who have? Why? How can you find support to become the person you want to be? How do you support others? How would you like to be a role model for others? Do you usually work successfully with others? Have you experienced feelings of competition or jealousy? Have you had positive/negative experiences in your work with others? What was your response? With whom do you work now? If you supervise others, how do you learn about their goals? How can you help them reach these goals? Does your work environment encourage mutual goal-setting and support? Have you tried discussing work issues with your co-workers? With others in your field? What was the result, or what do you think the result would be?

Responding to these questions as an individual might lead to some increased personal satisfaction in your work; discussing them with others in a women and work group could lead to more ideas for how to accomplish that—and to larger workplace and social change.

III

Only Connect: Technology, Consciousness-Raising and Feminist Activism

The Internet is as much a site of consciousness-raising for the Third Wave as meeting with speculums in someone's living room was in the Second Wave.[1]

— · — · —

In her 2007 article, Tracy Kennedy urges women to engage in "feminist virtual consciousness-raising."[2] Kennedy uses the model put forth by Kathie Sarachild, which shaped many CR groups in the early 1970s and is advocated in this book. This approach to feminist theorizing and action is based upon sharing experiences about our everyday lives and using common themes to develop a feminist analysis and action agenda for social justice.

It's no surprise that Kennedy sees such promise in electronic consciousness-raising. From its inception, the Internet has been touted as the ultimate participatory medium—a way to connect each to all, the mechanism for overcoming barriers of geography, physical ability, gender, race and class. The usefulness, and now the necessity, of computer technology in general and the Internet in particular have brought us so much information with such speed and convenience that these usually are lauded as wholly beneficial. Even among those who have some qualms, the technological "revolution" is an inevitable condition of living, as these everyday events in my own life reveal:

Item: I'm in my favorite coffee shop. Most customers are bent over their laptops, but next to me a couple is chatting. The woman was late, having missed her bus. She catches her breath, gets a coffee and begins to tell her friend about her technology woes, including the fact that she "must" get a website. The conversation soon turns to a story about her niece, who, at just two, already can use an iPad.

Item: My husband and I are at the Apple store to attend a class on the use of our new iPhones. As we are waiting for the instructor, an attendee notes that most of us have grey hair. He is right and several people mumble that they don't want to be "left behind." More stories follow of precocious children and grandchildren who possess mind-boggling technological proficiencies.

Item: My student scholar partner with whom I work at the Brandeis University Women's Studies Research Center tells me that she is in awe of her sister's decision to go "cold turkey" and not use any of her electronic devices so she can focus on her studies and graduate school applications. My companion wonders if it will be possible for her sibling to survive for even a short period without social networking.

Item: I am in a museum cafeteria. Two people are seated at a table, each engrossed in a hand-held device. Fifteen minutes pass before they look at each other and exchange a few words. I realize that they did not each take a spare seat at one of the crowded tables, as I had assumed, but have some relationship to one another. After a very brief conversation, each returns to their respective apparatus while finishing lunch. They leave together and I imagine they are probably off to view an exhibit with a narrative that can be downloaded onto their phones.

Item: I come across some old handwritten letters from my daughter and feel a pull in my heart. Brief e-mails took the place of these, and now the telephone conversations I enjoy so much are being replaced by text messages.

Surrounded by the evidence that technology is the very air we breathe, I want to believe that Kennedy is right: the Internet *can* revitalize the potent feminist organizing tool of consciousness-raising. Perhaps new technologies will also offer other, even more powerful models for achieving feminist social transformation.

Promises and Perils

In the spirit of consciousness-raising, this chapter is intended to encourage questions about our experiences in the electronic environment that surrounds us. It begins with a brief overview of the perils as well as the promises of the Electronic Age, looks at the inescapable reality that the digital environment is male-dominated, and turns to some feminist responses to technology—from practical efforts to strengthen educational and employment opportunities for girls and women in scientific and technical fields to cyberfeminist imaginings of applications that seek to break down barriers between people and machines. The chapter also reviews the ways in which today's feminists are using blogs and social networks, exploring if and how these inform and empower us as individuals and members of political and social communities. It concludes with a discussion of approaches to a "liberatory" technology that depends upon continuing to ask questions about the media-saturated environment, the answers to which may guide us to real improvements in the lives of all people.

Turning On, Tuning In, But No Dropping Out

Earlier technologies, such as radio and television, had enormous cultural impact, but they could be turned off. Most people are now required to be online in some way for school or work. And if you don't have a job requiring technical skills, you'll need to be online to find position openings and present yourself to potential employers. Barbara Safani, owner of a career advisory firm in New York, suggests that "having a blog can be a good way to show that you are a thought leader," and that a YouTube video of a speech you have given may be the critical difference in landing a job. Be sure you are LinkedIn, but beware what you put on your Facebook page, which surely will be searched by recruiters.[3] Our leisure time, too, is spent consulting big and small computer screens to check on what is "trending" and to connect to the information and relationships made possible by the World Wide Web.

Feminists seeking to end oppression and create a safe and caring world for girls, women, and all other people need to ask what kind of "connections" are being created. To a character in Ali Smith's 2011 novel, the Internet is "a whole new way of feeling lonely."[4] This fictional persona could have been one of the many respondents who told researcher Sherry Turkle how isolated they remain despite their many online "friends." Turkle, a psychologist and MIT professor, has written a series of insightful books on how human relationships have been shaped by technology. She recounts conversations with people who are deeply worried about how to present themselves online. Creating and updating a personal profile for social networking sites is a source of anxiety for all genders. Finding or photoshopping the most becoming picture of oneself is the first challenge. Decisions regarding whether to describe athleticism (or lack thereof) and/or idiosyncratic taste in music, books and films, or revealing that you are an omnivore or vegetarian, conjure fears of rejection. Efforts to be accepted and admired produce an Internet populated with "fantasy selves." Based on their own behaviors, few believe that others are presenting authentically. Whether one presents an authentic or inauthentic self, for some there is *no* self without the Net. I once attended a women's studies conference at which a faculty member reported a student's comment during a several-day power outage: "Who am I if I am not online?"

Turkle describes the thin and fraying line between an authentic self and one's cyberself. That electronic self may be establishing "relationships" with many people online while also losing the capacity for intimacy that is the foundation of real human connections. Dependence on electronic communication can make in-person conversations seem overwhelming. Turkle relates an exchange with an interviewee experiencing some tension in a college friendship. Rather than visit the person who lives next door, the student turns to her computer to discuss the rift.[5]

In her recent writing Turkle also expresses deep concerns about the willingness of her respondents to accept and even advocate robotic substitutes for human interactions. While women have often been limited by caretaking responsibilities, I wonder how many would agree with the notion that a cyber caretaker for the elderly or young is "better than no caretaker," as some futurists opine is forthcoming.[6]

Nicholas Carr is another astute critic of the electronic environment.[7] His assessment of how the pathways in our brains are being rerouted by today's information overload is relevant to the consciousness-raising approach advocated in this book. Carr reprises the work of the 1960s media guru Marshall McLuhan, who observed that it is not only the increased content delivered through new technologies—from Gutenberg's printing press to television and computers—but also the technology itself that reshape our ways of thinking, doing and being. Of the Web environment, Carr says, "It is so much our servant that it would be churlish to notice that it is also our master."[8] The many studies he cites corroborate his observations of his own behaviors. Carr notes that the Internet has limited the ability to focus, listen and read carefully, and to think deeply and reflectively. These skills are vital to developing a feminist analysis that can serve as a foundation for social action.

Even the critics of technology continue to advance grandiose promises and inevitability. How age, immigration status, joblessness, poverty, illiteracy, race, location, physical and mental ability, and gender affect one's place in the virtual world is seldom discussed. Nor is there adequate acknowledgment that corporate interests control the Internet just as they have other generations of technology. The do-it-yourself environment of blogs and YouTube provides expanding markets for business, and open-access advocates meet barriers when they challenge private investors. Questioning the assumptions that underlie Internet use and dependence is an infrequent practice, but one that consciousness-raising can stimulate as we look at our experiences with technology, share our responses with others, and develop strategies to bring together rhetoric and reality.

You've Got Males: Gaming and Shaming on the Internet

As with all efforts to create social change, the struggle to "become new" is both inspired and mired in what came before. Although women played a vital role in the development of computing, most histories of computing[9] offer a parade of the notable men, with important contributions of female techno-scientists all but ignored. In the rapidly changing world of technology, male domination is a constant.

At the turn of the millennium, Melanie Millar published *Cracking the Gender Code: Who Rules the Wired World,* revealing how dominant and subordinate relationships are perpetuated on the Web.[10] Much of her analysis was drawn from a careful assessment of the values and themes in the influential magazine *Wired.* My own review of recent issues reveals that few changes have occurred over the fifteen years that have elapsed since Millar observed the publication's message of male hegemony on each page. Then and now *Wired* aims its ad-laden issues at readers who see themselves as part of a select group who need or crave the latest electronic gadgets and apps—and have the financial wherewithal to purchase these for personal or business use. The covers of most issues feature a male icon, or icon-to-be, making it clear that men are continuing to lead us into this brave new cyberculture, in which, as Millar observes, "certain entities shape what other, less powerful, individuals and groups do, think, desire."[11]

Gaming is an example of the ways in which the less powerful yield to such "shaping." In the early days of computing there were mundane tic-tac-toe and ping pong–type games, but gaming became widespread and commercially profitable when military combat, space warfare and female sexploitation took hold. At the risk of being identified with the disempowered, girls and women enter the fray to become part of the play. "Female characters are hypersexualized and workers discomforted in an industry known for its fratboy culture," writes Leah Burrows in a January 2013 article in the *Boston Globe.* She quotes game developer Marleigh Norton: "If you are a woman in the industry, there are all these little signals that you are not part of the club, that this is not your tribe. After time, it wears you down." Women are only 11 percent of game designers and 3 percent of programmers—yet they are half of the customers. Burrows' piece includes comments from one gamer who says she has seen female players "harassed, hit on, and asked to show their breasts via webcams."[12]

In her earlier work, *Life on the Screen*, Turkle recalls logging on to a MUD (multi-user dungeon, or domain) and unintentionally leaving out gender in her description of her avatar. Another participant presenting as a male asked her if she was "really an it," after which numerous offensive posts appeared. "The innuendos, double entendres and leering invitations were scrolling by at a fast clip.... When much later I did try playing a male character, I finally experienced that permission to move freely I had always imagined to be the birthright of men."[13] The experience reveals both the ill-informed incredulity that an individual may be transgender and the easy dominance of males, whether real or pretend, in the cyberworld.

Opportunities for growth can come about as a result of assuming a false identity. Turkle reports that some men become more sensitive to what it's like to be female, leading to improved relationships with women. But in other cases real relationships suffer while a partner is experimenting online. Some respondents equate their mate's pretend connections with infidelity.[14]

While for some pretending in cyberspace, including gender traveling, is a game, others really need practical advice on ways to be the gender they "know" they are. Information and positive support about being transgender can be found on the Internet, but they often must be separated from the curiosity of those playing with gender roles.

The use of the Internet by all genders for dating—and rating—has become so routine that it isn't often a topic for either eyebrow raising or consciousness-raising, even though it offers much to ponder. *New York Times* columnist Alex Williams quotes an interviewee who opines, "The word 'date' should almost be stricken from the dictionary. Dating culture has evolved to a cycle of text messages, each one requiring the code-breaking skills of a cold war spy to interpret."[15] Instead of dating, people "hang out" or "hook up" for entertainment and/ or sex. Williams' article reveals that interactions over the Internet are leaving those seeking a long-term relationship wondering how this will happen. To some, meeting online, perhaps through texting nude pictures of one another, is liberating—that is, until video and photographic images begin to circulate widely on social media. The practice is used for "slut shaming" women and girls for whom sexual expression remains far more risky than it is for males.[16]

The most profitable Internet industry is pornography.[17] Feminists are by no means united on whether this is a bad thing. Like "sexting," it can be—or be packaged as—an expression of freedom and choice, but there are endless examples that it is the ugly opposite. According to Malika Saada Saar, president of the Rebecca Project for Human Rights, there is a "cyber slave market that is being built up by Craig's List and other web sites." This ugly phenomenon occurs worldwide. Women and girls and men and boys are trafficked for sex, labor, organ parts and other nefarious purposes, often pulled into the trafficker' network through online posts advertising opportunities for legitimate work and even that all but forgotten concept, romance.[18]

Digital Divides and Dead Ends for Girls and Women

Most women are at the bottom of the technological pyramid. They are the majority of data-entry personnel and assembly-line workers putting together the tiny components on which the huge technological endeavor depends. They are also behind the closed doors opened by a Public Broadcasting System *Frontline* report revealing impoverished women scouring dumps to create a livelihood. They inhale dangerously toxic lead for many hours each day while "literally cooking circuit boards to salvage the computer chips, which have trace amounts of gold."[19]

Yet glowing reports of the benefits of technology to women abound. Such positive views were presented in a two-day conference sponsored by the Radcliffe Institute for Advanced Study at Harvard University. The institute's conferences are noted for in-depth discussions and diverse opinions, but at this event the unqualified benefits of technology were celebrated by nearly every speaker.[20] A panelist touted progress for women in India, where girls are motivated to complete secondary school so they can qualify for work in call centers. Later in his remarks, he acknowledged that these jobs usually end when women become pregnant because there are no affordable child-care centers. That other temporary workers replace them helps economic growth, but does not provide a path to secure livelihood for women and their families.

One common myth is that technology will make it easier to combine work and family life. In the United States families earning very high incomes can afford the nannies and other household help featured in popular books and films—and it is these highly paid and positioned professionals who also benefit the most from telecommuting possibilities. For full-time workers who are in the upper echelons of an organization, occasional or frequent work from home offers welcome variety, savings of time and money for traveling, and other advantages. But most work from home doesn't follow that scenario. It is more likely that a harried caretaker juggles hours on the computer with household chores and child care, often offering the children their own screens to keep them amused while s/he is working.[21]

While there are variations depending on geography and industry, the technological development model of global capitalism creates an ever-growing market for exploited labor. Because women serve as a reserve labor force, recruited or discarded depending on workplace needs, their plights are manipulated to meet the needs of the global economy. Carla Freeman's *High Tech and High Heels in the Global Economy* illuminates the cycle of global production and consumption through studying women working in the information-processing industry in Barbados. In contrast to agricultural labor or standing on their feet in assembly lines, working in a cubicle at a computer terminal promises a "professional" identity. This idea is reinforced by a dress code. The "business attire" donned by these women workers masks the fact that their low-wage work offers little possibility of personal or career growth. As with clerical work in the past, capitalism and paternalism are perpetuated in the preference for "ideal" female employees whose docility and patience make them well suited for repetitive, deskbound work.[22]

Whatever the drawbacks, girls and women have their noses pressed against the window of wonders that technology offers. How do they arrive at the place where they have both the technical skills and critical insights to shape technology for positive purposes?

STEMming the Tide: Advancing Girls and Women in the High-Tech World

Notions that girls are innately less capable than boys in mathematics and science have been refuted repeatedly. Rosalind Barnett and Caryl Rivers are among many scholars who have documented the fact that girls and boys have equal aptitudes for math and science.[23] Yet even as females have begun to exceed males in school graduation rates and academic performance in many fields, the problem of gender inequities in technology education and career choices has not gone away.[24] Science, technology, engineering and math (STEM) initiatives in schools and organizations such as the YWCA and Girl Scouts[25] have thus been created to increase girls' confidence and achievement.

Although the underrepresentation of girls and women in the STEM fields continues, some women have broken the silicon ceiling. As women have entered workplaces as systems analysts, programmers and technical designers, information exchanges and networking also have proliferated on the Web and through in-person conferences and workshops. The earliest online community for women in computing was Systers, founded in 1987 by Anita Borg, a leading advocate for women working in science and technology. This forum has over 3,000 members in at least 54 countries around the world and invites "technical women of all ages and at any stage of their studies or careers to participate." Borg also founded the Institute for Women and Technology with the intention of "changing the world for women and for technology."[26] The mission includes finding practical solutions to energy, clean water, health, environmental and literacy problems. The organization hosts the annual Grace Hopper Celebration of Women in Computing Conference, named in honor of another pioneer computer programmer, U.S. Navy Rear Admiral Grace Hopper.[27]

Supporting the presence and advancement of women in male-dominated fields does not necessarily guarantee the furthering of a progressive feminist agenda. The long list of corporations supporting the annual Grace Hopper conference, including American Express, Goldman Sachs, Facebook, Google, Cisco and many more can suggest that, as in other efforts to break the glass ceiling, women seeking to shape an alternative vision are often "incorporated" into corporate capitalism. Walking the narrow path between accepting the support of corporations and adopting the values and goals of these organizations is another important reason to apply the CR process to an analysis of how technology affects our own lives and those of other women and oppressed groups.

Cyberfeminism

Feminist technoscientists were quick to embrace what they saw as the revolutionary potential of the computer revolution. As had occurred in other fields, female pioneers in computing were rediscovered and celebrated. For example, in *Zeros + Ones: Digital Women + New Technologies,*[28] Sadie Plant delivers a paean to Ada Lovelace, who is considered by some to be the founder of scientific computing.[29] Plant uses Lovelace as the inspiration for her notion that women, with their multiple perspectives of reality, nonlinear thinking and affinity for interconnectedness, can use the Web to disrupt the unitary perspective of Western men. Previously dismissed as "zeros" or "non-beings," Plant suggests that women ally with machines to challenge hierarchies and create a new world beyond any we have envisioned.

Another champion of technological innovation is Donna Haraway, who urges feminists to embrace the new possibilities that can emerge from the blurring of boundaries between mind and body, male and female, human and machine. According to Haraway, cyborgs, hybrids of machines and organisms, can offer feminists a way of seeing and being that challenges all limitations. Gender itself will become open to interpretation and action beyond previously defined social constructs.[30]

An Australian group, VNS Matrix, may have been the first to use the term "cyberfeminism" in its 1991 manifesto.[31] Many artists and writers became involved with this movement and created brash productions that transgressed cultural norms and expressed anger, irony, humor and paradox. Most cyberfeminists advocated a "just do it" approach, shunning theory-making in favor of using the technology in bold ways. There was agreement regarding the powerful connections of the machine to the female body, as expressed by the line "the clitoris is a direct line to the matrix."[32] But in keeping with postmodernism's scorn of confining definitions, as they continued their work they chose to say only what cyberfeminism is *not*. They issued 100 anti-theses, playing upon Martin Luther's famous 95 theses condemning the papacy and paving the way for the Protestant Reformation. These included the following: "Cyberfeminism is not a fragrance"; "Cyberfeminism is not a fashion statement"; "Cyberfeminism is not about boring toys for boring boys"; "Cyberfeminism is not only one language"; "Cyberfeminism no es una banana."[33]

More than twenty years after these utopian pronouncements, a collection of essays assembled by Radhika Gajjala and Yeon Ju Oh reveals that the promise of global communities collaborating to generate revolutionary ideas has fallen far short of these ideals. Contributors to *Cyberfeminism 2.0* observe the continued marginalization of women as shapers of cyberspace.[34] Women are vastly underrepresented in programming and other creative positions at the same time that they are often exploited subjects. The essays note the need to increase both physical access to computers and the capacity to use them in empowering ways, modest goals given the flamboyant rhetoric and extravagant hopes of the early cyberfeminists.

The Girls Just Wanna Network: CR and Blogging

Yet there are reverberations of the cyberfeminist bravado in the widespread use of social media by feminists. Susannah Feinstein, my student scholar partner at the Brandeis University Women's Studies Research Center and co-conspirator on this chapter, and I have spent countless hours exploring the potential of the Internet to promote and sustain a women's liberation movement. We focused on blogging, a favorite feminist tool, to determine to what degree CR, and the social and political advocacy and action it is intended to guide, is occurring on the Internet.

Feminist blogging and social networking are important "places where we realize we are not crazy and not alone," as Shelby Knox wrote on *Bust Magazine*'s blog.[35] In common with CR, most bloggers speak from their lived experiences. Thousands of diary-style commentaries from girls and women appear on the Net each day. And, as happens in face-to-face consciousness-raising groups, an *esprit de corps* occurs as posters learn that "what happened to me" also happened to others. Online sharing, celebrating, venting and commiseration can take place anywhere, ending the geographical and social isolation that affect many girls and women. Affirmations like "you're my new girlfriend" are frequent and understandable—and sound a lot like the easy assumption of "sisterhood" of an earlier generation of feminists.

Wherever one begins (perhaps with the more than forty sites on the "blogroll" of the mainstream feminist publication, *Ms. Magazine*), you'll soon be led to dozens of other blogs. Facebook, Twitter and other social media sites also connect users to blogs.[36] Here's a capsule summary of some of the blogs we crawl through regularly.

Many of the most popular sites are addressed to younger feminists. Feministing[37] is the award-winning blog founded by Jessica Valenti in 2004.[38] The blog covers both U.S. and international issues and seeks to connect feminists on- and offline to activist organizations and projects. The site's graphic is a silhouette of a curvaceous woman raising her middle finger, a variation of the naked lady leaning back on her hands that is sometimes sported on the mudflaps of 18-wheeler trucks. Like Feministing, Jezebel[39] is a commercial site, supported by advertisers. It was created in 2007 by its owner, Gawker.com, for the female audience that made up the majority of visitors to one of the other media sites owned by the parent company. The blog is about "Celebrity, Sex, Fashion. Without Airbrushing," and claims it "will attempt to take all the essentially meaningless but sweet stuff directed our way and give it a little more meaning, while taking more of the serious stuff and making it more fun, or more personal, or at the very least the subject of our highly sophisticated brand of sex joke. Basically, we wanted to make the sort of women's magazine we'd want to read." FBomb is targeted specifically to teens. The founder of this active site, Julie Zeilinger, now in the class of 2015 at Barnard, said that she created the blog in 2009: "In this case the 'F Bomb' stands for 'feminist.' However, it also pokes fun at the idea that the term 'feminist' is so stigmatized— it is our way of proudly reclaiming the word. The fact that the 'F Bomb' usually refers to a certain swear word in popular culture is also not coincidental. The FBomb.org is for girls who have enough social awareness to be angry and who want to verbalize that feeling. The FBomb.org is loud, proud, sarcastic ... everything teenage feminists are today."[40]

The camaraderie in the blogging community is revealed in Zeilinger's account of her early efforts to establish the blog. She initially emailed contacts at Feministing and Jezebel and received advice, support and referrals that led to thousands of new readers. All three of these blogs are quick to note misogyny and racism, but they are far less judgmental of the ways consumer capitalism is linked to sexism. For example, Feministing has an editorial team that determines content, and a moderator reviews posts for "anti-feminist" material, including that which is deemed to be racist, classist, homophobic, transphobic, ableist, dismissive of others' appearances or opinions, or offensive in other ways. Feministing acknowledges that, although they seek advertising in line with the site's mission, most ads are accepted. While the editors decide which posts are acceptable, it is assumed that readers have the ability to evaluate advertising.

Valenti retired in 2011 at age 35, her blogging success having led to book contracts and speaking engagements. She is often named as a spokeswoman for third-wave feminism, with its emphasis on popular culture and sexuality. Like her mentors, Zeilinger's tone is irreverent and "sassy," and she, too, has written a book (which she advertises on her blog). All three blogs have a similar self-referential, "clubby" tone that reinforces a feeling of being part of a "feminist" in-group.

Blogs are both self-branded and branded by others. Feministe is one of the oldest feminist blogs designed and run by women. Its masthead reads "in defense of the sanctimonious Women's Studies set."[41] The *New York Times* About.com lists Feministe in its top 10 feminist and women's rights blogs addressing civil liberties with this description: "Feministe is the Mayberry of feminist blogs. While many emphasize fierce debates and tough ideological questions, Feministe is a community—a friendly community with lots of cat blogging, shuffled iTunes playlists, and even a few antifeminist mascots. This is not to say that it's any less feminist, or any less relevant; just that it's less front line and more front porch."[42]

Our Bodies, Our Blog

http://www.ourbodiesourblog.org demonstrates how the Internet can expand the spirit, voice and benefits of second-wave feminism to new audiences in the United States and worldwide. Like the classic print resource *Our Bodies Ourselves*, the official blog of the Boston Women's Health Book Collective aims to "advance health and human rights within a framework of values shaped by women's voices and a commitment to self-determination and equality."[43] Every aspect of women's health care, from particular gynecological conditions and illnesses to sexuality, menstruation, menopause, pregnancy, breast feeding and much more, is offered. There is also coverage of public health studies affecting girls and women, many focusing on comparative data within racial and ethnic groups, and much information on health care policy. The site is well organized and professional, and through links provided to videos, articles, books and other blogs, users can find material that can answer specific questions, serve as a personal guide to good health, and inspire political activism on social policy. Most of the information comes from U.S. sources, but there are links to the OBOS global partners who, through small groups working in a CR-like process, have revised and translated the work to meet the needs of women in countries around the world.[44]

Our Bodies Our Blog conjoins the traditional research approach of gathering citation-laden articles with the ease of access and opportunity for immediate comments that the Internet provides. It exemplifies how one of feminism's most long-lasting and life- and institution-changing organizations can continue and enhance its mission through electronic means. Other long-standing feminist organizations, including NOW and Planned Parenthood, are also using social networks to get their messages to both established and new audiences.

Many feminist blog sites are gathering places for like-minded people to build community and solidarity around particular perspectives and identities. The Crunk Feminist Collective (CFC)[45] blog provides "a space of support and camaraderie for the hip hop generation feminists of color, queer and straight, in the academy and without." Drawing inspiration from black Southern culture and women-of-color feminism, the word "crunk" (a contraction of crazy and drunk) was chosen "because we are drunk off the heady theory of feminism that proclaims that another world is possible." Viva La Feminista,[46] founded in 2007 by Veronica Arreola, a Chicago-based activist, describes itself as being at the intersection of motherhood, feminism and Latina issues. The spirit of the blog is captured by this comment: "My feminism is not rooted in mothering, rather my mothering is fueled by my feminism."[47] Racialicious[48] blogs about the intersection of race and popular culture, with comments by and about Asians, African Americans, Latinas and Native Americans.

There are blogs for male feminists, too. The same About.com "Top 10 Feminist and Women's Rights Blogs" that listed Feministe also included Hugo Schwyzer's blog.[49] There are numerous misogynist bloggers, so Schwyzer was initially embraced by feminists eager to have male allies—until he began sharing his history of abusive behaviors, including engaging in sex with his students and plotting a murder-suicide with an ex-girlfriend. A religious Christian, Schwyzer seeks atonement and speaks of restorative justice, but many of his former supporters aren't buying it. One blogger who followed the controversy surrounding Schwyzer cautions, "The Internet has made it somewhat easier for male feminists to gain legitimacy, sometimes without necessarily deserving it and at an expedited rate. The movement may be too eager to latch onto men who 'get it' in hopes that they will serve as spokesmen to the rest of the world."[50] Schwyzer maintained his "feminist" blogging long after these revelations and criticisms, but in July 2013 he reported that he would be taking an extended leave from his blog.

Help Yourself—and Others

Self-help groups proliferate on the Internet. There are ample guidelines for accessing or creating an Internet group, exchanging information on everything from common hobbies and vocations to health and illness, including addiction to the Internet.[51] Sufferers report sleepless nights and the inability to limit the number of hours spent gaming, shopping or viewing pornography.[52] Groups discussing mental and physical illnesses abound. Some are moderated by professionals; more are forums for reaching out and offering advice from the "expert" perspective of one who has gone through diagnoses and treatments.[53]

There seem to be more plusses than minuses regarding the benefits of online groups. A close friend of blessed memory received much-needed support from a breast cancer support group. The connections became so powerful that members decided to meet in person in Arizona, and Joan chose to spend her modest savings on the trip. Shortly before the gathering was to take place, however, one of the members had a recurrence of her cancer. Her dependence on support from the group went beyond what some could give. The event was cancelled and the group soon disbanded. A happier result is the Internet version of a work group, akin to those discussed in chapter II. A young lawyer with whom I am acquainted engaged in Internet informational exchanges around work issues that eventually became a friendship network. In this case, undoubtedly because the issues initially discussed were not as emotion-laden, a face-to-face reunion was a success and strengthened the depth of the connections.

Bloggers and others exchanging information on the Internet resist cognitive dissonance. In common with choices most people make in their print and television news sources, they visit the sites where like-minded people can reinforce each other's outrage or enthusiasm. Those who differ with a post are often not seeking to shape discourse in a more nuanced way; rather, on sites with no editorial control, "f-bombs" are frequently dropped (and the "f" does not usually stand for feminism). After visiting many sites over a period of time, the polarization becomes tediously apparent—resounding cheers from believers in a posting, and reverberating insults from the detractors. Based upon my own surfing and the material reported in chapter IV, there is sparse evidence that the Internet is not yet a space in which to work out differences, find consensus and explore alternatives for action—all part of the consciousness-raising process advocated in this book.

Calls for quick action prevail over discussion and debate. Many sites devoted to or including feminist issues urge action, usually in the form of signing electronic petitions and letters and sending donations to fund continued organizing efforts. Some campaigns have produced specific changes. After receiving hundreds of protest messages, JCPenney pulled its fall 2011 sweatshirt with the message "I'm Too Pretty to Do Homework So My Brother Has to Do It For Me."[54] Following the company's decision, the blogosphere was filled with charges that JCPenney had yielded to the "politically correct" and that the protesters were humorless, "consumer Nazis," and so forth.

On a Hopeful Note

An acquaintance of Susannah's commented on a cause that no longer interested him: "That's so fifteen minutes ago." That dismissive remark is typical of some who are impatient to move on to the next thing that's "trending" online, but I think such individuals are in the minority. Most young people want to make a difference and are using the tools they know best. Rather than simply decry inadequate or misguided efforts, it would be helpful to acknowledge the positive impulses that underlie them. The small group, whether online or face-to-face, is a place to begin.

Social media sites are still fairly new forums. At the moment there is a large gap between personal sharing and the reflection and analysis needed to formulate considered action to challenge and reverse sexism and all forms of oppression. A new generation has the wherewithal to use technology, but it does not yet have the experience of organizing to create long-term, meaningful change. We have not had a major progressive movement in the United States for many years. There are calls for the adoption of tactics that earlier movements used with positive results—mass demonstrations, boycotts, speak-outs, strikes, sit-ins, and so on. Electronic communication can expedite these, but such actions are not in and of themselves valuable; they need to be chosen strategically and be part of a long-term plan that develops from and is sustained by participatory, grassroots organizing.

While it is unlikely that thoughtful strategies can be formulated among several hundred "friends," it is possible that small online working groups can engage in respectful dialogue and debate. The discussions on Google regarding the effectiveness of small-group work online suggest that much must still be done to capture the spontaneity, relational capacities and depth of interchanges of face-to-face connections. The Internet can be a vehicle to posit and implement a variety of short-term and long-term projects. The ongoing process of CR can help ensure that strategies are assessed and appropriately revised as participants learn from successful and not-so-successful efforts.

The controversies that emerged in response to SlutWalk offer an opportunity to consider how we can use the Internet in an anticipatory rather than reactive way. SlutWalk is a movement that originated in Toronto as a rejoinder to the comment by a police officer there that women could avoid sexual assault if they didn't dress like "sluts." The Toronto march in which women in skimpy clothing—and their supporters—gathered to confront victim-blaming led to a number of other such demonstrations in Australia, England, and several cities in the United States.[55]

Women of color were among those who proffered a range of objections. One black woman said, "We don't have the privilege to play on destructive representations burned in our collective minds, on our bodies and souls for generations." Another woman opined that using the word "slut" could not be subversive to the patriarchal culture that has provided its meaning: "the word 'slut' is hateful and violent and has never belonged to us. 'Slut' belongs to rapists and misogynists and pornographers." Yet another response critiqued the fixation of the SlutWalks on questions of individual choice: the "'I can wear what I want' feminism ... is intentionally devoid of an analysis of power dynamics." And there were many more.[56]

The rejoinders from some planners that "there were women of color on the organizing committee" reveals how much more reflection needs to accompany our activism. No person or even a number of people for whom dark skin is an attribute can speak for all who share that aspect of identity. Of course, the same observation applies to people with disabilities, various age groups, or members of particular religious and ethnic groups.

But the World Wide Web makes it possible to gather diverse responses *before* taking action. A call for suggestions on feminist blogs can provide an outline of a proposed action—for example, "This is an action we are considering for the following reasons.... Would this be a response with which you would resonate? Why? Why not? Who and what are we overlooking? What other responses might be more effective? Can you suggest individuals and groups with whom we could strategize and work?" A look at one city's planning for an upcoming SlutWalk reveals that criticisms are being heard and receiving responses, and comments are being actively solicited regarding the "many concerns" organizers know that people have.[57]

Small consciousness-raising groups on the Internet and in person are spaces in which feminists can have necessary conversations on the many different approaches that shape feminism and feminist activism. Engaging in the CR process can remind us of the line between feminism as fundamental social change and using women's issues as entertainment or a marketing strategy. This can help feminists move from acknowledging the role social media play in making us "realize we are not crazy and not alone" to understanding that those feelings of isolation and craziness are rooted in structural injustice.

Consciousness-raising on the Internet also has the potential to rectify the now-questioned notion of earlier feminists that CR was a kind of training ground for activism and, once experienced, did not need to be repeated. Electronic communication can bring women back to the consciousness-raising process again and again, enhancing opportunities for a sustained women's liberation movement. That is the approach that brought online feminist activists, some of whom founded the blogs described above, to a conference at the Barnard Center for Research on Women in June 2012. They produced a report titled "#FemFuture: Online Revolution" for Barnard's New Feminist Solutions series, detailing steps to affirm and strengthen "the online feminist world [that] constitutes both a 'communication arm' for the contemporary feminist movement and an inexhaustible force continually radicalizing and changing its institutionalization."[58] The planners know that there are many intersectional movements within feminism, that the need for funding will collide with the more radical versions, and that efforts to create a coordinated infrastructure may conflict with the decentralization that characterizes both feminist and online communities. Paradoxes abound, but the conference and published report have brought issues to the fore that can continue to be addressed in developing support for a women's liberation movement in the digital age.

Keeping the Feminism in Cyberfeminism

Shortly after the Cyberfeminist International conference mentioned above, one of the participants, feminist artist and activist Faith Wilding, prepared a considered response to the proceedings in an article titled "Where Is Feminism in Cyberfeminism?"[59] While praising the process that brought together women from eight countries and varied political, ethnic and social backgrounds to share ideas and leadership, Wilding is critical of the unwillingness of the attendees to take action that would lead to feminist praxis. The group even declined to define what they meant by "cyberfeminism," an explanation that Wilding believes is foundational to building an effective organizing strategy to achieve political goals. She also laments the lack of knowledge that younger women have of previous feminist movements, an unawareness that prevents building on past successes and causes a repetition of old errors while thinking that something new is being done.

Cyberfeminists believed they were breaking new ground, but those familiar with feminist history can hear echoes of the not-too-distant past. Haraway's work is reminiscent of the then-cutting-edge writing in the early days of the second wave of feminism. In her *Dialectic of Sex,* Shulamith Firestone embraced a future made possible by technology in which men would not be necessary to the reproductive process, thus eliminating the oppressive structure of the patriarchal nuclear family.[60] A sensation when it first appeared, Firestone was demonized for her searing analysis, and the author and her important contribution to feminist theory are remembered primarily for the controversy they sparked. The VNS Matrix statement can be viewed as a "stream of consciousness-raising." Its bombastic language recalls another second-wave writer, Mary Daly, who sought to reclaim words that had been corrupted by the patriarchy. (Daly's polemical works, including *Pure Lust* and *Gyn/Ecology*, valorized all things female, particularly, like the VNS statement, the most "essential" source of sexual power, the clitoris.)

Whether in the 1960s, 1990s or the present, the energy, intelligence, vision and creative ways in which feminists have challenged oppression is exciting to read and behold. But I concur with Wilding's call to her sister cyberfeminists to conjoin disruptive actions against patriarchal power with the creation of a thoughtful, flexible agenda for *feminist* change. Wilding urges that the potential presented by new technologies be connected to the "material, political, emotional, sexual and psychic conditions arising from women's differentialized social construction and gender roles" to build a worldwide movement for social justice and freedom for women.[61]

Liberatory Responses to Technology

I also share Wilding's belief that language informs action. From the first pages of this book, I've chosen to use words that can describe a vision of social justice, grounding my discussion in bell hooks' definition of "feminism" and Kathie Sarachild's explanation of "consciousness-raising." In the same spirit, I've selected the word "liberatory," meaning "tending, or serving to liberate."[62] Feminism and cyberfeminism are struggles against sexist injustice and call for a technology that is democratic, participative and inclusive, not only as a promise but also as a reality for women, for all people.

Consciousness-Raising Starts with Questions

A good place to begin envisioning and implementing a liberatory technology is to apply the consciousness-raising approach of sharing and asking questions. Exchanging our own experiences and insights about the present and potential, positive and problematic role technology is playing in our lives can lead us to choose and use what is empowering and take action against what is limiting and demeaning. Such questions might include the following:

How have our own lives been changed by new technologies? What technologies, old and new, do we use each day? Newspapers, television, books, e-books, land-line telephones, cell phones and other handheld devices? How much time do you spend on which technology each day? How much is related to your employment? How much to your life outside work or school?

How many jobs for women has information technology (IT) provided? Where in the economy and in various geographical locations are these jobs? Are you or other women you know working as data enterers, software designers, systems analysts, programmers, installers, assemblers, trainers, or telemarketers? What positions do you or they occupy in the organizations? Are these positions full- or part-time? With or without benefits? Has the use of computers and other technologies had an impact on your health or that of others you know?

The Internet is often described as an arena in which to dissolve distinctions of gender, race, ethnicity, class, age, geography and other categories. Is this your experience? How would you answer the question "How does technology advance the status of women worldwide?" What is your fantasy of technologies that could make a difference in your life and the world we live in, or would like to live in?

What information do you seek on the Web? Do you use the Internet to find out about health and sexuality? Do you use the Web for dating/hookups? Do you use the Web to learn about political and social issues, including feminism? Where do you go for information? What have you learned? How do you know whether the information is accurate?

How do you connect with other people on the Web? What words would you use to characterize conversations you've had with other people online? If you are a Facebook or other social network user, how do you describe the work and/or personal contacts you've made on the Web? How many friends have you made? Are there differences between these friendships and the face-to-face friendships you have? Has the Internet deepened your capacity for friendship?

Have you planned meetings through and/or on the Web? Have you planned actions on social issues through and/or on the Web? Do you use the Web for dialogue and debate? Have you used the Web to evaluate meetings and actions? To strategize and reach out to other groups? How does the Web facilitate the reflection, dialogue, debate, planning, and action (and then the repetition of this cycle) that is required for sustained social and political change? If this isn't happening to the extent that is necessary, how can we make it happen to build a stronger feminist movement?

Transforming Lives Through Information

Faith Wilding calls for coalitions of women with technical expertise and feminist understanding to form working relationships. She urges collaboration among academics, enlightened private-sector workers, community activists and others.

Shared reflections on the ways in which technology impacted their lives were foundational to the successful programs Virginia Eubanks created with women who resided in and/or frequented the Troy, New York, YWCA.[63] Eubanks began her work with a vision of providing computer skills to women. What she discovered was that most of the women already knew a lot about technology, and they also knew that it was not an empowering force in their lives. Many of the participants who joined the WYMSM (Women at the YWCA Making Social Movement) were employed in low-wage, physically taxing and sometimes dangerous jobs. Since much of the work was part-time most were still dependent on public assistance in which computing technology was utilized to monitor their lives. For one example, recipients of benefits reported that they faced the *back* of a computer when they visited social service agencies, and had little personal interaction with the person collecting data on their case. Such experiences had stifled feelings that political engagement would be an effective strategy for creating change in their lives or in the larger society.

When Eubanks got to know the real women in her program, as opposed to the "hypothetical" participants of her research proposal, she reframed her project. She shifted her focus from an emphasis on increasing technical skills to an exploration of the possibilities and barriers technology presents for meaningful citizen participation and social justice.

Eubanks utilized methodologies of Paolo Freire, Myles Horton and other community educators who used consciousness-raising, or conscientization, in their work with disenfranchised and oppressed people. (Their theories are discussed in chapter V.) She began with the lived experiences of the women involved in the WYMSM initiative. The insights that came from their shared analysis of everyday events shaped the three major projects: a Community Technology Center, an online Women's Resource Directory and the creation of a computer game called "Beat the System: Surviving Welfare."

WYMSM participants created what Eubanks calls "popular technology" based upon examining their lived experience. As they developed their tech center, electronic files of women's resources, and games to assist themselves and others in working with social service providers, they become engaged citizens. The technology will be different tomorrow, but the sense of agency, self-worth and political understanding reported by the program participants are attributes that can make a lasting difference in their personal lives and community activism.

The Troy YWCA initiative is an example of a successful effort by a small group of women working to apply technology in order to make a difference in their lives and to create feminist models and approaches that could empower others. Can their efforts inspire a broader group of women and their allies online and/or face-to-face?

Liberatory Libraries

Libraries are among the most promising settings for learning about the Internet and exploring positive ways in which technology can be applied to personal and societal issues. Public libraries exist to serve ALL people in the community. Indeed, one of the first destinations for newcomers to the United States is the public library. Many offer adult literacy, ESL and GED classes, book discussions, poetry readings, children's programming, homework help and guidance in the effective use of computers and the Web. Every library that receives government funding is required on a regular schedule to assess the needs of residents and create a plan to meet those needs. Although most people don't know about this process (and, unfortunately, many libraries perform the assessment and planning process in a pro forma way), this is a ready-made opportunity for feminists and other community activists to gain an active role in shaping their libraries' collections, programs and services that can empower individuals and enliven neighborhoods.

My own work as a librarian was changed by the feminist consciousness-raising process. Like Eubanks, I began listening to and learning from others. Rather than show and tell what *I* knew, I asked information searchers about the experiences and approaches they had in trying to locate resources. The process of asking questions about information follows logically from the consciousness-raising approach, and it can begin to reverse the feelings many express of being overwhelmed by data and uncertain about its reliability and pertinence.

To the questions about our relationship with technology listed previously, we can add others that will help girls, women and all people gather information that is useful to their own lives and communities: What interests and concerns led you to look for information on this topic? What do you know already? What more do you want/need to know? Where might you look to discover that? Do these resources satisfy your questions? Why or why not? If you're not satisfied with what you've found, where else might you look?

Most of my own career was spent in an academic library and I used these questions as the foundation for a course I developed with a colleague titled "Information Searching and Media Communication," through which students learned how to find, evaluate and present information. In the spirit of Wilding's suggestions for expanded collaboration, the course was integrated with three other first-year requirements, and students and faculty learned together how to gather and apply relevant resources to make learning meaningful and exciting.

Students became confident library users, but also discovered that information is everywhere—in social agencies, museums, and government offices, and also among groups and individuals with ideas and expertise. The students utilized the interview techniques they learned about through class readings and discussions, and developed skills in using technology—cameras and video and audio recorders—to capture, edit and present their findings, often in collaborative projects that allowed them to learn from and with each other. The latest developments in computer technology make such projects even easier to complete, yet success depends on continually questioning the assumptions and aspirations of your own and others' productions.

As the semester progressed, we added new questions to our searches: Who created and disseminated this publication or film or other media? For whom? And for what purposes? What motivated their approach to gathering and presenting the information? Would I have emphasized the same points? Does this information prompt a reaction? How will I respond? No one left the course without discovering that information is shaped by individuals and institutions with particular interests, and that we can interact with, challenge, and shape the information environment.

These very ideas have resurfaced in current discussions on teaching critical information-searching skills in the digital age. Essays in *Civic Life Online: Learning How Digital Media Can Engage Youth*[64] suggest that the techniques used in that class—taking a research-based position, structuring arguments, asking probing question and analyzing responses—are relevant now. Discussing approaches, findings and new questions in a group setting is a powerful way to enhance learning.

Information Searching as Consciousnes-Raising: Misinformation and Missed Information

Consciousness-raising not only informs the search process, but every information search can also be a consciousness-raising experience. As a dean of library services and professor of women's studies, I was eager to integrate "computer literacy" into the women's studies curriculum. After one of the first workshops held in the newly developed computer lab, I received a call from the head of Academic Computer Services reporting that students were accessing "porn." Yes, as soon as they typed in "women," the links appeared to numerous sites exploiting women. That particular CR exercise can be repeated by

Googling the word "women" right now. To quickly learn how racism and sexism are conjoined, Google "dating sites" and discover where to find "hot" Asian, black, Latina or other groups of women eager to date white men.

Even before the Internet, I was fond of saying (perhaps more often than my students wished to hear) that "too much is not enough." As the abundance and immediacy of messages increase, so, too, do misinformation and disinformation. Most information seekers are content with a little information, and many do not question whether it is accurate. Recently a conservative relative who is still trying to convert me forwarded to me a series of statements about the benefits of individualism and free enterprise enumerated under a picture of Bill Cosby. But these were not Bill Cosby's words.[65] Another example was the story of the exploitation of workers in Apple factories in China. While there are countless examples of poor labor practices in outsourced American manufacturing, National Public Television had to retract a story on *This American Life* because the specific allegations reported were not accurate.[66]

When information searchers seek documentation they are often led to the stories of the rich and powerful, usually white men. Coalitions of cyberlibrarians, archivists, historians, community organizers and others working for change can recover our past, capture our present and build our future through gathering oral histories, not only of recognized women leaders but also of the "ordinary" women whose lives are the foundation of the feminist movement. Loretta Ross, an activist nationally and internationally since the 1970s, and since 2005 the director of the SisterSong Women of Color Reproductive Health Collective, the largest multiracial women's network in the country, is a great model. After her life's work was assembled by archivists at the Sofia Smith Archives at Smith College, she and the staff realized how few other voices of women of color were in that and other collections. Ross subsequently began to gather the remarkable stories of her sisters whose courage and commitment shaped the women's movement.[67] Technology has expedited access to many of these documents, which are available online to those who have access to computers. Of course, one place where everyone can find that access is the public library.

Only Connect

Consciousness-raising is a tool to connect us, one to the other, small group to small group, small groups to a larger social movement. I've answered the question posed at the start of this chapter—"Can technology offer a new and, perhaps, even more powerful model for achieving feminist social transformation?"—with a resounding MAYBE.

Responses to technology have run the gamut from those who see limitless possibilities for technoscience to shape a positive feminist future to those who view it as a way to reinforce patriarchal divisions, and many, many others are positioned at various places along the continuum. But there is no one whose life has not been changed dramatically by the application of computers to every aspect of economic and social organization—and it is not going away. Women around the globe have experienced both the promise and the perils of technology. The challenge for those seeking to build a movement against sexist oppression is to ensure that technology's uses accentuate the former and limit the latter.

Feminists needn't be resigned to the inevitability of technological change and can approach new applications and their uses with some skepticism. At the same time, we needn't join an either/or camp. We can keep asking questions of technology and its impact on our economic, environmental and spiritual lives, and how technological "innovations" affect power relationships. We can assess technologies and their roles in society and insist that they be used in ways that serve people over profits.

We can become advocates for the kind of popular technology Eubanks proposes and modeled through her Troy, New York, project with YWCA women. We can get involved in shaping our local libraries using mechanisms that are already in place to ensure community participation. We can learn who is being served and how—and support these fundamentally democratic institutions so they can serve even more people more effectively. We can put technology in a larger context. Designing a webpage, making a PowerPoint presentation and similar skills and techniques are useful and important, but if you don't have anything meaningful and substantive to say, presentation graphics won't help. Blogging as a way to vent frustration has some value, but it is unlikely to build sustained commitments to feminist action that require thoughtful reflection and deeper conversations. We can learn from the past. Wilding urged cyberfeminists to refrain from ahistorical thinking that results in repeating the past while thinking you are creating the future. The fascination with the newest and latest obscures the deeper political analysis that is required to determine if and how technologies will be used to provide opportunities—or reinforce hegemonic relations.

The technotopians of today celebrate the computer and the World Wide Web as the means to spread knowledge and empowerment. But not that long ago public-access cable television's journey was also embraced as a site for free speech and community building. The trajectory of cable television from liberatory promise to commodification is being repeated with the Internet.[68] There is little debate on ways to regulate the commercialism and monopolization of all forms of communication. But perhaps it is not too late to consider how every form of information generation and delivery can be used to advance participatory democracy, and to shape and reshape policies and practices that support this. Community-supported television is still an option for organizers, just as newspapers, leaflets, magazines and other resources can be chosen as the right organizing tool for a particular action.[69]

Many college students are electing to study communications, a field that covers many topics, from writing, speaking, public relations, and advertising to using social networks to create and deliver information. Programs, especially at the community college and undergraduate level, emphasize applied skills. We can call for instruction, beginning in elementary schools, that explores critical thinking about the role of technology in a democratic society. Discussions can include access, free speech, whose voices are being heard and where, propaganda and opinion formation, censorship by government and commercial interests, breaches of privacy and more. Exploring such issues means that the promise of cyberdemocracy can be realized in the daily practices of a civil society.

Electronic Meetings AND Face to Face

Skype and other technologies permit the online face-to-face sharing of important information and exchange of technical skills. Video can maintain and broaden contacts, including global connections. Technologies do not yet provide the ease, intensity and emotional authenticity of in-person communication, although improvements are ongoing and hold promise for the expansion of CR on the Internet. But the intimacy of in-person connections will always be most effective.

Eubanks knew that the Troy, New York, YWCA would be the right setting for her work because of the powerful feeling of community she received from the weekly suppers held there. The power of small groups utilizing a CR approach was affirmed as the WYMSM activities developed: "The group's 'endless meetings' were not conceived specifically as outcomes or deliverables when we began the project, but in retrospect, group members agreed it was the meetings—the camaraderie, attention to process, willingness to share, and fellowship—that provided the most important, meaningful, and lasting impact of our collective work."[70]

Like Eubanks' YWCA project, the Cyberfeminists International conference described earlier utilized an organizing strategy characteristic of CR. As befits a group of pioneer technoscientists, a small ad hoc group gathered online input from others in organizing the event, shared and applied technical skills throughout the meetings, and remained in electronic contact as a "cyberfeminist cell" after the conference. But Wilding attributes the success of the meetings to the fact that discussions of technology were embedded in a collaborative feminist group process and states:

> The face to face interactions were experienced as much more intense and energizing than the virtual communications, and forged different degrees of affinity between various individuals and subgroups, while at the same time they made all kinds of differences more palpable. Brainstorming and spontaneous actions seemed to spring more readily from face-to-face meetings. The opportunity for immediate question and answer sessions and extended discussion after the lectures also enabled more intimate and searching interchanges than are usually possible through on-line communications. Most important, all presentations, hands-on training, and discussions took place in a context of intense debate about feminism, which produced a constant awareness of the lived relationship of women and technology.[71]

Conclusions

As I prepared this chapter I was struck by the contradictions of the Internet-driven world. After immersing myself in the blogosphere and reading extensively, my reservations about this supposed panacea grew. Then I read the "#FemFuture: Online Revolution" report and my enthusiasm returned—momentarily. Soon I was engaged once more in the concerns that have kept the dream of a feminist revolution from being realized. Whose "online revolution" is being put forth? To what extent did the visions of women of color, poor women, disabled women, old women, women outside the U.S. shape the definitions of terms such as "radical" and "transformative" used in the report? Did the 21 educators, writers and activists who created the report represent "online feminism," or an elite definition of that concept? Can funding by corporations be compatible with the radical and transformative?

There seemed to be one area of agreement among report-writers and critics. Consciousness-raising was cited as the tool to reveal and speak to differences and to explore ways to build honest, respectful human connections that can be applied to creating an electronic environment and feminist future that is liberating for all people.

IV

I and We: Consciousness-Raising, Mutual Aid and Participatory Democracy

The process of moving from the personal to the political is cyclical. Events in our own lives illuminate our understanding of the larger society, but the barriers to implementing a new vision frequently bring us back to our starting point. The material in this chapter blends hope and frustration: promising initiatives, occasional retreats, and painful pushbacks.

The chapter begins with a look at how feminism and democratic practices are intertwined and considers some obstacles to realizing democracy and a feminist vision, particularly economic inequality and token participation. Hopeful initiatives by feminists and their progressive allies include the promotion of active and authentic civic engagement, which has roots in women's associations, neighborhood groups and mutual aid. Yet many feminist insights and practices have been subsumed by other political movements or undermined by bureaucratic procedures. This chapter reaffirms small-group organizing and consciousness-raising approaches that can expose these usurpations and advance the participatory democracy that is an essential goal of the women's liberation movement.

Wrestling with Angels:
Feminism as an Expression of Democracy

The transformation was alchemical. A stunning lucidity arose, almost as if by magic, from the stark discomfort and pain we expressed. The resonance was so thick it was almost palpable. As woman after woman reclaimed her voice, we were giving the right of assembly a new meaning. But of course it was not the revelation of secrets or the expression of feelings by themselves that was transformative. As we spoke and listened, we were bringing a new framework to the discussion. Suddenly we could delineate a political meaning linking our stories together. We realized how many subjects considered personal had political significance. We began to see that even the trivialization of our concerns was a political act, depriving us of dignity and insight. One by one, as our secrets were revealed, a new picture of our lives was emerging, and with this a new way of seeing society. As we placed our own lives and the issues we faced at the center of the national debate, we were creating a new vision of the entire political landscape.[1]

Susan Griffin's *Wrestling with the Angel of Democracy* describes how feminism brought her to a deeper understanding of democracy. Griffin's book interweaves the story of her own life with reflections on American democracy, revealing how the personal and the political inform each other and become fused in the choices we make and actions we take as individuals and members of society.

Griffin's initial understanding of democracy was shaped by her parents' encouragement to express her opinions, ask questions, and be an independent thinker. Then came her mother's struggle with alcoholism and her father's inability to balance his work as a firefighter with the care of his two daughters. Each girl was sent to live with a different relative. Griffin contrasts her earlier upbringing with the "monarchy" of her grandmother's home, yet celebrates the religious tolerance she discovered there. Her intellectual growth developed from reading the books her beloved older sister shared and later the volumes recommended by the well-educated and politically active parents of a girlhood friend. She writes of discovering heroes, including Thomas Jefferson, Ralph Waldo Emerson, Walt Whitman, the Grimke sisters, Rose Schneiderman, and Frances Perkins, and the influence of jazz, civil rights and new left politics.

But it wasn't until Griffin discovered feminist consciousness-raising that she had a visceral experience of democracy. Her CR group was key to the process of finding a deeper understanding of the roots of perennial concerns and the sources of personal courage and political activism. She imagines that her experiences in the burgeoning women's movement were akin to those of the founders of the American Revolution who gathered at the Raleigh Tavern, exchanging differences, airing opinions, negotiating the terms of their independence, and "summoning the courage to stand by the truth."[2] In declaring "all men are created equal," the Declaration of Independence did not include slaves or women, but embedded in those words was a promise that later freedom struggles insisted would be honored. Griffin and other feminists and allied groups remain committed to keeping that dream of democracy alive.

Formal Democracy or Genuine Engagement?

Whether women will move beyond the formal democracy of the vote to genuine engagement in the political process is a critical question both in the United States and around the globe. In nearly every country in the world women now have full suffrage.[3] It is moving to hear stories and see pictures of women and other previously disenfranchised groups finally exercising the right to vote, but the images may mask an actual lack of meaningful participation. Women make up 51 percent of the world's population but are just 20 percent of legislative bodies.[4] Even if they have voting rights, many women, due to tradition, lack of education and other factors, do not exercise them. In some countries quota systems have been legislated or have been adopted by political parties as a mechanism to promote equal representation. As the numbers become more balanced, problems remain because women may not have developed effective political skills. While it is important to have all constituencies fully represented, defining oneself as female does not mean that a woman will advance a feminist social justice agenda. Under some quota systems wives and relatives of elected officials may be chosen for political posts on the basis of their docility and loyalty to family or kinship systems.[5] Social and political institutions that include women but do not reflect their needs or modes of participation often leave patriarchal arrangements unchallenged.

Income Inequality Means Gender Inequality

In 2011 the White House Council on Women and Girls issued the first comprehensive report on the status of women in the United States since 1963.[6] The document puts a woman's face on the growing gap between rich and poor across genders. A small percentage of high-earning women who are highlighted in the media suggests that women are "making it," but here are the facts: women are earning only 77 cents to every dollar earned by men; there is an ever-growing number of women raising children without a partner; single mothers are more likely to live in poverty; women continue to be concentrated in lower-paying traditionally female occupations and perform more household work, family care and unpaid volunteer work. Black and Hispanic women have the greatest challenges.

Louis Brandeis, the U.S. Supreme Court justice after whom the university where I am now affiliated is named, said this: "We may have democracy in this country, or we may have wealth concentrated in the hands of the few, but we can't have both."[7] According to the nonpartisan Congressional Research Service, the United States has the most unequal income distribution of all major industrialized nations, and the gap has widened since the 1970s, with the income of the top 1 percent increasing by 275 percent.[8] Between 1992 and 2007, the top 400 earners increased their income by 329 percent, while their taxes decreased by 37 percent.[9]

Detailed and disquieting statistics are presented in *The Unheavenly Chorus*, a thorough compendium of the decades-long trend of declining citizen participation in the political process due to economic inequalities.[10] The myriad participative organizations that represented a broad array of interests in an earlier United States have given way to powerful lobbying groups that are not membership-based; in fact, the majority have *no* members. The political influence of these groups is determined by money. The most effective have plentiful full-time staff working in their Washington offices. Once a major force in shaping political life, trade unions have declined precipitously. Organizations representing hospital workers, teachers and government workers are trying to hold the line on middle-class wages and benefits, but there is no mass movement that aims for solidarity across work areas and social classes. Unskilled workers and the poor, groups in which women are the majority, have no organized representation. *The Unheavenly Chorus* demonstrates that both wealth and political participation follow a generational pattern. Those with the greatest economic and social status are the most likely to be politically engaged, and their children inherit both income and political and social advantage. The authors conclude that "the disparities in political voice across various segments of society are so substantial and so persistent as to preclude equal consideration."[11] It is impossible to speak of women's equality and democracy without addressing the great and growing economic divide and how it is perpetuated by power arrangements that need to be revealed, analyzed and addressed—starting, as consciousness-raising does, with our own lives.

Drawing from Consciousness-Raising

According to Melissa Harris-Perry, "Citizens want more than a fair distribution of resources; they also desire—and are willing to sacrifice for—accurate, meaningful and mutual recognition of their humanity and uniqueness."[12] Consciousness-raising helps us understand the ways that sexism and other forms of oppression are embedded in social institutions. The process of looking at the meaning of their own experiences can lead people to resist repressive authority and work collectively to change their conditions. That is the message of Harris-Perry's book *Sister Citizen: Shame, Stereotypes and Black Women in America*.[13] The author utilized a consciousness-raising approach to gain responses from forty-three African American women regarding stereotypes or myths about black females that they felt other people may hold: "I then asked them to write down the 'facts' about black women as they saw them. They worked in 'focus groups' and had very lively discussions about both the myths and the facts. Although these women lived in different cities, were of several generations and had different economic and family circumstances, their discussions formed a coherent picture."[14] The groups independently described three familiar stereotypes: Mammy, Jezebel and Sapphire. Harris-Perry uses the metaphor of the "crooked room" to describe these shaming and oppressive stereotypes, which many have tried to escape by adopting what has become a new restrictive image—"black women with unwavering strength who are backbones of the community." This impossible expectation takes a heavy emotional and physical toll and fails to address the real struggles of black women "at the intersection of multiple forms of marginalization," which are often ignored by both black advocacy organizations and national party politics.[15] The book concludes on a positive note: through a shared understanding of their own experiences, black women can assert their own aspirations and paths as they continue their struggle for gender and racial equality.

Reshaping Civil Society Using Feminist Experience

From Aristotle's time until now sharing in ruling and being ruled has been the topic of lively intellectual discourse, if not always positive resolutions. Worldwide we are still searching for ways to engage citizens in determining what constitutes a good society and their place in creating and maintaining it. Many political theorists have joined in a call for encouraging citizen initiatives, revitalizing civic education (including public school civics classes), and reaffirming human relationships. Although women are often stereotyped for their attention to relationships, their skills and experiences in this area are usually overlooked by social theorists seeking to renew or create healthy civic societies. There are insightful exceptions, including work by Jane Mansbridge. In an article in *American Prospect*, Mansbridge reviews how feminist ideas have played a central role in discussions about deliberative democracy. Deliberative democracy is a technique that goes beyond simple voting to encourage authentic dialogues and consensus building that can challenge the rule of the majority and involve many voices in decision-making. She posits that two threads of feminism—nurturance and anti-oppression struggles—can be integrated in a deliberative approach to democracy. Deliberation is a theme sounded by many political theorists but, as Mansbridge maintains, is well suited to those with experience in the women's liberation movement, which sought "to integrate the nurturance, listening and emotional sensitivity of this culture into the politics that women had inherited from men."[16] Mansbridge does not consider women to be innately gifted with these qualities, but believes that their experiences, ways of approaching issues, and vocabularies can be particularly helpful in deliberative decision-making and should be explicitly sought and applied to this promising model. Mansbridge frames the concept as a way to bring about more, and more authentic, participation that can incorporate diverse opinions and honor the inevitable human conflict that is involved in political decisions.

Mansbridge's theories sound a common chord with the thoughts expressed by Sarah M. Evans and Harry C. Boyte in *The Civil Society Reader*: "Simply, democratic ideas only make sense in the context of democratic experience. When people begin to see in themselves the capacity to end their own hurts, to take control of their lives, they gain the capacity to tap the democratic resources in their heritage." The authors claim that democracy can continue only through people coming together in what they call "free social spaces."[17]

Free Social Spaces and Consciousness-Raising

Consciousness-raising groups are models of such "free spaces," the title chosen for Pamela Allen's primer on consciousness-raising cited in chapter 1. Consciousness-raising is vital for women who wish to be involved in political action. Efforts to reimagine the political landscape have been and are varied. Some women choose to engage in traditional politics, running for office and/or electing female candidates, promoting legislation to improve women's lives, and forming issue-oriented organizations to pressure political candidates and legislators; others seek to form alternative institutions and approaches to change; many work in both realms. Whatever the focus, small groups provide settings for women and others to discuss the conditions of their everyday lives, develop an analysis that grows from common aspects of their experiences and choose appropriate courses of action. CR groups are places where the elements basic to a functioning democracy can be realized. They develop a sense of membership, a place to listen and be heard, to practice reciprocity and discover other skills of effective participation that are foundational to political engagement.

Civil society, democracy and feminism, which claim many common values, need to be defined and redefined, shaped and reshaped, by the goals they advocate—among them inclusion across age, ability and economic circumstances, as well as broad and meaningful participation of all religious, racial and ethnic groups. And all need to be measured by daily practice. Communitarian impulses serve to inspire democracy; they can also reinforce parochialism, elitism and selfishness. Many conservative groups and movements (for example, the Tea

Party) embrace the same anti-establishment rhetoric and grassroots organizing techniques as politically progressive organizations. The Ku Klux Klan is one expression of a "community" organization that continues to exist to advocate hatred and even murder. Both fascist and Marxist-inspired governments utilized government-controlled mechanisms to give the illusion that citizens were participating in decisions with which they had no choice but to agree.

The consciousness-raising process involves asking questions about our experiences that can unmask the contradictions between statements of principles and the actual behavior of groups. It can be useful to begin with a look at ourselves. Although coalition building is an important objective, self-proclaimed feminists have often unwittingly, and sometimes consciously, yielded their theoretical insights and effective strategies to other groups, diluting the strength and promise of a sustained women's liberation movement.

The "Frame-up" of Feminism

Ignoring Feminism

The small consciousness-raising groups that fueled the second wave of the women's liberation movement stand out as proven settings for community building. Yet many women, including self-identified feminists, attach their concerns to other movements, often sacrificing their own agendas. The Occupy Movement, an economic justice initiative that began with Occupy Wall Street and spread across the United States and abroad, is a case in point. From the beginning of the occupations, women played a major organizing role, but they and other groups (among them lesbian, gay, bisexual, transgender and queer people [LGBTQ], people of color and individuals with disabilities) fought to ensure that the particular ways in which they experience economic hardship would be heard. But efforts to highlight that the "harms experienced by women as a result of global and national economic policies are, in aggregate, different and often far worse than those experienced by men" were largely ignored.[18] One LGBTQ commentator addressed leaders as follows: "We stand with the women and allies affinity group in the call for everyone to please examine and check their privilege. And we suggest that you think about the fact that heterosexualism is a privilege."[19] The lack of even a basic understanding of racism was observed by a writer on the Racialicious blog, who reported that some occupiers were making a comparison between student loan debt and slavery.[20]

Like many others hoping for the resurgence of a mass movement for social change, I supported the Boston encampment and attended a number of events. I was peripheral to the organization, so I do not know what sources the leaders drew upon to gain the wide participation they espoused. The visible commitment to horizontal decision-making was the practice of repeating aloud every comment made at General Assembly and many other meetings, a process that guaranteed that those who spoke were echoed, but did not ensure that the silent (or silenced) would have a voice.

I often wonder if an understanding of intersectional feminism that more cogently and explicitly linked economic inequalities with race, gender, age, disability and other oppressions could have turned this incipient movement into an effective mobilization against injustice. A "Statement of Principles" reveals the concerns of the "nondominant communities" within the Occupy Movement: "We worry that we already see this movement becoming a microcosm of systems of power and privilege that exist in the greater world."[21] Tragically, episodes of sexual assault, primarily against people identifying as women, were reported in several of the encampments, one major indication of the reasons for concern.

Though hardly a desirable way to build a movement, had Occupy continued, perhaps feminism would have benefited from the misogyny! Some participants began to speak out against what they saw as a repeat of the behaviors of male leaders in the student left of the late 1960s, whose trivialization of the issues raised by women—and women themselves—had led to a revitalized feminist movement. That movement was rooted in consciousness-raising, which brought about the realization that people cannot fight injustice if they ignore their own oppression.

Subsuming Feminism

Women's oppression and the ways that it can be addressed through political action require an understanding of a wide variety of theories and careful study of their applications. Feminism has found inspiration and incorporated the sometimes-overlapping perspectives of Marxism, other forms of socialism, humanism, liberalism, postmodernism and more. But just as with the Occupy Movement, the presumption that greater strength can come from allying with a broader political movement or intellectual framework often means that feminism is subsumed. I'll use anarchism as an example of this pattern because feminism and anarchism are frequently linked. Both share a commitment to end the power and domination of some over others and embrace a number of common approaches.

Although anarchism is often defined restrictively as a doctrine calling for the destruction of all government, both the term and the practices associated with it have evolved. According to Noam Chomsky, anarchism can be seen as "a historical tendency, a tendency of thought and action, which has many different ways of developing and progressing and which, I would think, will continue as a permanent strand of human history."[22] The nonviolent social or communal anarchist strand, like feminism, urges reciprocity, mutual aid and broad and equal participation of all people in decisions that affect them.

It was in an undergraduate Russian history class that I first learned about Petr Kropotkin, a Russian political activist whose theories were rooted in his background as a scientist. Kropotkin challenged Social Darwinists who applied Charles Darwin's theories of natural selection in the animal kingdom to human societies, leading to the widespread notion that humans thrived on hierarchies, conflict and competition. Kropotkin did not refute Darwin's findings, but believed they were not the driving force within human history, unless it was necessary to oppose oppressive institutions that denied the more natural tendency toward cooperation. He demonstrated that there were many examples of animal species whose social behaviors allowed them to survive, thrive and develop stronger communities by joining together. Humans, too, he wrote, flourish through collaboration in freely formed groups without top-down control, pointing to practices of indigenous cultures and the organization of pre-industrial production.

I revisited Kropotkin's *Mutual Aid: A Factor of Evolution*[23] in graduate school. Although Marxism and anarchism were not part of my doctoral program in education at Boston University, the late Howard Zinn kindly provided a happy detour from the prescribed curriculum by welcoming me to his course on those topics. I had been inspired by Zinn's words at peace demonstrations and other events, and I knew he was an ally and advocate for feminism. That semester I rediscovered the connections between feminism and anarchism that had intrigued me when I first read Peggy Kornegger's article, "Anarchism: The Feminist Connection," in 1975 in the Boston-based journal *Second Wave,* of which she was an editor.[24] Kornegger discusses historical events in which authority and hierarchy were replaced by cooperative forms of associations. She offers as examples the collectives that formed during a brief period in the Spanish Civil War when autonomous small groups combined into larger federations that equalized wages, shortened the work week, and produced better products than the previous exploitive system.

Kornegger's discovery of anarchism led her to link retrospectively the alternative institutions rooted in feminist consciousness-raising groups, such as clinics, women's centers, and shelters, to communal anarchism. Small-group organizing within feminism has corollaries to anarchist activism, but the projects that were realized and sustained by feminism grew from the women's liberation movement, few of whose members would link their activism to anarchism. Kornegger does not claim that the influence of anarchism led to the feminist forms of organization, noting instead that "this development is usually intuitive." She also acknowledges that "[a]narchist men have been little better than males everywhere in their subjection of women." But rather than celebrate feminism as the transformative theory that can challenge such misogyny and has offered dramatic examples of effective practice, Kornegger urges that feminism be incorporated within the anarchist philosophy.

Reclaiming Feminism: Everyday Activism in the Neighborhood and Beyond

Political scientist Martha Ackelsberg also explores anarchism in her work, which queries "whether, why and under what circumstances political authority is necessary," but her theories give priority to feminism rather than anarchism.[25] Ackelsberg applied her understanding of women's roles in anarchist organizing during the Spanish Civil War and precursor events to other studies of women's political behavior. Her insights reveal that women's lives merge the public and private, workplace and community. Their experiences as mediators between the home and the marketplace, for example, negotiating with landlords and vendors as well as employers, gives them a different kind of wisdom and potential power than is understood in most political analyses. As many second-wave women's liberation movement activists acknowledged through consciousness-raising, they do not fit tidily within either the liberal understanding of self-interest as the chief motivator or the socialist notion of class solidarity as the means to overcome oppression. Both within class, racial and ethnic networks and across them, women become politically conscious through relationships and networks that develop from the everyday issues and concerns they discover they share with others.

Ackelsberg acknowledges that the need for connection is not limited to women, but it is women who have performed the bulk of the work in building and sustaining communities. Her recommendation of a new political paradigm based on how people experience connections as individuals and members of communities links to other feminist models that, like consciousness-raising, begin in small groups that can shape larger social change.

Mutuality in Human Relationships

Jane Addams, the co-founder with Ellen Starr of Chicago's Hull House, defined democracy as "mutuality in human relationships."[26] Her vast array of civic, educational, recreational and health initiatives began with small groups created in response to community needs. For example, a kindergarten was created after a neighborhood mother asked Jane to care for her child so she could go to work; immigrant clubs were founded to celebrate the cultures of new arrivals to the United States who felt the pain of separation from their home-lands. Dozens of volunteers, some of whom lived at Hull House, interacted with the community, teaching literacy skills, developing programming, bathing children and preparing the dead for burial.[27]

One of my favorite authors, Grace Paley, an acclaimed short story writer and poet, found her sources of inspiration and insight in the women in her neighborhood with whom she struggled for better schools, playgrounds and social services—and for equality in their intimate relationships. The deep insights and large truths of her wonderful short stories often begin with an "everyday" interaction within the urban neighborhoods and households that are the settings for her narratives.[28] Paley carried her grassroots style of activism from her city block to national and international organizing for peace and justice.

From Self-Help to Mutual Aid to Systemic Change

In her biography of Mary McLeod Bethune (1875–1955), Joyce Hanson notes, "As feminist historians have become more interested in political history, they have worked to redefine politics as 'any activity [that] includes all community work which is oriented to change through multifaceted goals including service, support, public education and advocacy.'"[29] Bethune grew up in a south-ern culture in which examples of mutual aid were abundant (such as cotton-picking parties, church activities, financial assistance, lay nursing and midwifery). She took those everyday practices to her work, initially identifying with Booker T. Washington's approach to instruct black people in leading exemplary lives—with the example being the white people who were the benefactors of many of their efforts. She founded or became active in a variety of educational proj-ects, including the school that eventually became what is now Bethune-Cookman University.

Bethune's dedication to personal and community "self-improvement" evolved into social activism as she gained a deeper understanding of the systems that produced racism and economic injustice. Attacks on the moral character of black women, their exclusion from the 1893 Columbia Exposition and other instances of racism helped Bethune understand and join those who were impa-tient with a gradualist approach. She concluded that democracy should live up to its principles and began joining with African American women of all political persuasions, rather than just those aspiring to move a privileged few blacks into the middle class. Soon she was working across racial lines at local, state and national levels, and even internationally, to support many of the same causes for which Addams campaigned—voting rights, anti-lynching initiatives, child labor reform and the World Court.

Yet Bethune did not abandon the approaches of mother's clubs, benevolent societies and women's mutual aid associations, the purposes and techniques of which are similar to those of CR groups. These provided women with a supportive environment in which to face everyday challenges and discover the leadership skills and confidence to enter decision-making and shape an enlarged political agenda. Bethune is an example of what can occur when women "change their ideas about the causes of their powerlessness, when they recognize the systemic forces that oppress them, and when they act to change the conditions of their lives." Hanson sees Bethune's legacy in womanism, a term that Alice Walker and others use to describe the activism that grows from black women's experience and "incorporates racial, cultural, sexual, national, economic considerations for *all* people."[30]

From Mutual Aid to Activism Today

The benefits of interdependence motivate people of all genders, races and ethnicities to form groups around common concerns and interests. With the notable exception of Alcoholics Anonymous, which has about a ⅔ to ⅓ male predominance,[31] women are the majority of those involved in what has become known as the "self-help" movement. But self-help can be reframed as mutual aid, and mutual aid can lead to collective action for social change.

Phyllis Silverman, who has done extensive research and practical work in the area of grieving, emphasizes that the benefits of bereavement groups can increase when "mutual aid" is the approach.[32] Her perspective is that grief and loss are an inevitable part of living. Sharing one's own situation in a CR-like setting with those who also are experiencing grief can offer insight, support, and the opportunity to provide comfort to peers at a time when it seems that one's own resources are depleted. Silverman's initial work focused on widowhood; more recently she has been working with children who have lost loved ones. While the children meet together to talk and engage in writing, art making and other joint projects, their parents, older siblings and other caretakers meet simultaneously to discuss their grieving process. Having lost a four-year-old brother when I was eleven, I am a strong advocate of The Children's Room, the center Phyllis helped create in the Boston area. There were no such services that my grieving family knew about; at the time they probably didn't exist. I felt guilt about my own survival and lonely and helpless as I watched my parents struggle. Consistent with consciousness-raising, Silverman's work has moved from the personal to the political. In a consumer-oriented culture, grief counseling has become a subspecialty in the psychotherapeutic and social work fields. She and some of her colleagues have challenged the "medicalization" of life-cycle events, urging professionals to question their own need to provide therapy instead of encouraging small mutual-aid groups that do not require professional leaders and support.

The epidemic of breast cancer has spurred countless support groups for those living with the disease. Many of these have moved from only offering encouragement to interrogating accepted treatments and approaches to prevention. In *Pink Ribbon Blues*, Gayle A. Sulik documents the branding of breast cancer by fundraisers allied with corporate sponsors and suggests that beribboned merchandise and hundreds of walkers clad in pink are obfuscating the lack of progress in finding a cure for the disease. She observes that women are now questioning familiar mantras, such as "early detection," that emphasize mammography, although it is unclear whether this is as effective as advocates suggest.[33]

The "Think Before You Pink" campaign was initiated in 2002[34] by Breast Cancer Action, an independent, nonprofit organization based in San Francisco that has disclosed the connections between marketing and medical diagnoses. The group raises questions about corporate marketing around breast cancer, including asking how much money from "pink ribbon"–adorned products actually goes toward breast cancer research, what kinds of programs are supported and whether the company can ensure that its own products are not contributing to the disease. Breast Cancer Action coined the term "pinkwashing" to describe companies that claim to care about breast cancer by promoting a pink ribbon product, while at the same time producing or selling products that are linked to the disease. Examples include cosmetic companies, yogurt and drink manufacturers, and producers of clothing and jewelry. Activists have achieved results; for example, in August 2009 General Mills, the producer of Yoplait, stopped using cows treated with recombinant bovine growth hormone (rBGH), which has been linked to breast cancer.[35]

These efforts reveal the effectiveness of political activism that is rooted in the everyday reality of women's lives. The Women's Community Cancer Project at the Cambridge, Massachusetts, Women's Center is a New England counterpart to the San Francisco group.[36] Founder Rita Arditti died in 2011 of metastatic breast cancer, a disease with which she had lived since 1979. Just months before her death I attended a lecture she presented detailing the social and economic factors of breast cancer, including the fact that black women have a 37 percent higher breast cancer death rate due to lack of access to treatment and care, and urging that discussions of cancer move from genetic dispositions and personal behaviors to underlying political issues. The organization advocates environmental research spearheaded by such groups as Alliance for a Healthy Tomorrow, which is trying to replace toxic chemicals with healthy alternatives, and urges that such efforts be featured in every march and rally.[37]

More recently, red ribbons have begun to appear on products in a new campaign aimed at women that focuses on heart disease. This prompts the need for an investigation of the latest way that pulling our heartstrings diverts attention from activism—and a new slogan, perhaps "Use Your Head Before You Red."

Mainstreaming: Indication of Success or Barrier to Feminist Change?

It is apparent that consciousness-raising and grassroots approaches of moving from personal experience to social and political activism are still powerful models. A task of feminism today is to make explicit the connection of current efforts to earlier organizing efforts and determine what can be learned from the achievements and errors of the past that can inform today's social justice initiatives. Women's liberation depends on being aware of the tributaries that feed into the mainstream, which are often unseen when creative responses to issues become incorporated into the prevailing views of the dominant culture. Consciousness-raising provides an opportunity to reveal that the political agenda of earlier generations of feminists has not been implemented fully (and, in some instances, not at all). Like those who are thinking before "pinking," we need to examine critically what may be inadequate responses to more complex problems and be sure that institutions do not become focused on their own self-perpetuation rather than the issues they were created to address. Seeking unity of process and goal is another area in which feminism and democracy fuse.

Over lunch with a dear friend, we recalled the excitement of helping to create early feminist organizations. As we formed new collaborations to take action with others on shared concerns, the values and approaches discovered in the small CR groups went with us. We practiced rotating tasks and sharing skills, bottom-up rather than hierarchical decision-making, and collaboration in place of individualism. The emphasis was on implementing changes that demonstrated that ends and means were one. Beverlee remembered the counseling center she and some colleagues began in a church basement. Their approach coupled the insights of feminism and the radical therapy movement in a model of change that placed individual struggles within a social and political context. In that same period I was redefining my work, finding ways to conjoin feminism with my education and experience as a librarian and joining other women in establishing a campus women's center and women's studies program, as well as a community women's school. We were part of a widespread movement that created numerous rape crisis hotlines, battered women's shelters, health projects, women's schools, bookstores, art collectives, campus and community women's centers, and other feminist organizations that responded to the lived experiences of those who initiated and used them.

When I moved to a new community and was asked to serve on the board of directors of the New Bedford, Massachusetts, Women's Center, I was gratified to find the same approaches in place. Lines between those providing and receiving services were blurred. Board members volunteered to work at the battered women's shelter or staff the rape crisis hotline. Paid staff and board members together planned and carried out community outreach and fundraising projects. The New Bedford Women's Center remains a strong organization. Today's excellent leaders care deeply about the community, but many are not *of* the community, as were the director and staff in earlier years. Like many action projects that often developed from the energy and analysis discovered in the small CR groups, the center became "mainstreamed," which can be a mixed blessing for feminist organizations. These had come into being as, one by one, group by group, women broke silence and spoke to the experiences of their daily lives. The issues they raised, including disparities in health care between men and women, violence against women, and economic deprivation that affected women and children disproportionately, soon became widely acknowledged social problems that led to legislation and government and private funding. Grassroots neighborhood organizations became established institutions staffed by college-degreed professionals whose credentials were required by funding agencies. Reporting structures were instituted and the anti-hierarchical ethos of the founders yielded to bureaucratic structures. Even the technique of consciousness-raising became professionalized. The practices of small groups became a model that was taken into traditional organizations, particularly social agencies.

Institutionalizing Change: An Oxymoron?

As a feminist committed to small-group, participative approaches to leadership, I tried, with mixed results, to transport CR methods to the settings in which I worked. When I took the position of dean of library services, I supervised a large staff within a bureaucracy in which competing for funds, positions and power was the daily agenda. Instead of working directly with students, faculty and community users of the library, as in earlier jobs, I had to discover effective ways to represent and advocate for those constituencies. I was able to hire talented staff members whose dedicated and creative work with students, faculty and community library users made the organization shine. Within the library I had some success in flattening the pyramid. Instead of permanent department heads, we moved to elected chairs. The rotating leadership provided opportunities for librarians to have the experience of guiding a unit—and to earn a department chair stipend during their stints. I searched the state organization chart for positions that would provide more growth opportunities for media technicians and library assistants than their current classifications. I introduced a consensus model of decision-making in the meetings of the chairs who reported directly to me. In retrospect, I realize that a few staff members understood and embraced my enthusiasm for a participatory organization; others, who were accustomed to being told rather than asked what to do, went along because I was the "boss."

At the time I was hired, I reported to a dean of faculty who shared many of my progressive political views. His departure and a changing climate throughout higher education meant that being an administrator was less about advocacy and more of what I sometimes called being the "surrogate oppressor." My responsibility became focused on pleasing the layer of the bureaucracy above me, rather than the staff, students and community. In 40 years of working in higher education I observed an enormous growth in administration (often justified by the need to be "accountable"). As the years passed, my colleagues and I spent an increasing number of hours preparing lengthy reports to which there were sometimes no rejoinders. Decisions were often made with little regard for the data we were asked to gather.

Following the rules was the path to using my position on behalf of others. I took care to follow the detailed evaluative criteria in guiding and assessing my staff. When the new dean of faculty (a position soon retitled vice president for academic affairs) insisted that I could recommend only one of three people who had requested promotions, I balked. They had been hired at the same time and each had earned the increase in rank and salary according to the specific standards by which they were to be judged. I won promotions for all of them, but it was clear that nurturing and advancing capable people who made an important difference in the quality of our students' educational experiences was not the way to win favor with my boss. "Holding the line" by limiting the advancement of those lower in the hierarchy (while high-paying administrative jobs proliferated) was commended. Marketing and public relations—looking good—became as, or more important than, doing good. In an increasingly hierarchical and contentious environment, I was grateful that my appointment allowed me to teach. Yet the egalitarian spirit and practice of the women's studies program (marked by frequent potluck suppers for faculty and students, collaboration with the Women's Resource Center and active connections to community agencies) also began to yield to bureaucratic pressures. As the struggle for status and resources became more demanding, such feminist practices were no longer givens.

A Feminist Issue: Democracy or Bureaucracy?

I campaigned enthusiastically for Barack Obama; yet I knew that it was a willing suspension of disbelief that led me to think those "HOPE" posters signaled a new vision of American politics. I support any action that can improve the quality of life for people who are suffering, but my own hope for the maintenance and growth of democracy resonates with those who continue to find ways to involve citizens as agents of change rather than clients of bureaucratic agencies. The intentions of the Obama administration are detailed in the introduction to the Report on Women referenced earlier: "The initiative furthers three governance themes of the Obama Administration: (1) pursuing evidence-based policymaking; (2) catalyzing the private sector, including private researchers, to partner with the government in analyzing data and formulating appropriate policies; and (3) pursuing an all-government and all-agency approach to addressing special issues affecting Americans."[38] Interlocking structural relationships among private and public organizations may meet some temporal issues, but an ever-growing and increasingly complex bureaucracy is not the answer to women's liberation and social justice for all.

Bureaucracy is a feminist issue, as Kathy E. Ferguson argues in *The Feminist Case against Bureaucracy*.[39] Ferguson and others who have studied the responses of social service, educational and medical agencies reveal the routinization and regulation of care and the increased dependence of clients—and workers—on the bureaucratic order. Women are the principal clientele of social services and the front-line staff in most agencies. All workers are subjected to administrative structures that limit their authority and autonomy, but women are seen as well suited to obeying orders and providing "care," often limited by the strictures of the bureaucracy to filling out forms and offering formulaic responses. Ferguson writes, "The capacities for compassion, and for self-assertion, for solidarity as well as confrontation, need to be seen as possible dimensions of *human* behavior, not as male or female traits. But as long as there are groups of people who hold institutionalized undemocratic power over others, femininity will continue to be a trait that characterizes the subordinate populations, and the vision of a liberated community of autonomous individuals is denied. This, if nothing else, should show the importance of linking the feminist critique of male dominance to a larger set of criticism of all power relations, including those manifested in administrative hierarchies."[40]

I see myself in Ferguson's words: "[M]anagers who break ... rules and seek to humanize, perhaps even democratize, relations within their offices are posing a fundamental threat to the organization; even if their offices function effectively, they are subverting the hierarchy, undermining the official value system, attacking the organizationally defined identity of other managers, and propagating relationships within the organization that are antithetical to the legitimated ones."[41]

CR Groups and Support for Resistance

Hierarchical organizations have long been the norm; countering them requires "chutzpah," not to mention the support of feminists and others trying to apply their political vision to their daily lives. Without the camaraderie and counsel of feminists on campus,[42] and the groups mentioned throughout this book, I would not have been able to challenge the institutional structures to the extent that I did. Yet even as I like to think of myself as a change agent, my own limitations, coupled with the absence of a strong social movement and the ongoing consciousness-raising that had nurtured my earlier work, made me become satisfied with the "too-small" changes.

Building Feminist Community and Practicing Democracy

"Our feminist survival is dependent on maintaining frequent, ongoing and active contact with a feminist support group or system."[43] Consciousness-raising allows practitioners to develop a critical analysis of the underlying factors that produce our daily reality and helps us determine how to respond to those that perpetuate subordination and exploitation. CR groups can provide a setting for self-reflection in which shortcomings can be named and contradictions addressed. Articles critical of feminist practices were discussed at length in my CR group, and also in women's organizations and women's studies classes, resulting in new awareness and appropriate, if not always consistent, change. One frequent comment that requires continuing discussion is "women do it, too," often said when observing deficient conduct. As has been noted several times in this book, internalized oppression often keeps women and other oppressed groups identifying with and adopting the behaviors of the very systems that are limiting them. Such remarks also equate feminism with a male vs. female struggle rather than a movement to fight the interlocking oppressions that

people of all genders, races, physical abilities and other identities experience—
and sometimes reinforce.

Practicing Democracy

American democracy has shifted from the direct democracy of the town
meeting, where each (originally each male) citizen had an opportunity to speak
on every issue, to representative forms of governance. Increasingly, power is
concentrated in the hands of fewer people—and, usually, the most affluent.
In my own community there have been recent proposed revisions to the town
charter that remove hiring authority from elected boards such as the Board of
Library Trustees or Recreation Commission. My response to the ostensible
effort for "increased efficiency" is that this takes another little piece away from
governance by the people. I expressed my concern at meetings and in an op-
ed piece for the local paper,[44] noting that the lack of citizen involvement that
justifies such actions lies not only with Joe and Jane Citizen but also with the
bureaucratization and administration that has made "constituency input" perfunctory. Sometimes the decisions already have been made before public opinion is sought. Ersatz democracy promotes lack of interest and even despair.
While postmodernists might decry any agenda of hope, I continue to believe
that using the freedoms still available to us can counter prevailing trends. I
think the answer to a lack of participation in a democracy is more democracy—authentic involvement in the shaping of organizations and institutions.

Real Meeting

When Martin Buber wrote that "all real living is meeting," he was not thinking of sessions held to rubber-stamp administrative fiats, but of deep mutual
engagement, soul-to-soul connections, and a commonness of need and spirit.
He envisioned economic and social justice in "communities of communities"
that could respond "to the living, personal, human being."[45] Susan Griffin's
discussion of consciousness-raising evokes Buber's vision of meeting. She feels
that CR impacted political gatherings regardless of whether people were aware
that they were applying this feminist technique: "Instead of acting simply as
arenas for debate, with the practice of breaking larger assemblies into smaller
groups, and allowing everyone present to say something about her [or his] life,
meetings have encouraged a deeper level of connection between all the participants and at the same time have become more democratic."[46] Although I
think the phenomenon of meeting in small groups has myriad roots, I agree
with Griffin that the CR model fostered a depth and honesty that enhanced

the authenticity of discussions in many other settings, from families and workplaces to religious and social institutions.

My bookshelves include a number of titles on feminist group processes and I never stop trying to learn new ways to become a more effective group member. A battered copy of *Living Our Visions: Building Feminist Community*[47] sits next to Starhawk's *Empowerment Manual*.[48] These volumes invite us to dream of organizations—and a world—in which social justice is the purpose and collaboration is the mode. "They are groups of peers, working together for common goals, collaborating and co-creating. Such groups are at the root of democracy, and participating in them can be a liberating, empowering, life-changing experience."[49] Starhawk explicitly applies the consciousness-raising model to offer guidance in creating organizations in which power and authority are balanced with responsibility, and trust with accountability.[50] She offers explicit advice and examples on how women can come together around strong values; choose to work in circles, or webs, rather than in pyramidal structures; share information and skills; celebrate difference; learn to be deeply attentive to what is both said and unspoken; and create a decision-making structure that can engage the participation of all who are affected by an organization's policies and services.[51]

The authors of *Living Our Visions* invite us to ask the simple questions WHY, WHAT and HOW.

WHY: The vision statement of a group or organization lets people know why they should join and provides the standards by which decisions can be judged. Starhawk states, "Successful groups form, articulate and maintain a common vision." She observes that in many collaborative groups vision is assumed rather than articulated. Starhawk also notes that progressive entities, such as anti-war or anti-racism organizations, often are formed to *oppose* oppressive circumstances, but shaping a group's vision provides an opportunity to think positively.

WHAT: Specific goals grow from the group's purpose and inform the daily work on projects and tasks that leads to the realization of vision. Long-term and more immediate goals need to be articulated and ways determined to measure accomplishments.

HOW: For feminists and others working to promote democracy, the ways in which the work is carried out are closely related to the activities. The slogan "the process is the product" was second only to "the personal is the political" in some of the feminist groups with which I was involved in the late 1960s and 1970s. While sometimes group members can become impatient with too much attention to process, building authentic connections and relationships is not at odds with attention to tasks. Being faithful to a process delineated and embraced by group members provides an impetus to work and a real example of alternative ways in which organizations can function.[52]

Authentic Participation

I've been involved in many planning efforts within the academic institutions where I worked, and in community agencies and feminist organizations as well. Some are recognized quickly as perfunctory exercises, but even when there is a deep intention to involve and energize people around a revised mission and new or reaffirmed goals, these have often fallen short in gaining authentic participation. Sometimes the failures are due to the fact that people do not know how to get involved. Feminist and other progressive organizations need to be sure that members and potential members have opportunities to share their particular strengths and learn new skills, including effective participation. Meeting facilitators need to keep learning ways to involve participants in planning agendas, setting time frames for discussion, and ensuring that members become more comfortable in engaging in conflict and difficult conversations, without which individuals and groups cannot thrive and grow.

Political action will involve feminists in many groups, from small grassroots organizations to national initiatives for change that do not function with the explicit commitment made by CR group participants to inclusion, support, confidentiality, respectful listening and shared reflection and analysis as a basis for action. Most of us do not work in settings where we can share our dreams of the quality of life we would like for ourselves and others. Yet carefully, consciously, and with the support of others who share our values, we can take the experiences discovered within intentional communities into traditional institutions, offering alternative ways of making decisions and carrying out tasks, engaging in and resolving conflict, and recognizing contributions of those who are not always seen and honored. Consciousness-raising approaches also can be applied in interactions within families, intimate relationships, friendship networks, neighborhoods, and social and spiritual communities.

Sometimes it is best to aim for small changes. I've served on numerous boards and committees in which it is second nature for me to introduce processes I learned through CR. For example, I might ask that we begin the meeting with a "check-in," though I might not always use that term. I try to link the suggestion for a brief go-around with the mission of the organization, perhaps asking, "Has anything happened this week that made you feel proud of your work as an educator?" or "Maybe we can take a few minutes to hear how the recent storm [or other significant local, national or international event] has affected you and your family before we discuss the agenda." Beginning a meeting with an opportunity to share a personal experience invariably builds community; it also allows members to see one another as Buber's "living, personal, human beings." Starhawk's book has dozens of exercises for beginning meetings, from meditation to poetry reading to physical exercise.[53] Sometimes these are appropriate and incorporated with ease and enthusiasm; at other times even feminists object to too many "touchy/feely" activities.

Electronic Democracy

An earlier chapter of this book reviewed the possibilities of consciousness-raising on the Internet and whether and in what ways technology has provided opportunities for girls and women to advance their economic and social positions.

The participatory democracy that is indispensable to a women's liberation movement requires in-depth information that is often at cross-purposes with a cyber environment saturated with celebrities and consumerism. While the Internet potentially could change many lives in dramatic ways, corporate interests have a controlling interest in electronic communication. Promised transformations have not occurred and evidence mounts that technologies can be used to control as well as liberate. Yet the claims continue that technology promotes inclusivity and is a great equalizer, and I want to support policies that can make me believe in these arguments.

Before the Internet can be considered as a new democratic tool, physical access to electronic devices and the skills and confidence to use them must be extended to everyone. Those championing—or selling—the computer revolution seldom ask who is left out due to race, ethnicity, immigration status, joblessness, poverty, illiteracy, physical and mental ability, and gender. The employed working and middle classes are stretched financially with the purchases—and regular upgrades—of the hardware and software required to be part of the everyday world of technology. Few people look at how much of their income is spent on cable, Internet and phone services, many of which duplicate one another but are deemed necessary because of the belief that 24/7 access from any location is required.

Even when electronic tools are available, many people do not know how to go beyond the information that immediately pops into view, so the new "worlds" that can be opened through knowledgeable use of computers remain beyond reach. There are less obvious exclusions, too. Ever-changing techtalk is one example of the gulfs that exist amid heightened promises of egalitarianism. To frequent Internet users, "textisms" such as "l8r," "brb," "ftf" and "meating" reinforce the easy camaraderie of their Web associations. To those outside this community, these "simplifications" seem arrogant, elitist, or just incomprehensible. Less technologically savvy users, including elders who are not accustomed to "playing" with language and immigrants who are trying to master the basic principles and inevitable vagaries of a new tongue, are woefully disadvantaged.

When I started to write this book I had concerns about online security and privacy. Hearing from Amazon and other vendors that I might like this or that book or product based on previous purchases or searches felt more intrusive than helpful, but knowing that my own government is monitoring my telephone, e-mail and postal transactions is more than annoying—it is alarming.

At the same time that the invasion of privacy has dampened the confidence of many citizens that our government will uphold the basic premises of a free society, the utopian promises of e-democracy continue, such as using smartphones to express opinions on legislation. With less substantial dialogue and more opportunities to express quick reactions, these new applications may be a variation on the television polls to "voice your choice." Issues such as whether the ball team should have traded a particular player assume equal importance with climate change or tax policy. And will "citizen opinion" expressed by a computer click in a poll developed by a partisan group register with public officials?

Feel-Good and/or Do-Good Clicking

In the late 1960s "click" was a word that was used to describe the "aha" moment when a woman became aware of sexism. Examples abound: a husband accompanies his wife to the event at which she is to give a speech, but the person at the registration center assumes the man is the presenter; a man comes into a roomful of women and asks, "Is anybody here?" Did that happen decades ago? Yes! But *Click* is also the title of 2010 volume in which a new generation of women shares how they came to their initial understanding of sexism, racism, or other forms of oppression.[54] In the age of social media, "click" has taken on a double meaning. The Internet allows immediate and widespread sharing of information, including reports of injustices. Some believe spreading the word about an injustice *is* activism, and raised awareness is certainly a first step in creating social change. But it is hardly enough. In many cases, "feel-good clicking" and "slacktivism" (performing some easy task, often from a seat in front of the computer, without serious engagement in the cause) prevail over serious debate, strategic thinking and careful planning. Clicking on a site to add one's name to a petition or ordering a T-shirt to support a cause cannot produce profound social change. The "kony2012" campaign is a particularly troubling example of misguided activism.

A Click That Didn't Quite Click

With over 100 million views within a six-week period in 2012, a YouTube video calling for the capture of the Ugandan warlord Joseph Kony broke the then-record for "going viral" on the Internet. The video reported that Kony abducted 30,000 children in Central Africa and forced them to be child soldiers in his Lord's Resistance Army (LRA). According to the website http:// invisiblechildren.com, which sponsored the Internet campaign mounted to hunt down Kony and protect and rehabilitate the children affected, young girls were routinely raped and children were coerced to attack communities in the remote border regions of South Sudan, the Democratic Republic of the Congo, and the Central African Republic and even to kill members of their own families.

For a short time the "kony2012" film and fundraising campaign were a widely recognized phenomenon, supported by celebrities and spread across college campuses. The website quickly linked information about Joseph Kony to the "Kony store," with bracelets, bags, bumper stickers, buttons and a $30 organizing kit for sale. A story on a feminist blog was among the reports that revealed that the largest portion of expenditures went to "advocacy and awareness" rather than planning and delivering services to victims.[55] The Invisible Children website is still actively seeking donations and sponsored a "Fourth Estate" conference in California in summer 2013, as it had in previous summers. The conference fee was $495. The website for the conference reports the average age of attendees is 16, suggesting that Kony is not the only one recruiting children.[56]

Despite the conferences and continuing Internet outreach, the Kony campaign is yesterday's news. The Internet played a role in exposing the campaign's shortcomings just as it stimulated the initial video and calls for donations. Yet perhaps it was not the disclosures of alleged misinformation and malfeasance that caused the demise of kony2012. It may be that people stopped caring about the atrocities and moved on to the next thing that went "viral." The story is important for feminists and others interested in using the Web to advance progressive goals. Activists need to continually assess the legitimacy of the causes touted on the Internet and weigh the appropriateness of joining in a fleeting trend that can derail steady progress toward social justice.

Sustaining Democratic and Feminist Initiatives

YouTube, Twitter, Facebook and other social media were used in the early stages of the Arab Spring in Tunisia and Egypt to bring masses of people together to protest, and eventually overturn, repressive regimes; it is less clear how successful they are in moving from immediate responses to committed, long-term action. To take just one sad example, women were celebrated for their technological savvy in organizing demonstrations against the tyrannical dictators, but they have had a very limited role in shaping or participating in the governments that followed the successful routing of the dictators.[57] Some new, and supposedly more democratic, Middle East governments are implementing laws to regulate and censor Internet use, as Jacey Fortin reports in the *International Business Times*.[58] But censorship is also an issue in the United States, prompting an unusual consensus of concern from the left and right about increased restrictions that are justified as countering cyberespionage, preventing child pornography, and protecting intellectual property rights and "national interests."[59]

Feminists need to take a leading role in addressing these issues if the promise of electronic democracy as a means to shape a women's liberation movement is to be realized. Meeting in small groups to share and question our daily experiences, including the information and perspectives presented on the Internet, is one way to incorporate thoughtful analysis into sustained efforts for change.

Keep Asking Questions

Consciousness-raising groups can utilize the questions Melissa Harris-Perry asked her respondents in preparing *Sister Citizen*, and add many more in order to build an inclusive, effective women's liberation movement that models and supports a democratic society. Here are some that might start the process:

How do you think others see you given your particular skin color, ethnic background, gender, class, religion, physical ability and other characteristics? How do you see yourself? How are these definitions and impressions reflected in political inclusion? Have they been barriers to full participation? In what ways? What thoughts and values come to mind when you hear the word "democracy?" Do you feel that you live in a democracy? How do you define citizenship? What do you think are the rights and responsibilities of citizenship? How do you practice citizenship? Did you have a civics/civic education course in school? Do you recall what it included? If you did, or didn't, do you think such a course would be a good idea and what would you include? Have you heard the term "civil society?" What does it connote to you? What kind of world would you like to live in? How can you realize that vision?

What issues concern you the most? Do you consider yourself to be politically active? Do you support candidates based upon their commitment to these issues? Do you vote? How else do you express your political hopes? How else might you do so?

Are you involved in local organizations or neighborhood groups? Volunteer activities?

Do you have conversations about political issues? With whom? Would you consider your grandparents, parents, or other members of your family to be politically active? What expressions of their activism can you cite? Did they inspire your own involvements?

Do you use social media to gather information about political and social issues? Do you use social media for political activism? How? In what other ways might you use the Internet for political activism? What are the limitations?

V

Consciousness-Raising in the Classroom and Beyond

*I now understand why feminist consciousness-raising groups
in the 1970s were so effective in generating women's energies.*

— · — · —

This was one of numerous favorable responses by her students to Estelle Freedman's use of small groups in the "Introduction to Feminist Studies" course that she teaches at Stanford University.[1]

This chapter shows how CR and women's studies were once nearly synonymous; gives examples of how the approaches to teaching and learning rooted in consciousness-raising have been applied in college and university classrooms, including my own; and suggests some possible reasons why they now are used less often. I urge that the technique be revisited, revised, and revived both in the classroom and among women's studies program planners so as to create and sustain a feminist community of teachers and learners. CR is an important tool for learning in settings beyond the academy, too. The CR methodology and kindred processes can support many learning environments that inspire personal and social change.

When Women Ask the Questions

Early in the second wave of the feminist movement, the consciousness-raising process, through which thousands of women came to identify with the women's liberation movement, spread to college campuses and shaped a new academic field—women's studies. I was lucky enough to be among those who advocated for and team taught one of the earliest women's studies courses at

104

Salem State College (now University) in Massachusetts. Neither I nor the other course developers had academic preparation in the field because there was not yet a discipline called "women's studies"—we were creating it. It was in developing, teaching or taking women's studies courses that we made discoveries that are now common knowledge, but were stunning revelations at that moment in time. We unearthed forgotten female writers and learned how sexism meant that those few women who managed to become literate and find time for the life of the mind and pen frequently had to write in secret; male pseudonyms often were adopted to gain the interest of a publisher and an audience. We studied how psychological theories based on notions of an essential female nature confined women to limited roles; "hysteria" and other mental illnesses were thought to be the result of challenging their appropriate sphere. We found out that women "didn't count" in economic analyses, although no economy throughout recorded history would have been possible without their reproductive and productive labor. Of course, there were some "exceptional" women, with unusual family encouragement and financial resources, whose art work, writing and scientific discoveries changed the world. As we brought their work to the fore, we wondered how many more contributions could have been made if educational opportunities had been available to women from all class backgrounds and ethnic and racial groups.

It's hard to impart the excitement of planning those first women's studies courses and programs, which incorporated the materials that we discussed almost as soon as they were written. Sometimes we used the mimeographed articles that we exchanged in our CR groups; soon many of these pieces were collected in the early anthologies, such as *Sisterhood Is Powerful*,[2] that we assigned, along with special issues of academic journals and articles from the new feminist newspapers and journals that began to be published (and soon films by feminist filmmakers). My training as a librarian helped identify resources for our incipient program at Salem State and I am proud of the work my sister librarians have done from the start of the women's liberation movement of the late 1960s and early 1970s to track down, catalog and disseminate sources.[3]

There was a lively exchange of ideas and intellectual energy—and joy and laughter too—in the circles of women meeting over coffee or potluck suppers to plan what should be included in the foundational introduction to women's studies and feminist theory courses. In the first women's studies classes, students and faculty engaged in the consciousness-raising process together, discovering how every discipline could be reshaped when women are the subject of inquiry and, as Marilyn Boxer titled her historical account of women's studies,[4] *When Women Ask the Questions*. A consciousness-raising approach meant asking more and ever-deeper questions about how knowledge is created, what becomes important to know, and how traditional ways of learning might be altered to reach and empower more people.

Many of the insights that were shaped in the discussions among those who participated in the burgeoning programs were developed and articulated in journal articles and books, so teachers and learners in the growing field of women's studies had a recorded body of thinking and practice to build upon. The National Women's Studies Association (NWSA) established in 1977, became a meeting place to exchange ideas on course content and pedagogy. The NWSA mission embraced the connection between theory and practice, research and service, affirming campus women's center staff as feminist teachers and promoting civic engagement informed by feminist theory.[5] As electronic resources came into use, a Women's Studies List (WMST-L)[6] provided an e-mail site for women's studies scholars to exchange syllabi, teaching approaches and strategies for building women's studies programs and women's centers and to share ideas for linking these to activist projects beyond the academy.

Feminist Teaching and Learning: Roots and Branches

"CR groups were like the sun coming out," said a panelist at a conference on feminist pedagogy.[7] Consciousness-raising provided a new light by which to reread and reinterpret models of democratic and liberatory education. Among many others, these include Progressive-era philosopher John Dewey (1859–1952)[8]; Marxist-inspired critical educational theorists such as Peter McLaren, Henry Giroux and Maxine Greene[9]; and advocates of alternatives to formal schooling such as Ivan Illich.[10]

Paolo Freire's work was perhaps the most influential on my own thinking. His *Pedagogy of the Oppressed* was published around the same time that women's studies programs were developing on college campuses.[11] Freire used the technique of *conscientização*,[12] or "conscientization," in teaching Brazilian peasants to read, a requirement that had to be met before they could vote. Like participants in feminist consciousness-raising settings, the peasants discovered "the word and the world" through sharing experiences around what Freire called "generative themes" from everyday life. In the course of becoming literate, they also became liberated. They were able to transcend negative self-images and begin to name and create a vision of the future that challenged conditions they had previously believed were unchangeable.

Praxis, often used as a synonym for practice, is given deeper meaning by Freire. His definition—"reflection and action on the world in order to transform it"—resonates with the consciousness-raising approach threaded throughout this book. Freire critiqued the "banking system" in which teachers deposit the pieces of information students must accumulate to be considered educated (as I had done for most of my learning from kindergarten, but was learning to challenge). Like feminist education, Freire's model involved learning in one's community. Instead of turning against each other, students created solidarity through sharing and examining their common plights, and they became participants in the process of changing their lives and the institutions that had limited them.

Freire described how dominated people mimic the behavior of the powerful: "To be is to be like; to be like is to be like oppressor." That simple summary of a familiar pattern has stayed with me and helped me resist the dominant culture that had "an outpost in my head,"[13] the internalized oppression that Audre Lorde[14] and other feminist theorists observed.

Kathleen Weiler has written about the limitations of both Freire's and early feminist pedagogy, noting how binaries of oppressor/oppressed relationships fail to account for the fact that in various situations people can occupy both roles. She describes how feminists have expanded Freire's framework to validate personal experiences that may not fit into an encompassing theory, to analyze how oppressions intersect, and to explicitly address power and authority in learning environments.[15]

It has taken some time—and important, reiterated and insistent critiques, especially by lesbians and women of color—for those of us who thought our initial women's studies courses were transformational to acknowledge serious limitations. Early courses were developed with the assumption that addressing the oppression of "women" would result in ending all expressions of dominance. Although it is true that women experience political, economic and social subordination in all countries, cultures and religions, the ways in which gender roles intersect with other forms of oppression to shape the experience of individuals and groups was unexamined or explored only superficially.

Transforming Knowledge

I return often to Elizabeth Minnich's *Transforming Knowledge*[16] to keep these issues before me. Her book weaves in the three components Weiler cites as characteristic of feminist teaching and learning—speaking from varied experiences, understanding intersecting oppressions, and exploring power and authority.

Minnich's analysis reveals that the omission of women, native peoples, and some racial and ethnic groups from the standard curriculum is not a benign oversight. Knowledge is created and promulgated by elites and systematically excludes those who are not part of the dominant culture. The privileging of the voices of those elites diminishes or, more often, negates other voices, and demands a substantive change that involves examining the power relationships at the root of most curricula.

Minnich's call for transformation utilizes a consciousness-raising process that begins with examining the daily experiences in her own life and encouraging her readers to respond and contribute their stories. Minnich exposes the errors in thinking that must be challenged in the effort to develop a new way of constructing knowledge. I've asked my students to consider with me the common philosophical mistakes she outlines, including the following: 1) faulty generalization—arriving at universals based on the experiences of too few; 2) circular reasoning—basing continued devaluation and exclusion on the initial faulty generalizations; 3) mystification—keeping hidden the hierarchical determinants of the exclusions; and 4) partial modes of knowing—ignoring the specificity of history, location and other considerations in our construction of knowledge.

Transforming Knowledge summarizes well the inadequacy of adding "and she," "and African Americans," "and Jews," and so on to the "he" who represents the standard by which "others" are measured. She notes that "if we act now as if ... all we need do is assert our gender-, race-, or class-blindness, the awful weight of an old, fully developed, very powerful meaning and power system will ensure that in critical ways 'human' will continue to be conflated with 'man' and 'man' with a particular group of males. *Saying* we are now inclusive cannot make it so. It will take a while to transform what has been developing for millennia."[17]

Today most women's studies courses claim to incorporate an intersectional approach. Yet the deep "ruts" of internalized belief systems need to be exposed continually through ongoing consciousness-raising—the in-depth examination and analysis of the varied and changing experiences of women across class, culture and location.

Frances Maher and Mary Tetrault discovered this fact as they were conducting research for *The Feminist Classroom*.[18] They adjusted their theoretical lenses as they acknowledged how their own status as relatively privileged, white college teachers had influenced their initial thoughts about what they would discover. Their openness, self-criticism and ongoing reassessment (characteristic of consciousness-raising) resulted in an illuminating book about "positional pedagogy." They profile seventeen professors from six very different campuses and disparate "cultures," a term the authors use to encompass the behaviors, values and attitudes that we inherit, and that change with our personal and social paths, geographical locations and other influences. Although all the faculty members defined themselves as feminists, the ways in which they and their students constructed and shared knowledge varied greatly depending on their institutional affiliation, race, ethnicity, and other combinations of identities, revealing and affirming that many interweaving threads shape and strengthen the feminist classroom.

Consciousness-Raising in the Classroom

Intersectional feminist pedagogy is based on very real contradictions within our individual life experiences and choices, and it acknowledges interpersonal and intergroup conflicts. Consciousness-raising can be an important technique to apply to the difficult dialogues that are called for by today's feminist educators. Yet instead of reexamining and reshaping the technique that is the foundation of women's studies, there has been a move away from the practice and even the term itself.

Barbara Winkler describes the phenomenon: "While shying away from the term, many Women's Studies educators still embrace specific goals of CR in the classroom."[19] Her accurate statement suggests that the students who claim "I'm not a feminist, but ..." might be learning their behavior from their teachers. In striving to reject the simplistic or totalizing constructs of early women's studies courses and to embrace the new, some have abandoned language that describes women's struggle for equality, agency, dignity and justice, including the word "*feminism*."

Winkler herself uses the term "consciousness-raising," outlining a revised form that incorporates an intersectional model of social identities. She encourages students to examine how a range of often conflicting identities affects them personally and reinforces social and political power. Winkler calls for a deeper analysis of familiar techniques and texts, including the late African American poet and essayist June Jordan's classic article, "Report from the Bahamas,"[20] in which the author confronts her class privilege when she vacations at a Caribbean resort, and Peg McIntosh's always relevant *White Privilege and Male Privilege*[21] reveals that what seems so obvious to white women about sexism is not as apparent to them in regard to racism. (See below for further discussion.)

Coalitional Consciousness

Winkler's approach is reinforced and expanded in Cricket Keating's excellent article "Building Coalitional Consciousness."[22] Keating brings back the question posed by Kathie Sarachild, whose model of CR informs this book: "Who/what has an interest in maintaining oppression in our lives?" But Keating urges that this be asked in a way that pays close attention to racial, class, national and other pertinent histories. She calls for an examination of how these interact to maintain power relations not only over but also among women. Keating outlines steps in what she calls "coalitional consciousness building." This revision expresses new values and ways of seeing across diverse populations, which Keating contrasts with "raising" a dormant awareness of sexism that characterized earlier women's CR. Let me briefly describe the steps: step one, locating experience with attention to diverse histories; step two, examining the multiplicity of oppressions and resistances to their recognition and interactions; and step three, coalitional risk-taking that includes women challenging power relations among themselves in order to build coalitions for change.

Along with some of the faculty and students who shared their teaching and learning with Maher and Tetrault, Keating questions the women's studies classroom as the safe haven promised in early second-wave CR, insisting that the path to coalition will be a rocky one. Her reshaping can help us learn from the past and structure potentially contentious, yet honest, engagement within respectful parameters.

Creating "Free Space" in Small Groups Outside the Classroom

Keating's approach requires conditions that go beyond the confines of the classroom in a one-semester course. Although still limited by the standard term, Estelle Freedman responds to some constraints, including professorial authority and confidentiality, by moving the consciousness-raising process out of the classroom.[23] As a component of her introductory course, Freedman creates "free space" where difficult conversations can occur outside the classroom.

She describes one semester when she divided her class of 66 men and women into thirteen leaderless groups that met biweekly to respond on a personal level to the three weekly lectures and extensive reading. For example, following a lecture on race and feminism, students were asked to address how their personal experiences of race, class and ethnicity affected their responses to what they were learning. In another session small-group participants shared reactions to the assignment the class had received, which was to write a letter coming out to their parents about their sexual identity. Students were expected to keep a journal on these independent meetings and summarize their experiences in a final, ungraded paper. Gathering face-to-face in small groups to question together the meaning of their experiences, to weigh contradictions, and to posit and assess courses of action gave students an opportunity to engage in a more intimate and profound exchange. Many found it to be the highlight of the course.

Teaching and Learning About Women: Applying the Theory

When I received a joint appointment as dean of library services and professor of education at UMass Dartmouth, I had an opportunity to develop a course in which I could share my thoughts and experiences on the feminist teaching and learning process with students who were preparing for careers as educators. The course was cross-listed with women's studies, and it attracted students from many majors with diverse backgrounds, interests and experiences. It seems appropriate to revisit "Teaching and Learning about Women" in this chapter on consciousness-raising in the classroom. Patricia Hill Collins uses the metaphor of the "three-legged stool" to describe teaching women's studies—content, critical thinking skills and emotional learning need to be in balance.[24] Often the stool teetered as I tried to maintain equilibrium. Here are some of my recollections on what it was like to plan and deliver the course.

Beginning a Conversation: Creating the Learning Setting

My own education had emphasized content and critical thinking and was delivered in lecture halls or classrooms with the teacher at the front and the students in rows. Participation in consciousness-raising groups inspired me to think a lot about how to create an environment for both emotional learning and critical thinking. I initially taught "Teaching and Learning about Women" as a seminar course in a typically sterile conference room. We transformed the conference table into a "kitchen table" around which we shared good snacks, and even better conversation, about the texts and our lives. If this sounds like a stereotypical "female" way of creating a welcoming learning environment, I accept the nomination. I often think of the visit from a student who came to my office before she graduated and told me that being served tea by a professor was the best experience she had at the university. (One of my own best college memories was joining two or three other classmates for an evening discussion at a history professor's apartment; even my embarrassment at breaking a china cup doesn't take away from the pleasure of that recollection.) A comfortable setting and personal kindness are not at odds with learning but increase the motivation to perform challenging intellectual work.

Teaching *about* teaching made it even more imperative to be explicit about the pedagogical approaches I would be using. In the first meeting of "Teaching and Learning about Women," I gave students some articles that had helped me shape the course. I used Nancy Schniedewind's "Feminist Values: Guidelines for Teaching Methodology in Women's Studies"[25] and Carolyn Shrews-

bury's "What Is Feminist Pedagogy?"[26] Discussing the articles at the outset
and referring back to them throughout the semester gave a fuller appreciation
and understanding of what I hoped we were about, as did Adrienne Rich's
wonderful essay "Reclaiming an Education."[27] I joined Rich in encouraging
students to *claim,* not merely *receive,* their education, bringing their own experiences and ideas to classrooms rather than accepting a curriculum that often
excluded them.

We grappled together with issues of authority in the classroom. As the person who was responsible for outlining the course and grading performance, I
had to look carefully at the ways in which I could or could not share authority.
Although I professed that I didn't want grades to be so important, I confronted
and shared the fact that I didn't want my course to be known as "an easy A."
I had many conversations with myself and some with trusted colleagues on
how to structure a course that offered substantial learning experiences through
carefully chosen texts and learning approaches. I also brought students into
the decision on how the class would be graded. Here's what was decided: Each
week students prepared a learning journal based on responses to a detailed set
of questions on the material assigned. The questions were prepared so students
could share personal experiences as well as summaries and interpretations. I
assured students that whatever they wrote would be confidential; what they
wished to share in our class discussions was their choice. All students participated in a group presentation and had the choice of a final project or paper
that could be prepared independently or with other classmates. If these assignments were completed with reasonable attention to college-level writing skills,
the A grade—not an easy one—was achieved. Some students wrote a dozen
pages each week; others much shorter journal entries. Some students came
into the class having taken a number of women's studies courses; others were
newer to the ideas presented. My goal was that we would learn with and from
each other and all grow in understanding—including me. I also began using
a check-in as the semester progressed to get a sense of what was working and
what wasn't and to make changes. I used a detailed anonymous course evaluation to fine-tune the syllabus, assignments and teaching strategies each semester.

Authority is not limited to the professor-student relationship. A stated value
of the classroom was that all would be heard and respected by recognizing, as
Cricket Keating emphasizes, that power dynamics also exist among "peers" in
a classroom. Rather than seeking unanimity, we strived to make the particular
experiences and perspectives of students of various and intersecting ages, abilities, class statuses, genders, religions, skin colors and ethnicities central to our
discussions and analyses.

What to Teach: Choosing the Content

I tended carefully to the affective, but I worried mightily about the content, too, and how to structure assignments so as to encourage the analytic skills that are necessary for successful learning—and to build a women's liberation movement.

One of our first texts was Toni Morrison's *The Bluest Eye*,[28] a poignant and provocative novella revealing the confluence of race, class and gender oppression. Early on we also viewed Julia Reichart and Jim Klein's classic film, *Growing Up Female*,[29] one of the first made during the resurgent women's movement and an excellent conversation starter for exploring what has changed and what has not in the socialization of girls. We returned throughout the semester to the themes, content, questions and contradictions raised by both.

Since this was an education course, I chose as a centerpiece Jane Roland Martin's *Reclaiming a Conversation*.[30] I was chagrined to realize that, although I had taught courses in the philosophy of education, I had not used Martin's insightful book until I developed a course that was to be cross-listed with women's studies. Feminist teacher, heal thyself! Martin discusses how five thinkers—Plato, Jean-Jacques Rousseau, Mary Wollstonecraft, Catherine Beecher and Charlotte Perkins Gilman—envisioned an appropriate education for women. We invited these authors to participate in a learning adventure with us. Let me briefly introduce them and summarize their theories.

PLATO (CA. 427–347 B.C.E.)

Some feminist scholars in the burgeoning women's studies programs found documentation for Plato's "feminism" in Book V of *The Republic*, where he stated that women could be trained as guardians, the leaders in his ideal state, because the innate intelligence and reason required for that elite role were not dependent on gender. However, despite his insistence that gender was a "difference that made no difference," many other passages of *The Republic* decry "womanish" qualities in men and assign stereotypes to women that today continue to limit female participation in the life of the mind and the governance of social institutions.

JEAN-JACQUES ROUSSEAU (1712–1778)

It was many centuries before another philosopher offered opinions on women's education. In what he considered his most important and best work, *Émile*,[31] Rousseau detailed the learning trajectory to prepare a *man* to become a decent, contributing citizen who could maintain the moral values necessary to a functioning civil society. Key to the success of Rousseau's educational plan was keeping boys from the corrupting influences of the world, instead spending time exploring nature with a dedicated tutor who would guide them in learn-ing, not by mastering sets of facts, but by developing physical and mental skills required to function in the natural world. The last chapter of *Émile* is devoted to "Sophie," the prototype female who, by nature, is destined to be Émile's sub-servient helpmate. She, too, has a prescribed education, the very opposite of a man's. Females need to "learn many things, but only those which it becomes them to know," including coyness, charm, domesticity, virtue and submissiveness.

MARY WOLLSTONECRAFT (1759–1797)

Wollstonecraft, often called the mother of modern feminism, concurred with Rousseau that an informed, educated citizenry was necessary to maintain civil society. But she questioned how women could raise sons capable of rea-soning if they were considered incapable of doing so. In *A Vindication of the Rights of Woman*,[32] she asserted that "to be a good mother a woman must have sense, and that independence of mind which few women possess who are taught to depend entirely on their husbands. Meek wives are, in general, foolish mothers.... If children are to be educated to understand the true principle of patriotism, their mother must be a patriot ... make women rational creatures, and free citizens, and they will quickly become good wives, and mothers; that is—if men do not neglect the duties of husbands and fathers."[33] Wollstonecraft urged that the same education offered to men be extended to women, and not only women of privileged backgrounds.

CATHERINE BEECHER (1800–1878)

Beecher embraced Rousseau's notion that women had special qualities that made them particularly suited to their roles of mothers and teachers (a vocation then limited to single women; if they married, they could continue to impart to their children the knowledge and Christian values they had transmitted in the classroom). Beecher founded seminaries for girls and, following Woll-stonecraft in this regard, urged a curriculum that would include subjects such as higher mathematics and Latin, which she had to teach herself. While insist-ing that women's intellect should be appreciated, she cautioned against "exces-sive" mental stimulation. She maintained that women were equal to men, but opposed women's suffrage because it would cause "the humble labors of the family and school to be still more undervalued and shunned."[34]

CHARLOTTE PERKINS GILMAN (1860–1935)

An artist, social theorist, journalist, economist, fiction writer and champion of women, Gilman flatly denied differences in intelligence between males and females, stating, "There is no female mind. The brain is not an organ of sex. Might as well speak of a female liver."[35] Gilman described the flawed bargain whereby women exchanged sex and domestic labor in order to receive economic support, and urged that women be educated for meaningful work. She suggested that the repetitive and isolating tasks of homemaking and childcare could be performed by sharing duties in collective settings. While many of her ideas were progressive and she described herself as a humanist, Gilman also espoused racist, anti-immigrant viewpoints rooted in the Social Darwinism of the time.

How to Teach It: Assignments and Classroom Experiences

Education students had seldom looked at the educational philosophies repeatedly cited in their texts through the lens of gender, and the prescribed education curriculum did not cover Wollstonecraft, Beecher and Gilman as the important educational philosophers they were. These three writers tried to advance learning opportunities for women; yet the patriarchal values of the "foundational" theorists were unwittingly incorporated and perpetuated in their concepts.

We reflected on the ways in which class, race, ethnic and other biases were shaped by educational philosophies. Most theories rested on the assumption of a hierarchical society and recommendations were clearly addressed to the "elites" who would occupy a place at the top of the social pyramid. We looked at the "ideal" republic and observed that Plato assumed nursing and childcare would be the job of servants whose "natures" were suited to these tasks. The education of Rousseau's Émile clearly was aimed toward those few who could afford a private tutor to prepare them as male leaders of civil society. Later writers challenged Plato and Rousseau, but many of their ideas remained unquestioned. For example, Wollstonecraft urged that women have their own representatives in government, but did not suggest that women *be* those representatives. And although it seemed that Gilman's views on gender roles were diametrically opposite from Beecher's, both saw women as a "civilizing" force. That theme returned us to Jean-Jacques Rousseau, who felt that one of a woman's most important functions was to curb men's overwhelming sexual urges.

How and what we knew about the philosophers covered in Martin's book became part of the learning in the class. Plato and Rousseau had been included in courses taken by most class participants. Only students who had taken other women's studies courses knew about Wollstonecraft, and occasionally someone recognized Gilman, not as an economist and political philosopher, but as the author of the novella *The Yellow Wallpaper*.[36]

As students researched the philosophers for their assigned papers and projects, they discovered that material about Wollstonecraft, Beecher and Gilman more often focused on their personal lives than on their intellectual contributions. They quickly found information about Mary Wollstonecraft's affairs and her tragic death just a few days after the birth of her famous child, Mary Wollstonecraft Shelley, the author of *Frankenstein*. The demise of Beecher's fiancé was frequently cited in writings about her. As is often the case with women, being unmarried requires an explanation. Charlotte Perkins Gilman's mental breakdown following the birth of her daughter and her choice to give the upbringing of her child to her former husband and his new wife are explored in detail in books and essays about her. We talked about the fact that, even today, women in the public eye receive intense scrutiny and judgment when they step out of prescribed "feminine" roles. Occasionally, students found information speculating on Plato's possible homosexuality and acknowledging Rousseau's bizarre personal life, which he revealed in detail in his autobiography, *Confessions*. But most books and courses that discuss the theories of these intellectual "giants" do not review their biographies in depth, and certainly do not dismiss their work because of their personal idiosyncrasies.

Continuing the Conversation: More Texts and Techniques

Even in a small class, I followed Estelle Freedman's suggestion for "free space" outside the classroom. As we read Martin's *Reclaiming a Conversation*, we formed five groups, each of which designed its own presentation to illuminate the insights of one of the philosophers covered in the text. When students in the class took on the role of teachers, they often discovered strategies for explicating the material that I had never considered. Along with an opportunity to showcase their special skills, they got to know others in the class more personally, and they discovered and encouraged aspects of personality that hadn't been revealed. There were many memorable moments; as I write, I am thinking of one occasion when the quietest student in the class played Sophie in a skit and became an outspoken, brazen reversal of Rousseau's ideal of the docile partner intended for Émile.

Performance and personal sharing were not the typical experience of most students but, as occurs in consciousness-raising groups, it soon became easy to relate the material to our own lives. After the presentations we rearranged the groups and formed new CR circles to discuss how the theories regarding a suitable education for women and girls that had been put forth over the centuries affected our own educational experiences and choices. Those of us who had suffered through the mandatory home economics courses offered by many public schools acknowledged—and sometimes damned—Beecher's legacy as we exchanged stories about those classes. Mine was creating the required skirt that was revised so many times that it could only have fit a toddler, and turned me off sewing forever. Some students talked about their experiences in what had morphed into coeducational "home ec," where the boys in the class were uncomfortable and insulting. Others had positive responses to courses that taught family life skills to young men and women. With Gilman's theories in mind, we considered ways in which such courses could be an exploration of how an ideal home, family and community might work, and how changing notions of gender roles could shape these.

Some of choices of texts and techniques were more successful than others. One semester I assigned Virginia Woolf's *Three Guineas*[37] to demonstrate that quality higher education for women was a fairly recent and hard-won phenomenon. Most of the students in the course held jobs to support their tuition and were the first generation in their families to go to college. They had trouble identifying with Woolf's context—the elite British university system that primarily served the male offspring of the well-to-do and then made a few places available to women from the same class background. A wiser selection to show how difficult it was for women, particularly women of color and working women, to become educated is the wonderful 1986 film, *Women of Summer*,[38] which chronicles the innovative summer school for working women held at Bryn Mawr College from 1921 to 1938. The film weaves footage from a reunion with scenes from the summer sessions that might have been informed by the feminist theories on pedagogy from the early days of women's studies. Faculty and students created projects jointly; barriers were defined and challenged, including the admission of the first African American student; and factory workers took part in discussion groups with visitors like Eleanor Roosevelt and Frances Perkins. The documentary also reveals the limits of experiments that threaten the privileges of those in power, as many of the benefactors withheld their donations when the students became activists—participating in a local strike and joining in demonstrations against the Sacco and Vanzetti trial and execution. These scenes prompted conversations on how organizing initiatives in our own campus and local community by minorities, immigrants, workers, and other groups are supported only to the point that those who hold power feel their control is not threatened.

We spent a lot of time in the class discussing adolescence. Many of the students had recently been in that part of their lives; others were parenting and a few were grandparenting adolescents. However distant from the actual experience, we all could remember the struggles we faced. I used a variety of readings popular over the years, including Mary Pipher's *Reviving Ophelia*,[39] an anthology of writings responding to that book,[40] *Schoolgirls* by Peggy Orenstein,[41] and others. We queried whether the experiences thus reported described the reality of particular students and what was left out or seemed exaggerated. Ethnic differences, immigration status, age, economic circumstances and other issues emerged in our conversations.

I reviewed Carol Gilligan's work *In a Different Voice*[42] to provide background for a detailed discussion of *Women's Ways of Knowing*, by Mary Belenkey and others,[43] and shared the critiques of these books. Some reviewers charged that the researchers generalized findings based on a small and narrowly representative sample; others cautioned against the authors' valorization of certain "female" traits and "natural" proclivities, as Beecher and Rousseau had done. But over the years most students in diverse classrooms found that much of the material about "women's ways" of learning and living rang true.

Based on interviews with 135 subjects, the authors of *Women's Ways of Knowing* posited five learning perspectives: 1) silence—the blind following of authority; 2) received knowledge—listening to, trusting, and emulating experts; 3) subjective knowledge—listening to one's own voice and feeling that one's "gut" can provide the most valid information; 4) procedural knowledge, which the authors divided into "separate" and "connected," the former relying exclusively on reason, and the latter coupling analysis with listening and empathy; and 5) constructed knowledge, merging what is important to the knower with what is learned from others. Learners utilizing the last perspective recognize that knowledge is contextual and changes as we continue to integrate personal responses and analytical assessments to gain and share new understanding.

Students spoke of how they saw themselves in these perspectives, acknowledging that, in some ways, their learning had followed a straight trajectory, and, in other ways, they had moved, and were still moving, back and forth among the perspectives. They found inspiration in the description of constructed knowing and, in later class experiences, noted how we were individually and collectively "constructing" knowledge by offering our opinions and values along with analyses of the material and developing new models.

After our discussion of *Women's Ways of Knowing*, I showed *Educating Rita*.[44] I often wonder whether Belenky and her colleagues had viewed this film before writing their book. Students wrote insightful journal essays chronicling how the film's protagonist Rita, a hairdresser studying through an adult learning program, moves through each of the learning perspectives. We talked about how the book and film both suggested that constructed knowing was the goal, reinforcing hierarchical notions of moving up a ladder and explored who and what is left behind in that climb and at what price.

The students I taught in this and other classes remain with me: some greet me with a hug when we meet in the supermarket; many continued to drop by my office after they graduated; some invited me to their weddings; more have moved away but occasionally keep in touch. Twenty years after she took "Teaching and Learning about Women," one of the students wrote me a letter from Alaska, part of which I quote below:

> Dear Dr. Freedman (Janet),
>   I am a former student of yours—I think from 1990 or 91, at UMD. You were the Dean and I took a Women's Studies class with you, in a room connected to your office. We read *Women's Ways of Knowing* and we kept journals. I just read something about mentors and you immediately came to my mind. You were a really important person at an important time in my life! I think you made a difference in my life by being so authentic, and caring, and valuing my voice, and my experience. I will love to have the opportunity to create an atmosphere for my students, like you did for us, but I have not yet had that opportunity. I wanted to tell you that you had a lasting impact on me as my teacher. THANK YOU!! I hope you are happy and well and realize what a good and caring person and leader you truly are!

Jen shared that she is now a mother and an associate professor of library science. She is thinking of developing a research project using *Women's Ways of Knowing* as a framework.

Twenty years later, I can still see Jen's face and hear her voice.

Building Coalitions for Change: Consciousness-Raising, Commitment, Community

The call to reveal pervasive, shifting and internalized relationships of power and privilege is a repeated theme of the books and articles cited above, as well as much other postmodern and feminist writing. Yet there are few "how to" responses to redress these realities.

Peg McIntosh's *White Privilege: Unpacking the Invisible Knapsack*[45] is an exception and I used it in most of my courses. Written in clear language and offering examples that can be considered for self- and group reflection, McIntosh reverses the approach taken in many discussions of racism by changing the focus from the disadvantaged to the privileged. The invisible knapsack is a metaphor for the unearned benefits that come from simply having white skin or meeting other societal norms that do not have to be considered by those who fit them, but are the yardstick by which those without the advantages are measured. McIntosh lists some of these, from easily finding cosmetic products that suit your complexion and hair to being free to wander through a shopping mall without fear that you will be suspected as a shoplifter (students inevitably add more to this list). McIntosh's work is remarkably effective in shifting the conversation from disclaimers of "I am not a racist" to a larger discussion of how we can still be part of a social order in which systemic racism is pervasive even when as individuals we do not use or tolerate overt racist language and behaviors. The piece also provides a means to understand how white skin privilege and male privilege are linked. Women who ask "why don't they get it?" about men who don't seem to have any insight into their misogynist behaviors begin to see that they, too, may be "clueless" about advantages they haven't earned. If unacknowledged and unchanged, the benefits accorded by skin color, age, class, being able-bodied or other privileges lead to self-deception, social complacency and oppression.

Beginning to unlearn timeworn responses and develop a critical, social change model cannot be accomplished quickly. For over a quarter-century Peg McIntosh has guided a project on creating an inclusive curriculum. SEED (Seeking Educational Equity and Diversity) is a year-long reading and discussion program designed to change teaching practices and curricula from the elementary schools to higher education.[46] I participated in a SEED project at UMass Dartmouth that brought together a group of people from diverse personal backgrounds and varied disciplines, from fine arts to engineering, who were committed to working on our own racism. Through a year of sharing personal experiences and studying disability oppression, ageism, Islamophobia, racism, anti–Semitism and gender bias, we came to know each other at a deeper level and became a "community within a community." The experience made us more effective in our classroom practices and more capable of collective action for deeper institutional change. The SEED program is just one of many groups that are based on learning through the analysis of shared experience.

What's Wrong for Women with What's Right

Feminist advocacy of equal educational opportunities for girls and women was given a dramatic boost by Title IX, a provision of the 1972 Education Amendment Act. The legislation opened many faculty and administrative positions on college campuses to women, dramatically increased opportunities for girls and women to play sports, ended quotas for undergraduate and graduate school admission of women, and required schools and colleges to implement policies to protect against sexual harassment and violence.

Title IX is a favorite target of the conservative right. Efforts to weaken it have been launched in Congress, the courts, and the executive branch, justified by the spread of misinformation reporting that men are harmed by women's gains. The Independent Women's Forum (IWF), a so-called nonpartisan organization that states it is "home to some of the nation's most influential scholars—women who are committed to promoting economic opportunity and political freedom,"[47] is one of the most active groups trying to reverse the purpose of Title IX, often in the guise of a new brand of feminism.

Like other conservative organizations, the IWF studies feminist and progressive positions carefully and then revamps these to fit its agenda. Self-defense has been and is an important concern for women; the IWF's approach, in keeping with its support for the NRA and other pro-gun lobbies, is to encourage women to arm themselves. The IWF stresses that education and sports programs should respond to the "different strengths and preferences" of men and women. Despite such overwhelming evidence as the 2012 Olympics, in which female athletes dominated medal awards, the organization maintains that males prefer to engage in athletics more than women, so they should have more programs. Adherents of the organization emphasize "family values." They have attacked as "vulgar" Eve Ensler's *Vagina Monologues,*[48] which presents the testimonies of women of all ages and backgrounds who have been victims of oppressive sexism. The IWF wants its adherents to challenge the Ensler-inspired "V-Day" commemorations that take place on many campuses, replacing them with a holiday that celebrates dating and courtship leading to traditional marriage and family roles.[49] According to the IWF and similar groups, giving girls and women equal opportunities has caused men and boys to suffer.

Right-wing attacks have also been leveled at the SEED program. "Wake Up America!" reads the headline of one post on the Stop Seed website (April 30, 2012): "Seeking Educational Equity and Diversity (SEED) is a program that works behind 'closed' doors by using various mind control techniques to steal America's innocence, and further their agenda of transformation. Nazi Germany had their 'Hitler Youth,' the Middle East has their 'Madrasas' and America has its SEED Program." Among the "mind control" techniques enumerated are "encouraging people to want to do something wonderful for the world," reading journals, sitting or standing in circles, promoting relaxation, role-playing, sharing experience and using humor.[50]

If it's not humorous, it's at least ironic that the contributors to the Stop Seed website are cautioning against humanism and Marxism at the very time that the academic theorists they so distrust have rejected these "grand narratives." As a long-time practitioner and advocate for women's studies, I feel caught between the attacks from the right and the discourse of the postmodern intellectual environment.

W(h)ither Women's Studies?

Consciousness-raising is about asking questions, and women's studies faculty, students, and the communities their work is intended to serve all depend on continuing to ask questions based on a feminist framework. We have just begun to formulate—and are far from finding—the answers to such questions as the following: What is a good education for girls and women? How do we create that? How does this contribute to building a global movement dedicated to the support and advancement of women? How are we expressing our commitment to social justice in our daily lives on our campus and in the community?

I have several thoughts on how we have come from the transformational time when "women asked the questions" to a place where it is considered limiting rather than empowering to focus on women's lives. Since the very purpose of this book is to revive the practice of consciousness-raising, it is apparent that I believe women's studies programs lost their way when faculty stopped utilizing the reflexive political process of CR and no longer shared the technique with students or modeled and applied it in community activism.

From 1970, when both San Diego State College and Cornell University established women's studies programs, there are now over 900 undergraduate and graduate programs worldwide, including Europe, Latin America, and Japan.[51] With the recognition of women's studies as a legitimate academic field came an attendant focus on the administrative and organizational tasks that could maintain its legitimacy and increase its importance. In other parts of this book I've observed that other activist projects have also become victims of bureaucratization and a focus on self-perpetuation. It is difficult to resist this phenomenon without ongoing consciousness-raising.

Although I sometimes wear a T-shirt with the message "I'll be postfeminist in the postpatriarchy," it is simplistic and foolish to blame an interesting body of scholarship for the fact that women's studies, the analytical and activist "mother" of postmodernism, has now been relegated to the old-age home. In many ways, those of us who created the early programs hoisted ourselves on the petards of our own complacency. We stopped asking questions about our behaviors and did not reflect deeply and collectively on what would be lost and gained by our decisions and who would be the beneficiaries of our choices. We stopped doing consciousness-raising.

Other things took priority. Negotiating academic life involves making choices. Women's studies faculty have obligations to the department in which they are hired—and which has the largest role in determining promotion and tenure. So from the start research and publication in the "interdiscipline" of women's studies conflicted with disciplinary priorities. For example, the decision to prepare a presentation for the National Women's Studies Association, a setting in which many discussions on feminist pedagogy, women's centers and community activism took place, had to be measured against giving a paper at a conference within one's narrower subject specialty.

As usually happens when the once marginalized become more mainstream, women's studies faculty began to organize their own hierarchies of who and what was in or out. Postmodern analysis came to be seen as more "serious" scholarship than that based on experience. Search committees seeking the "cutting-edge" scholars wooed theoreticians trained by other institutions caught in the same cycle of postmodern promotion. Indeed, it now would be hard to locate new faculty whose graduate school focus was on making women's studies "the scholarly arm of the women's liberation movement." This is too bad—because our own experience as women in all areas of political, social and personal life should have warned us that this would happen.

At the time that women's studies programs were proliferating, it didn't seem possible that they would be vulnerable to being absorbed into a larger framework. Most women's studies faculty had responded to the critiques within the discipline that challenged a unified notion of woman, and changes were incorporated into modes of teaching and research that emphasized an intersectional examination of women's experience. What wasn't anticipated was that the very word "women" would be questioned. Now the "larger" framework of gender and sexuality studies is in the process of establishing its legitimization, a confounding dilemma for a theoretical framework that is about delegitimization.

What's in a Name?

Extensive energy has been expended within the women's studies community on changing names—and directions—of programs to respond to broadened understandings of gender and sexuality. I have followed the discussions, including reading the postings on the debate on WMST-L[52] from the 1990s through 2009. Initially those who wrote felt that the name changes were an effort on the part of college and university administrators to respond to conservative criticisms of exclusivity and political correctness, but soon the comments were overwhelmingly coming from a "post" perspective—poststructuralist, postmodern, and, yes, postfeminist. There were critiques of "essentialism," some harsh judgments of identity politics and radical feminism, and an "out with the old, in with the new" tone.

Eventually many women's studies programs added gender and sexuality to their titles; in others women's studies has been subsumed into a gender and sexuality program. When I tried to find the New York University Women's Studies Program, the new Gender and Sexuality Program came up—neither the program title nor the description include the word "women." From the website of the Princeton University program: "As many of you know, the Program in Women and Gender Studies now has a new name, to reflect the new developments and changing focus of scholarship in the field. The Program in Gender and Sexuality Studies will, as our director Jill Dolan states, 'continue to honor its history in women's studies through our courses, our programming and our scholarship, while broadening our scope to include gender and sexuality writ large.'"[53]

I applaud the shift from an essential "woman" to a recognition of the differences among women and agree that the term "gender studies" incorporates men who experience oppression based on race, class, sexuality and other intersecting identities. I also understand that transgender cannot be addressed when *women's* studies, no matter how broadly defined, is the descriptor. Yet I feel that the alacrity with which (sometimes former) feminists have embraced gender and sexuality studies comes at least in part from the process so accurately described by Freire through which power (in this case, academic power) is sought by "being like" those who have it. I have recognized this pattern within myself. Because I want to be seen as knowledgeable and up-to-date, I have often stifled my opinion that many postmodern insights are overstated, repetitive, often incomprehensible and sometimes silly. Yet it is hard to resist being caught up in the groundswell.

The enthusiasm for "post" theories borders on sycophancy. I recall attending a Harvard conference in 1998 sponsored by the Center for Literary and Cultural Studies.[54] Much of the discussion was interesting and informative, but I came away appalled by the way some in the audience greeted Homi Bhabha, Judith Butler and several other speakers. I almost expected arms to be waving in rock-concert style for the "stars."

I observed the same phenomenon when I attended a lecture at Boston University in January 2013 given by a prominent writer on queer studies. There were many followers in the audience, along with some whose puzzled expressions suggested they may have been attending on the recommendation of faculty, perhaps as a course assignment. The talk was delivered by Harvard Law School professor Janet Halley, to whom I wrote the following letter a few days after the event. I am including it in this chapter because it expresses the hard place I find myself in when people reject their pasts to become champions of their new discoveries, a pattern that has greatly affected the women's liberation movement.

Hello Janet [Halley],

From one Janet to another I want to thank you for your very thoughtful presentation at the Eve Sedgwick Memorial Lecture at Boston University last Thursday afternoon. Your remarks were a tribute to your dear friend and colleague and, because you had taken such care and consideration with the subjects you discussed, to your audience as well.

I was the person who questioned why your theoretical perspective requires a critique of feminism, or "dominance feminism," as you described it. Is it possible that, in trying to "become new," we have created a "straw woman"—the feminist (the word is sometimes hurled in derision) who must be attacked in order to advance a new way of seeing/being? This "feminist" is described, not as a participant in a growing, evolving liberation movement that has continually absorbed new insights and approaches to activism, but as a cartoon figure who is standing in the way of recognizing that there are middle ranges, axes of sexuality and many forms of power and agency. While "queer theory" has certainly advanced some of these ideas, they were part of feminist discourse even before Butler and others developed them more fully and brought them to center stage in academia.

I appreciated your retrospective allusions to your "women's concerns" group at Hamilton College, where you were among the "young turks" against "Mr. Chips." As you recalled in your talk, this was a period of the women vs. the men, and "the Jews and friends" against the "W.A.S.P" establishment. You noted that some called Kirkland, the women's college that eventually merged with Hamilton, "Kikeland." But it seemed to me that you then dismissed as "Manichean" and almost embarrassingly naïve your efforts to oppose the structural oppression that seemed apparent at that point in Hamilton's history, and separated that Janet Halley from the person you see yourself as today.

Like you, I was part of a feminist "awakening" in an academic setting. I began my career at a public college in the late 1960s. There were very few women faculty, gross inequities in pay and routine condescension. A group similar to your women's concerns group at Hamilton organized to address these, and also urged the establishment of a day-care center for students and health services responsive to women. We worked on and beyond the campus to combat racism and classism (when we started in the late 1960s gay rights were not on the agenda because, initially, the lesbian women within our group were not out) and also on reproductive issues, welfare rights and other social justice issues.

Over the years I and other feminists made some colossal mistakes that I think relate to your critique. For example, at the same time we were advocating a revolutionary social order, we placed hope in Affirmative Action Offices. We lobbied for what turned out to be another oppressive layer of institutional bureaucracy. Rather than the diversity we thought such an office would support, yet one more well-paid administrator was appointed to comply (barely) with the letter of the law through such actions as perfunctory diversity trainings and, in the name of affirmative action, enforced surveillance of search processes that justified lessening the autonomy of faculty in choosing their departmental colleagues. Your talk alluded to the overkill of some sexual harassment policies, and I am certain that formal governance structures and NGOs have supported strategies that do not consider the myriad circumstances of people's lives and are limited in many other ways.

But why do legitimate critiques and appropriate responses based on new insight have to involve "taking a break from feminism?" Why can't we learn from the discovery that our analytical framework was too narrow, and continue to develop new vision without trivializing a movement that, though flawed, has created real change in real lives? If we have to demonize, why not choose the global capitalism that destroys agency and "middle ranges" in ways that are obvious each time one logs on to the Internet and discovers that "freedom" has become equated with the freedom to consume products we don't need and information we cannot believe.

They say on Twitter, "just asking," but I AM asking. I wouldn't have raised these issues if I hadn't been thoroughly impressed with the breadth of your background and the quality of your superb presentation. I hope you'll respond.

Cordially,

She didn't.

Learning from Our Past

As I stated in my letter to Janet Halley, I think it is a mistake to reject the past rather than learning from it.

I value the postmodern criticism of "meta-narratives" that attempt to define and struggle against oppression through a single "totalizing" framework. Yet I think it is valuable to read and reread Marx and other socialists, study the philosophical traditions of liberalism, investigate the theses of theologians, evaluate scientific methodologies, and consider how these and other approaches developed and how they have been used to both enlarge and control human potential.

I think we still need to talk about women. Women's studies programs grew from, and really have just begun to respond to, the lived experiences of women around the globe. Today many initiatives that grew from consciousness-raising in and out of the classroom, including anti-violence programs, welfare rights, and access to birth control and abortion, are being threatened in the United States. Women throughout the world are struggling with poverty, health challenges, rape and murder at this moment.

In advocating feminism, I am inviting a conversation on ways to combat sexist oppression, racism and homophobia. I am embracing a place from which to ask questions, grow in understanding and change perspectives as new insights arise, including many that come from postmodernism. Working with a definition of feminism as the continual unfurling of new vision, I think it is possible to accept, weigh, interrogate and reject what does not fit with my thoughts, values and feelings—and remain open to changing with more learning, with more consciousness-raising.

Feminist education is distinguished from other liberatory models of learning when practitioners of all genders and backgrounds are insistent on striving for processes that can continue to enlarge understanding and possibility, as opposed to a unity of belief.

The approach is captured by the words that the late self-identified feminist

Howard Zinn used when he addressed artists, educators and other cultural workers: "What most of us must be involved in has to not only make people feel good and inspired and at one with other people around them, but also has to educate a new generation to do this very modest thing: change the world."[55] While people around the block and around the world are struggling for justice and dignity, the repeated postmodern rejection of "utopian" ideas, often from the comfortable platform of a tenured professorship, can be seen as arrogant. Many of the intellectual constructs are interesting and empowering, especially regarding issues of sexual and gender expression, but it is important, even *essential*, that women's studies programs keep at the fore the actual experiences of those who identify or are identified—and oppressed—as women.

Teaching Activism

Many women's studies faculty define their activism by the act of teaching and research; they leave it to others to carry out the implications of theory beyond the classroom. I was fortunate that throughout my career I had opportunities to merge feminist theory and practice in daily experience. For many years Juli Parker, the director of the UMass Dartmouth Women's Resource Center (now the Center for Women, Gender and Sexuality), taught "Introduction to Women's Studies" as part of the job description for the position and provided a foundation for students to discover the connection between their work in the classroom and projects on campus and in the community. Even before I left library administration to teach full-time, we had many discussions on teaching approaches and worked together on numerous projects with women's studies students. When I became director of the women's studies program, I kept office hours at the center and developed many joint programs, some supported by grants. Through relationships we had forged with allied groups working to end sexism, racism and homophobia, we were able to lead students to volunteer, and sometimes paid, opportunities in a community agency or within the university, including on the center's staff. The personal and political change model of consciousness-raising helped a diverse group of students and staff link theory and practice, and build the cohesion necessary to come together and organize with other campus and community groups to address conditions that required action for change. The benefits of the model have been recorded in an article in *Women's Studies Quarterly*.[56] Looking back at this partnership, I am gratified that Juli and I were able to practice what Patricia Hill Collins calls "public sociology."[57] Our work deepened the possibilities of the "service learning" that many courses require by offering students the opportunity to share and analyze their experiences and consider ways to work not only *for* but also *with* the groups their projects served.

When I left the university the daily working partnership between the center director and the director of women's studies was not sustained. The director no longer teaches the introductory course that reinforced women's studies as the theoretical basis for feminist activism. Part-time faculty are recruited for the "Introduction to Women's Studies" course and the content and pedagogy often change. Conversations with a number of women's center program directors who meet annually at the National Women's Studies Association conference reveal that campus women's studies programs and women's centers occupy separate, and often unequal, spheres, with practice occupying a lesser role. (These conversations took place at the November 2011 NWSA conference in Atlanta, Georgia.)

Consciousness-raising, the very approach that was the foundation for the phenomenal growth and collective energy of the second wave of the women's liberation movement, is still practiced with or without the label CR, but it is seldom used today by faculty in women's studies programs as a tool for self-reflection and program assessment. One of the results is that it has been difficult to see and acknowledge that a shift from "we" to "I" has affected our women's studies classrooms and programs, as well as other campus services that grew from a feminist analysis. At one time there was a thriving Returning Students Association at UMass Dartmouth, which brought together the mostly female students who were juggling family and job responsibilities along with their pursuit of an academic degree. The gatherings of the group yielded support, friendship and collective energy to advocate for improved services for students who didn't fit the profile of the traditional undergraduate, including a campus day-care center. The activism that led to establishing a child-care center was coordinated by a campus Committee on the Status of Women, which brought together faculty, clerical workers, students, administrators, and even one or two feminist members of the Board of Trustees to formulate a proposal that was presented to that body. The proposal grew from telling each other about our lives within and outside the workplace, finding common bonds and determining appropriate action. Whether or not a person was actually struggling with the issue of affordable child-care, the creation of a center needed by workers and students became the concern of all.

The Returning Students Association no longer exists, although unemployment has brought many older students to the classroom in search of new skills, and a couple of years ago the childcare center at the University of Massachusetts Dartmouth ceased operation. Had faculty continued to meet regularly with women from all segments of the campus and our allies within and beyond the university, would these and other services still be available? Has the absence of ongoing CR made it difficult to analyze other challenges and construct a feminist response to them?

Learning Everywhere

Through participation in the CR groups to which I belonged, I discovered that many of the most powerful educational experiences take place in settings outside traditional classrooms and campus environments. I took the CR model to other settings, including some described in this book, with the conviction that sharing and analyzing everyday events could provide a foundation for social action.

The approaches used in feminist classrooms are not limited to colleges and universities. They've been used by community organizers, librarians, social workers, K–12 teachers, staff members of women's centers, health care advocates and many others. Not long ago I met with two feminist activists who have worked for many years in the New Bedford, Massachusetts, community. One of them brought a packet of leaflets listing the array of activities offered by the New Bedford Women's Center and YWCA in the 1970s—CR groups, discussions on child care, finances, health issues and organizing strategies. The offerings were reminiscent of the topics covered by the Salem State College Women's Center and the North Shore Women's School, a community skill-sharing collaborative in which I was involved at the same time in another part of Massachusetts. We recalled the countless hours spent preparing and mailing fliers and brochures, and regretted the irony that now that electronic communication makes it much easier to get the word out, the events and projects that bring women and their allies together to build a movement for systemic social change are fewer. This book is written with the awareness and hope that this can change.

Myles Horton's Highlander School is another inspirational project that expands the boundaries of the word and experience of "school" as most of us have known it. His work resonated with my growing vision of feminist pedagogy when I discovered it many years ago, and it is a valuable source for all who envision communities of teachers and learners wherever people gather to work for social justice. Just one example of the influence of Highlander was Rosa Parks, who attended a workshop at the school five months before she refused to move from her seat on a Montgomery, Alabama, bus. Horton was involved in two major social movements—labor and civil rights. Those who are uncomfortable with the stalled growth of feminism will find comfort in his advice on how to avoid disillusion in times when there is not a mass movement. He cautions against both blind faith in existing systems and romantic radicalism, urging social change advocates to stay the course by keeping a "slow burning fire," rather than yielding to all-consuming anger at social injustices.[58]

Keeping Hopeful for the Long Haul

While I was writing this book, I was able to connect with several of the women who were in the consciousness-raising group described in the first chapter. One has had a career as an innovative secondary school teacher and curriculum developer, and another is a psychotherapist whose practice was among the first to serve the needs of the LGBTQ population in the region where she works. Another member, Patricia Gozemba, and I worked closely on a number of projects when we were both employed at Salem State College.

Before Pat and I got together, I reread her book *Pockets of Hope*,[59] co-authored with Eileen de los Reyes, which highlights settings (including High-lander) that demonstrate liberatory models of learning. When I told Pat about this book on consciousness-raising, she said it sounded a lot like what she sought to impart in *Pockets of Hope*. We recalled how the CR approach was applied in our work, including the design of a collaborative approach to the first-year experience that involved several faculty members. Students picked up on the sense of community and engagement we faculty were discovering through small-group interactions. The students gathered in their own groups to support each other in their individual and team projects, and their creative responses to our assignments helped us continue to reshape the program, a process Myles Horton called "multiplication."

Although I left Salem many years ago, Pat and I continued to apply similar approaches to our work in and out of classrooms. In different places, with different constituencies, we've practiced "multiplication," collaborating with others in groups that form pockets of hope. The separate, but somehow joined, paths that connect me with my former student who wrote from Alaska, with the people with whom I worked in the past, and with new colleagues at the Brandeis Women's Studies Research Center where I'm now a part of a community committed to research, creativity and activism, all provide hope for the long haul.

VI

Spirited Women

Consciousness-Raising: A Tool to Challenge Patriarchal Traditions and Create New Meanings

> "i found god in myself
> and i loved her
> i loved her fiercely"
> —*Ntozake Shange*, For Colored Girls[1]

— ·—·—

Shange's words have stayed with me ever since I heard them in a production of *For Colored Girls* offered at the university where I was working. The amateur performers from the campus and surrounding communities captured the longing for a feminist spirituality so well that I'm sure a professional cast could not have left a deeper impression. As I was beginning this chapter, I recalled how that evening symbolized the search to discover an often hard-to-define spiritual dimension, or "inner life," within or beyond the strictures and hierarchies of patriarchal religions.

In her essay "Holy Listening" Barbara Eve Breitman quotes theologian Nelle Morton, who used the words "hearing into speech" to describe consciousness-raising groups in which women gathered to listen to each other's stories, offering "a hearing engaged in by the whole body that evokes speech—a new speech—a new creation."[2] Breitman recalls her own experience: "It was a presence of life and energy, of passion and honesty. It was a presence that empowered and emboldened. It was creative and erotic. We felt filled with knowledge and vision. We experienced healing and were pointed toward justice. We sensed that, collectively and in extended community with other women engaged in similar endeavors, we were giving birth to a new vitality, creative and conscious."[3]

In the "spirit" of consciousness-raising, this chapter draws upon my own experiences seeking ways to fuse my feminism with the Jewish traditions that shaped and continue to inspire my life. I have been fortunate to have met other women who are engaged in similar searches within their own faith traditions. CR approaches have helped us to explore and heal contradictions, and have likewise been used to build interfaith understanding and social action work. I have also drawn upon my joyous participation in a women's spirituality group that met three or four times a year for over twenty years. Among the dozen members from various religious backgrounds are several who taught me about "New Age" practices that combine Eastern religions, meditation, psychology, and other influences. Since many feminists have celebrated goddesses and explored witchcraft, I will briefly touch on these spiritual strands, too. As in previous chapters, questions and concerns will be raised.

Rejecting and Reclaiming

My initial response to feminist critiques of patriarchy was to reject religion in general and my own in particular. I clearly remember a gathering of faculty at Salem State College (now University) at which we discussed *The Church and the Second Sex*, by Mary Daly,[4] then a theology professor at Boston College. Her book critiqued the misogyny of her Catholic faith tradition, which, she revealed, used the myth of the "Eternal Feminine" to keep all women docile, create self-sacrificing mothers, and deny religious women the opportunity to serve as priests or contribute in an active way to their tradition. The reactions of the Catholic Church hierarchy and her college administration, including attempts to fire her, pushed her further into a radical feminist analysis.

In *Beyond God the Father*, Daly exposed the patriarchal practice of identifying women with the sexuality and evil of the material world, and associating men with a transcendent Supreme Being. She attributed the "unholy trinity" of race, genocide and war to a perverse sense of God as a static noun, rather than a verb—an evolving, growing, "human becoming."[5] Daly's early work was influenced by, among others, Paul Tillich, a Christian existentialist theologian, but she soon abandoned all forms of Christianity and built her work around the "Otherworld" of female experience. I heard her speak several times, always in awe of her amazing intellect and her unwillingness to become a heroic figure to other feminists. She firmly rejected adulation, preferring her audience to embark on their own voyages far from patriarchal limitations.

As a Jew I knew of the prayer Orthodox Jewish males recite each day thanking God that they were not born Gentile, a slave, or female. I had been told that the prayer was not intended to insult these groups, but rather to bless God for the privilege to pray, an honored obligation from which the other categories are exempt. But as a new feminist I found it hard to accept that my religious tradition contained such an edict, whatever the rationale. I had long struggled with my notions of God and religious observance, and, influenced by the critiques of religion by progressives and feminists, I set aside these quandaries to focus on feminist activism.

Yet I soon began to miss the celebrations and rituals of my own faith tradition. If it was feminism that made me turn away from Judaism, it was also feminism that brought me back. Through study with Jewish feminist scholars, participation in a Rosh Chodesh group described later in this chapter, and involvement in the National Women's Studies Association Jewish Caucus, I found a way to blend "Jewish" and "feminist."

Womanspirit Rising

The feminist processes highlighted in this book have helped "spirited women" to reshape spiritual practices that have marginalized women within and across faith traditions for many thousands of years. Consciousness-raising and small-group interactions have been utilized to both challenge and redefine the male-shaped precepts and practices of institutional religions—and also to recover and reclaim pre-patriarchal beliefs and rituals.

The CR process is woven through the classic anthology on feminist spirituality, *Womanspirit Rising: A Feminist Reader in Religion*, edited by Carol P. Christ and Judith Plaskow.[6] Defining experience as "the fabric of life as it is lived," the authors explain that "[t]he image feminists have in mind when they say *experience* is the consciousness-raising group," in which women whose roles have been shaped by "norms or preferences for female behavior expressed by men" begin to discover and give voice to what has been stifled. They describe the process in language already familiar to readers of this book: "In consciousness-raising groups, every woman's experience is heard, and judgment is not immediately made as to whether certain feelings are good or bad, appropriate or inappropriate. Women are encouraged to speak what has not previously been spoken. Often this speaking leads to the discovery of shared experiences."[7] Christ and Plaskow observe that there is relief in knowing that previously censored feelings, such as the occasional dislike of one's own children or lack of pleasure in sex, are not unique.

The feeling of jubilation in making deep and honest connections with other women is often followed by a critique of ideologies that have supported women's oppression and a determination to create alternatives. *Womanspirit Rising* contributors take many different approaches to healing the mind/body separation that informs much religious theory and practice. Most of the writers urge a questioning of the male-identified God, a revision of theology to value and celebrate women's history and experience, and new language and rituals that incorporate the feminine.

In a follow-up volume titled *Weaving the Visions: New Patterns in Feminist Spirituality*,[8] Plaskow and Christ recall the joyful exhilaration of early feminist consciousness-raising. But, in retrospect, they also acknowledge that a presumed sisterhood among all women obscured important differences. The newer work reveals the tensions in their own close relationship as each moved in a different direction, Christ toward embracing goddess spirituality, and Plaskow toward feminist reformation of Jewish tradition. *Weaving the Visions* includes a more diverse range of experiences and incorporates new approaches to methodology (*how* we learn the meanings of these experiences). In observing and lamenting the racism, anti–Semitism, class and other oppressions within the women's spirituality movement, the authors reveal that not all who call themselves feminists share a common sensitivity and commitment to others' struggles.

Many of the provocative thinkers who contributed to these important volumes, including Rosemary Radford Ruether, Elisabeth Schüssler Fiorenza, Dolores Williams and Riffat Hassan, have continued their analyses and enlarged their visions to explore intersections between race, gender, sexuality and culture.[9] Expanding theories continue to shape profound changes in individual lives and institutional practice, as my own journey exemplifies.

Jewish and Feminist

The connection of Judaism and feminism over the last forty-five years is stunningly presented in *Jewish Women and the Feminist Revolution*, an online multimedia exhibition created by the Jewish Women's Archive.[10] A timeline reveals that the growing feminist movement of the 1960s involved many women from Jewish backgrounds. To mention a few: Shulamith Firestone, author of the controversial *Dialectic of Sex*[11]; Adrienne Rich, poet, essayist and activist; Heather Booth, a founder of Jane, the underground Chicago abortion service; publisher Florence Howe, whose Feminist Press brought back many long-forgotten classics as well as new feminist works; and Gloria Steinem and Betty Friedan, who spread feminist ideas to a wide audience.

Jewish feminist calls for radical social change soon were applied specifically to Judaism. The archive timeline highlights the development of an analytic technique—consciousness-raising. The CR practice of gathering in small groups where shared experiences and insights can be examined and utilized to inform action has been woven throughout the tapestry of Jewish feminist change. Small groups for study, prayer and sisterhood include Ezrat Nashim, which derived its name from the women's section of the sex-segregated Orthodox synagogue, but also translates as "women's help." That ten-woman group prepared the "Call for Change" presented to the Conservative movement.[12] Another is B'not Esh, the "daughters of fire" collective, founded by Judith Plaskow and other academics, which has met for many years and has birthed similar groups within and beyond synagogues dedicated to celebrating feminist spirituality.[13]

The most common offspring of these is the Rosh Chodesh group, which celebrates the first day of the new month in the Jewish lunar calendar, a holiday with special significance for women, whose menstrual cycles follow the phases of the moon. Its roots trace back to the honoring of the righteous women who, according to the biblical book of Exodus, refused to contribute their jewelry to the creation of an idol in the shape of a golden calf.[14]

For many years in my southeastern Massachusetts community women of all ages and across the spectrum of Jewish identification joined together each month to celebrate the New Moon. Although there was no imperative to share personal experiences, over time we discussed what it was like to grow up Jewish, to be a Jewish mother and daughter, to challenge male leadership in Jewish institutions, to celebrate belated bat mitzvahs, to be Jewish women in the workplace, and more. Among the meetings I remember most was one in which the conversation was as warm as the cozy kitchen where a participant taught us all to bake challah; at another the visiting mother of one of our members shared how her Jewish values of progressive politics and *Yiddishkeit*, which loosely translates as a Jewish way of life, were supported by Workmen's Circle activities. During yet another session, we responded to the isolation a member felt in acknowledging and celebrating her daughter's lesbian identity within parts of the Jewish community and committed ourselves to working for inclusivity. Knowing that our gatherings were being replicated by women in many other places made us feel part of a vital movement.

Small groups once again made an important difference in a course I developed at University of Massachusetts Dartmouth on "The Jewish Woman," so titled to refute within the first class session the notion that there was such a recognizable composite, despite the images of chicken soup, Jewish American Princesses, overbearing Jewish mothers, and other stereotypes that participants (including the teacher) brought to the learning. Filled with students from varied religious, ethnic and racial backgrounds, we often formed smaller CR components, so class members were able to respond to often-controversial material at a deeper and more personal level and also to develop meaningful action projects to further explicate the texts. Among these were the creation of *midrashim* (commentaries on selections from the Bible), the revision and creation of prayers that drew on their own varied traditions, a presentation comparing the stereotype of the JAP with other racial and ethnic stereotypes, and the organization of the first women's seder at the university. The seder has become an annual event, with co-sponsorship by campus religious groups, the multicultural center, environmental organizations and many others whose diverse experiences have enriched our university community's understanding of the myriad and continuing struggles for freedom.

Teaching women's studies brought me to the National Women's Studies Association and membership in the Jewish Caucus, established in 1983. The caucus expanded my understanding that within the words "Jewish" and "woman" were multiple experiences and identities that shaped our being and becoming. For a number of years, the caucus sponsored a pre-conference day before the start of the annual conference, during which we discussed how being a Jewish feminist varied depending on one's class background, geographical location, sexuality, disability and other variables. Our CR exchanges of personal stories led to shared understanding and action. We became aware of stereotyping and anti–Semitism within the women's movement—and within ourselves. The caucus also held a Shabbat service and organized sessions and panels on the diverse experiences of Jewish women, from which numerous books, articles and new courses grew. After several years of inactivity, I joined a few other members to petition NWSA to reestablish the Jewish Caucus as a constituent group of the organization, which was approved at the 2011 annual conference.

I am proud to be a strong supporter of Keshet, a grassroots organization dedicated to creating a fully inclusive Jewish community for gay, lesbian, bisexual and transgender Jews, directed by Idit Klein.[15] *Keshet,* a Hebrew word for both "rainbow" (the LGBT symbol) and "bow" (an instrument for action), is a model not only for Jews but also for any individual or group whose refusal to be the other, the outsider, can reshape and revitalize in positive ways what has been seen as immovable and unchangeable. The organization produced a wonderful documentary film titled *Hineini,* which translates as "Here I Am" and highlights the courageous action of one young woman who was determined to create a gay-straight alliance at her Jewish high school.[16] The film illuminates how difficult dialogues within a community can lead to greater understanding and connection. Keshet has merged with Mosaic, an organization with affiliates in Denver and San Francisco. Although the growing organization has a national and international political agenda, the CR process of individuals sharing their stories in small gatherings remains a principal organizing technique.

My own experience offers a very partial view of the mosaic of connections between Jewish and feminist identities. Of course, I have an even more superficial understanding of the search to fuse feminism with faith traditions other than my own—but enough to keep me reading and learning and exchanging thoughts with friends and acquaintances so I can deepen my knowledge.

Catholic Women and Spiritual Leadership

Over many centuries Catholic religious women have been inspirational models of the supportive communities advocated by feminism. E. Ann Matter has written about medieval nuns. In their cloistered environments, they were able to enjoy an autonomy that escaped most women of their era and experience spiritual, intellectual, and, according to the author's research, sexual connections. Although the experiences of nuns varied, Matter cites many nuns who became religious thinkers, poets, musicians and composers.[17]

The tradition of quality education for nuns produced the first female academic leaders in the United States. Most Catholic colleges were founded by women's religious orders and led by members of those orders for decades. When I first became an academic administrator these Catholic women deans and presidents were sources of admiration and advice. As Catholic colleges became co-ed, male priests and lay leaders replaced nuns, and now female leadership is at an all-time low, even as more women are gaining presidencies at non-sectarian institutions.

"Where Have All the Women Gone?" is the question posed in an article in *Inside Higher Education* by Libby A. Nelson.[18] One answer is that they have turned from administration to activism. Two of my close friends have "sister sisters." Unlike my childhood memories of the teachers at the parochial school near my home who wore wimples and black habits, or the often caricatured nuns in motion pictures who entertain us with their "nunsense," these "women religious" (the preferred nomenclature for today's Catholic sisters) bear no outward signs of their affiliation. In contrast with their cloistered foremothers, they are out in the world advocating for social and economic justice; many consider themselves feminists.

Fifteen hundred members of the Leadership Conference of Women Religious (LCWR) represent more than 80 percent of the 57,000 Catholic women religious in the United States. Their webpage describes their mission as "inspired by the radical call of the Gospel, led by God's Spirit, and companioned by one another."[19] Since 1998 the Leadership Conference of Women Religious has organized "think tank" sessions to explore ways to apply both spiritual reflection and social analysis to issues calling for the systemic transformation required for real change. As in other consciousness-raising settings, the collective wisdom and power of the group challenges complacency and stimulates insights.

One participant notes that "systems thinking will prevent us from uncon-sciously employing the same mental models that are causing the problems that we want to solve."[20]

Many Catholics and other advocates for the outstanding work being done by women religious for and with immigrants, youth, the physically and mentally disabled, and the poor would like to see these church leaders perform duties now limited to priests, including conducting mass. Instead, the Vatican has denounced the LCWR for advocating "radical feminist" ideas. The Congregation for the Doctrine of the Faith has issued a mandate aimed at bringing the alleged mis-creants into line. The Vatican's "Congregation" claims that the LCWR is under-mining Roman Catholic teachings on homosexuality and birth control and promoting "radical feminist themes incompatible with the Catholic faith." It also reprimanded the nuns for hosting speakers who "often contradict or ignore" church teachings and for making public statements that "disagree with or chal-lenge the bishops, who are the church's authentic teachers of faith and morals."[21]

In an interview on National Public Radio[22] Sister Pat Farrell, the president of the LCWR, responded to the phrase "radical feminist themes": "Sincerely, what I hear in the phrasing … is fear—a fear of women's positions in the church. Now, that's just my interpretation. I have no idea what was in the mind of the Congregation of the Doctrine of the Faith when they wrote that. But women theologians around the world have been seriously looking at the question of: How have the church's interpretations of how we talk about God, interpret Scripture, organize life in the church—how have they been tainted by a culture that minimizes the value and the place of women?"

In her article in the *Boston Globe*[23] Farah Stockman traces the activism of women in the church back to the late nineteenth century, when a group of nuns set up schools in malaria-infected southern Africa. Stockman notes that pre-vious efforts to limit nuns' activities have resulted in breaks from the church by several hundred sisters; the Congregation for the Doctrine of the Faith might lead the vast majority of U.S. nuns to become independent of the Vat-ican. LCWR President Sister Pat Farrell continues to express hope for a "third way" that would allow the women religious to negotiate with the Vatican. Whether this model of creative tension will keep the women religious within the Vatican structure is not yet known, but it is clear that many agree with blogger Thomas Fox's assertion that, working from the bottom up with the poor and afflicted whom they serve rather than as subservient, unquestioning followers of the hierarchy, Catholic sisters, supported by one another, will change the course of church history.[24]

In an Easter Monday message in 2012, Pope Benedict XVI expressed an appeal for women to have a more visible role within the church.[25] Pope Benedict has since been succeeded by Pope Francis, who, in an interview on July 29, 2013, said that women have a "special role" in the church, but would not be ordained as priests.[26]

Both religious and secular proponents of women's "superiority" have used presumed compliments to limit females to only those roles that are deemed by the patriarchy to be worthy of this elevated status. The members of the LCWR have declined such flattery, believing that their "right place" is wherever people need help. Their vision and commitment grows from, and is nurtured by, their community of sisters.

In preparing this chapter, I had a long conversation with "sister sister" Mary Behan, SSJ, who had read some of my work. Our conversation strengthened my respect for the life of prayer, meditation, loving connection to her community members and social activism that infuses her daily existence with meaning. She spoke in a deeply personal way, but without anger, about the Vatican's response to her activism and that of her colleagues. Her reaction is as follows: "Listen—and do what you know is right."

As I've observed within Jewish denominations, challenges and changes in the Catholic institutional structure have expanded spiritual vision and enlarged opportunities for its expression. The hierarchical structures that prevailed when Sister Mary first became a nun have changed dramatically. Then a permanent mother superior answered to a bishop; now a president is elected by each chapter in her order every six years. The president works with a leadership team, and numerous committees have been created for maximum participation. Mary talked about how her community of women religious has grown through using a process similar to consciousness-raising, which she describes as "small groups to share personal experiences and support."

Although Mary works with some young nuns, the number of women who make a lifelong commitment to religious life has dwindled. The consciousness-raising gatherings include not only women religious but also lay Catholics who, while not dedicating themselves full-time to religious life, have taken more limited vows of faith that allow them to combine family and work with spiritual activism. Other women who do not wish to take vows also join the groups to share their spiritual explorations and find individual and collective strength in their work for social justice in their immediate communities and beyond.

Muslim Women and Feminism

One of my first encounters with Muslim women came when two of my college dorm-mates returned from the summer break dressed in long skirts and head coverings. They had become part of the Black Muslim movement.

What I began to learn about the Muslim tradition was within the context of the civil rights and black liberation movements through reading and discussions about the differences between the separatist black movement espoused by Malcolm X and the approach to integration advanced by Martin Luther King, Jr. I knew little of how the Nation of Islam advocated by Elijah Muhammad, Malcolm X and Louis Farrakhan resembled or differed from beliefs and practices of Muslims throughout the world.

Fortunately, my colleagues at UMass Dartmouth, Shaukat and Parveen Ali, introduced me to many Muslim traditions. Shaukat was a member of the political science department and Parveen the author of an important book, *Status of Women in the Muslim World*.[27] Although she traveled frequently to visit family in Pakistan, the women's studies program utilized her abilities and willingness to lecture and teach when she was in the area. It was through small gatherings in which the university's feminist community and its allies shared the stories of our lives that my knowledge and understanding of Islam, and the status and struggles of women within that faith tradition, grew.

Parveen's commitment ran in the family. Her sister Riffat Hassan is a renowned Islamic feminist scholar of the Qur'an who has taught at Harvard, Oklahoma State University and the University of Louisville.[28] The women's studies program and other campus partners brought Hassan to the university, where she presented an eye-opening talk that, like her prolific writing, contrasted the deep commitment to human rights expressed in the original words of the Qur'an with cultural practices that have oppressed Muslim women.

Her feminist critique of patriarchal misinterpretations of Islam began by happenstance. As the lone Muslim faculty member at Oklahoma State University, she was, by default, the adviser of the Muslim Student Association. The adviser was required to address the organization each year. Although her knowledge of her religion was deep and broad, Hassan was given the topic of women's role in Islam, which they assumed was her area of expertise. She was dismayed at the obvious sexism of the members of the all-male group, but decided not to challenge the assignment. In an article in the *Harvard Divinity Bulletin,* Hassan recalls, "I began my research on the subject more out of a sense of duty than out of any deep awareness that I had embarked on perhaps the most important journey of my life. The more I saw the justice and compassion of God reflected in the Qur'anic teachings regarding women, the more anguished and angry I became at seeing the injustice and inhumanity to which Muslim women in general are subjected in actual life. I began to feel that it was my duty, as a part of the microscopic minority of educated Muslim women, to do as much consciousness-raising regarding the situation of Muslim women as I could."[29]

Hassan acknowledges that "for Muslim women, kept for centuries in physical, mental and emotional bondage, analyzing their personal experience is probably overwhelming."[30] She identifies with Christian and Jewish women who also have gone back to the original sources and discovered that many interpretations that reinforce the notion of male supremacy are not validated by careful textual analysis. In her speaking and writing Hassan poignantly reveals that many women know from their life experiences that they are discriminated against by patriarchal Muslim structures, but are uncomfortable identifying with Western secular culture, principally because many people, including feminists, offer "pity" to Muslim women, instead of providing support to those who wish to question practices and misinterpretations of the tradition while retaining their place within it.[31]

Womanist Spirituality

Many feminists of color have rejected misogyny within their traditions while honoring the joyful expressions of faith and support for daily living that religious institutions also offer to women. Theologian Linda E. Thomas explains that womanist theology explores both the positive and the negative aspects of African American women's relationship to institutional religion and the larger American culture, affirms the positive aspects of African American women's spiritual experience, and "talks back" to both white feminists and black male liberation theologians.[32]

While black theology responded to racism, and feminist theology to the oppression of women, womanist theology deals with the everyday reality of African American and other women of color. It reveals how patriarchy, racism, classism and other complex and interweaving forces affect women, men and children.[33]

Womanist theorists and practitioners draw upon the stories of grandmothers, mothers and their own lives. The writing and practice of womanists exemplify the CR model advocated in this book, which drew inspiration from the civil rights struggle. In asking the questions "who and what has impacted our lives from earliest days ... who has been excluded from what is known and how might we see the world differently if we acknowledge and value the experiences and thoughts of those who have been excluded?"[34] womanists seek to rediscover and revalue the voices that have been silenced. Insights on the distribution of power, wealth and social privilege can be uncovered by listening to the "direct speech of women in our midst ... whether poor or advantaged, literate or 'Ph.D.ed.'" Although centered on the experiences of African American women, the goal is to unite God talk and God walk to improve the lives of women of color and all who are oppressed throughout the world.

I asked a friend who is the associate pastor of a local Bethel A.M.E. Church about womanism. Her answer reflects a point made frequently throughout this book: no one descriptor can encompass the experiences and aspirations of any group. As a Jamaican American she brings some different perceptions to the search for affirmation among women in her church where congregants are 80 percent female but the pastorate is nearly all male. Many A.M.E. congregations have a women's outreach program that "seeks to minister to the whole woman and her unique spiritual, emotional, physical, fiscal, social, and psychological realities as a Black woman in America. Activities include: Bible study, prayer teams, seasonal retreats, conferences, seminars, fellowships, a book club, sisterhood-building outreach projects, health and fitness classes and workshops, an investment club, financial management classes and workshops, and a mentoring program linking younger and older sisters in fellowship and support."[35] As such efforts *for* women are translated into activism *by* women, she predicts there will be a change in the current male-dominated leadership.[36] As a teacher, counselor and parent, as well as a pastor, she is also hoping that there will be a more generous approach to spiritual practice that will transcend the growing tendency toward fundamentalism and the distrust and hatred some people direct toward those who have different ways of believing.

Returning to the Goddess

"We all come from the Goddess and to her we shall return," is the beginning of a pagan chant attributed to Z Budapest.[37] Despite numerous positive examples of feminist transformations of religious traditions, many feminists have not been able to reconcile the male-defined authoritarianism and misogyny of organized religion with their feminist values. The search for a meaningful spiritual life has led a sizeable number of feminists to seek inspiration in practices they have discovered, or can hypothesize took place, before the establishment of patriarchal religions. Elinor Gadon's *Once and Future Goddess*,[38] a comprehensive anthropological study of goddess worship, is a preeminent example of the scholarship that has informed the reclamation of the role of women in religious practice.

An example of the ways in which goddess spirituality has been applied in a contemporary setting is *Cakes for the Queen of Heaven*, a curriculum developed for the Unitarian Universalist Association by Shirley Ann Ranck[39] to explore "women's power—past, present and future." First issued in 1995, it is used in its original and revised editions by Unitarian churches and other groups, and is taught in small gatherings of women akin to consciousness-raising groups.

Ranck utilizes her background in psychology and religious studies to trace the shift from goddess worship to patriarchal religions. She documents how the journey from Goddess to God obliterated many thousands of years of female and shared gender power. Ranck also reveals that the Goddess was not completely forgotten as this transition occurred. She suggests that the image of Mary is a key example of the ways that traditional religious practice retains its roots in goddess symbolism: "The Church used her to satisfy the need for a female presence in Christianity but also to keep women in a subordinate position."[40] Ranck states that the New Testament mentions Mary only to emphasize the divine conception of Jesus; yet she has been and continues to be celebrated in both great works of art and everyday worship. The veneration of Mary in artistic production reached its pinnacle in the fifteenth and sixteenth centuries. The Protestant Reformation attempted to end the honoring of Mary, abolishing nunneries and reinforcing women's subordination in other ways. Yet Mary is still a central aspect of religious faith in many parts of the world.

Witchcraft

Witchcraft continues, too, despite a lengthy history of persecution of presumed witches, 80 percent of whom were female. Many cite the notorious *Malleus Maleficarum* (translated from Latin as, *Hammer of the Witches*), authored in the fifteenth century by German Catholic clergyman Heinrich Kramer, as the guidebook that influenced witch trials for over 300 years. This book outlined ways to disclose who was a witch and detailed methods of torture. According to Kramer and the many who believed him, females, who were by their very nature "weak" and carnal, were more likely to be practitioners of witchcraft.[41]

Circles of women have formed to reclaim witchcraft from its misogynist history. The process of reclamation includes celebrating the female body and sexuality, embracing women's relationship to Mother Earth, validating mother-daughter connections and respecting the wisdom of women that grows with age. Reclaiming challenges the notion of the Divine as male and calls into question religious systems that justify power *over* women, who, with Eve as exemplar, have been seen as the sources of temptation, promiscuity and disorder.

In *Drawing Down the Moon,*[42] Margot Adler provides a comprehensive history of "Witches, Druids, Goddess Worshippers and Other Pagans in America Today." She describes the transformation she herself experienced through participation in a gathering, not at Stonehenge or another setting associated with ancient spirituality, but in Staten Island, New York. Women joined together to bless the Goddess, each other, the feminist movement, and struggling women around the world. Her story is one of hundreds told by women who feel that their participation in a women's spirituality circle is a kind of "home-coming" to a place where they can integrate body and soul, receive energy from other women and support one another in becoming whole.

Small groups, some known as covens, are the setting for explorations of various expressions of Neo-Paganism. Like consciousness-raising groups, membership is usually limited to twelve or thirteen and the participants meet in a circle. With slight variations, similar rituals involving candlelight, flowers, edibles, libations, music, dance and chanting occur wherever Neo-Pagans gather to celebrate. Adler quotes from a priestess who stresses the common themes that cut across differences in the deities honored, the traditions drawn upon and the rituals practiced. Many Neo-Pagans express a fusion of feminism and the Craft. They "view earth as the Great Mother who has been raped, pillaged and plundered, who must once again be exalted and celebrated if we are to survive."[43] Adler observes that Neo-Pagans appreciate anarchism, pluralism, polytheism, animism, sensuality, passion and pleasure. They share a belief in religious ecstasy and the goodness of this world—and the possibility of many others.

Starhawk (born Miriam Simos) is another well-known proponent of Neo-Paganism and the goddess movement. A self-described witch, ecofeminist and social activist, she has authored several clearly written volumes that are "bibles" for those wishing to incorporate goddess-centered spirituality into their lives.[44] Starhawk rejects the idea of the Goddess as the female counterpart of the male ruler. The Goddess doesn't rule the world—she *is* the world, within and around us. Starhawk explicitly advocates using consciousness-raising, and her advice will be familiar to those who have read earlier chapters of this book: "Consciousness-raising techniques can ... be very effective. We may go around the circle, letting each person tell why she or he came to the group and what she or he hopes to get out of it. Everyone is allowed to speak for a limited period of time without interruptions, so that quieter people are encouraged to express themselves and more voluble individuals do not dominate the conversation. Questions and comments come after everyone has had a turn to speak."[45] In common with CR groups, a coven's success depends upon building strong interpersonal connections based on trust.

Along with consciousness-raising exercises, Starhawk's books include poetry and rituals, meant to inspire and guide women wishing to embark on a personal and collective spiritual journey to bring the Goddess into their lives. Doing it "right" is not a concern. There are no rigid guidelines—except perhaps to be open to experimentation. She encourages innovation: "Do something once, it's an experiment. Do it twice and it's a tradition."[46]

The familiar backlash against those who challenge convention has been leveled at Neo-Paganism, which is often caricatured and trivialized. For example,

Sandra Miesel, writing for the Catholic Education Resource Center, asserts, "The feminists see witches as the natural enemy of patriarchy, rallying around them as Old Leftists did around the leaders of the Spanish Republic. For them, as for pagans, playing the politics of victimization strengthen solidarity." She also scorns "those of a Green Stripe," such as ecofeminists, who celebrate the historical role that women played in medical treatments and midwifery.[47] Their healing skills, regrettably, were often dismissed as "witchery."[48]

Helen Berger, a sociologist of religion and author of four books on witchcraft, has followed the remarkable growth of paganism and chronicled both the common practices and variations in beliefs and rituals. She notes a similar pattern of generational "rediscovery" in paganism and feminism. Despite ancient antecedents, modern practitioners renew the "click" experience of new feminists. As one of her interviewees noted, "everyone comes into Paganism" and "makes it up all over again."[49]

Opening to the Spiritual Experience

As part of an ongoing discussion group of greater Boston Jewish feminists, I attended a lecture by Israeli scholar Rivka Neriya-Ben Shahar, a young Orthodox Jew who spent a semester at Harvard University on a Fulbright grant. Rivka spoke about what she saw as the "revolutionary" Amen meals, ritual gatherings of women that are taking place throughout her country. As the meals proceed, both the special benedictions over the various food items and the stories that women are invited to share about personal challenges and accomplishments, such as childbirth, recovery from illness or finding employment, are followed by a resounding "Amen."[50]

I must admit that my initial response was a bit incredulous, even condescending. I have replayed my reaction and realize that I often judge stories of spiritual transformation with a suspicion that may be preventing me from being as open as I might to exploring these possibilities in my own life. Perhaps this is another instance of the patriarchy having "an outpost," not only in my head, but also in my heart, that has led me to overidentify with the "rational," secular viewpoint of many male progressives.

In fact, when I heard the excitement in Rivka's voice and saw the incredible light in her eyes as she recounted the Amen sessions, I realized she was experiencing many of the same feelings that I had—and have—when I am in a safe space to share my dreams, hopes, passions and commitments with other women whose reciprocating energy makes me feel that real change is possible. Rivka suggests that Israeli women are creating a "new women's religious culture" through combining traditional blessings over food with the sharing of personal experiences characteristic of the consciousness-raising process. She theorizes that the Amen meals conjoin the insights of the source material for her work—Judith Butler's concept of "doing gender" and Orit Avishai's notion of "doing religion," which "focuses on the authentic religious subject that *chooses* its religious conduct, experiences, and complex identity."

Being outside the Israeli Jewish culture, I was not fully aware of the wide range of religious—and secular—expression embraced by women of various ethnicities, ages and socioeconomic backgrounds. According to the attendees interviewed by Rivka, the Amen meals that have proliferated in various locations and group formations have offered uniquely stirring experiences. The ritual, separate from male-defined and dominated traditions, unites participants as women, and as Jews, in settings where they can define what provides spiritual meaning and feelings of empowerment. As she has collected data on the "Amen meals," Rivka has discovered that other faith traditions have similar gatherings. "It seems that the creation of a new women's religious culture is a more widespread phenomenon, not just restricted to Jewish women. For example, a somewhat similar ritual is the 'Sofre' ritual in Iran. Iranian women come together, sit on the floor, eat, and pray. In the center they put a tablecloth on which they place various foods—fresh fruit and vegetables, cakes, and sweets. Generally, the goal of the Sofre is to ask something from God. Like the Amen meals, women promise: 'If my son will be healthy, I'll make a Sofre.' They invite an ayatollah's wife and study the Koran together. And, like at the Amen meals, they bring home something fresh and sweet."[51]

Breaking Bread and Healing Divisions

Breaking bread together can build community and trust. In an era when fundamentalism is widespread, gathering in small groups—initially to feed our bodies, and eventually, perhaps, to see that there is no one "right way" to nourish our spirits—can be a step on the road to intergroup understanding and social action.

Rahel Wasserfall has worked for nearly a decade with the International Summer School on Religion and Public Life (ISSRPL) which brings together people from different religions for an intensive two-week practical experience in respect for diversity. Finding a way to appreciate and incorporate the symbolic and literal dietary requirements of the forty participants in the annual program is what she calls the "hidden story" of the program's success. "Learning to live together differently starts with learning to sit at a communal table together," Wasserfall states. As in small, consciousness-raising groups, personal stories become the source of the intellectual themes explored in the school, among them the contentious issues of minority-majority relations, purity vs. impurity, exclusion vs. inclusion, and collective work for justice.[52]

Drawing upon daily experience to build larger understanding and positive action for change is illustrated in the popular book, *The Faith Club*.[53] Following the terrorist attacks of September 11, 2001, three mothers—a Palestinian Muslim, a Jew, and a former Catholic, now an Episcopalian—decided to meet to write a children's book that would affirm the shared elements of their traditions. They soon discovered that they needed to address their own stereotypes, fears and concerns. They began what became a three-year exploration, during which they discovered issues and questions about their own faith traditions as well as those of their colleagues. Their gatherings were far from the perfunctory interfaith services or breakfasts that take place in many communities. Instead, they had deep, soul-searching conversations, arguments, rifts, rages and times of hopelessness and disillusion. The authenticity of their interactions and the profound changes that were the result of their sharing are reminiscent of the responses of women who have participated in CR groups.

Rather than a children's book, the authors' discussions, dialogues and debates produced an inspirational work for adults that is a springboard for forming consciousness-raising groups around issues of religious differences. *The Faith Club* website links people to a blog, offers a kit of guidelines and even connects people who want to start their own groups.

Bringing the Past to the Present

Among the many pieces of wisdom that my feminist spiritual journey has offered is that a feminist transformation does not mean that the shaping experiences of the past cannot be brought into the present. The wonderful memoir by Helène Aylon, *Whatever Is Contained Must Be Released*,[54] captures this concept beautifully. Aylon's personal journey begins with a deeply religious upbringing in an Orthodox Jewish home, the required attendance at an all-girls yeshiva, marriage at age eighteen to a rabbi, and devotion to husband, children and tradition. After her husband's tragic illness and death when she was just 30, Aylon "reinvents" herself. Through her unique talents and energy, and inspired by the feminist movement, she becomes an internationally recognized artist and an activist for peace, social justice and the environment. One of her most controversial pieces is "The Liberation of G-d" (1996), an installation of Hebrew Bibles in which she has inserted pages of vellum over the text and highlighted by hand in bright pink every passage in which women are rejected or unrecognized or violated. Yet, having revealed the misogyny within her tradition, Aylon remains a committed Jew. She explains, "You see, I need more than Women's Liberation; I need Jewish Women's Liberation. I stay [within Judaism] because I sense a beauty intrinsic in what I perceive to be the Foremothers' input that has not been recorded, nor honored, nor acknowledged. These particular aspects of Judaism [that very well might have originated with women] I would never let go of."[55]

Speaking from Experience: A Women and Spirituality Group

More than twenty-five years ago a friend called to tell me about a gathering of women taking place near her home in New Hampshire. The purpose of the weekend workshop was to explore ways to meet the challenges of balancing work, family, and relationship transitions. An experienced facilitator who had taught in a graduate program from which two of the participants had graduated was to guide the workshop. We each contributed to her modest stipend. One member of the group offered to host the gathering. We brought our sleeping bags and spread out on whatever floor space we could find. Meals consisted of what turned out to be a delicious and balanced blend of our potluck contributions.

Each of the women knew one or several others, so we began in the spirit of friendship. After a wonderful weekend of empathic listening to each other's life stories and an exchange of tears, laughter and lots of creative energy and insight, we were already a community. As our time together drew to an end, the workshop leader said she'd like to meet with the group again, not as a facilitator, but as a participant, to build on the discoveries we'd made together.

When we met for the second time, "spirituality" became a unifying theme that was threaded throughout our weekend gatherings for more than two decades of meetings. I was teased about my oft-repeated remark that I was "spiritually incorrect." I had not yet read Starhawk, Adler and other proponents of a New Age spirituality and had not participated in rituals inspired by pre-patriarchal cultures. I was initially self-conscious about practices unfamiliar to me, and concerned about the appropriation of sacred traditions that were not my own. These reservations remained, but I acknowledged that resistance to "new-age-y stuff" came from critiques from others rather than my own experience. With each gathering I became less self-conscious and judgmental. Along with growing friendships, I discovered the benefits of meditation, enlarged my capacity to connect "body and soul," and enriched my connections to the beauty and rhythms of the natural world.

Many of the women in the group lived much closer to nature than I did.

Three had homes "off the grid," in a land trust where each person or family had a small private dwelling, but shared a road leading into the property, as well as a beautiful, large, jointly created pond, equipment, and friendship. They used electricity sparingly through photovoltaics and heated their homes with wood. One, with a little help from her friends, had built her own home in the community. I had grown up in urban and suburban neighborhoods and loved being surrounded by trees and wildflowers. Time spent in their homes, one of which could be accessed only on snowshoes or cross-country skis in the winter, offered a very different experience—and an appreciation of other ways of living that women could and did choose.

Initially we met four times a year, sharing the seasons of our lives as the calendar turned. We supported each other through separations and divorces, the challenges of raising children, the mixed emotions of watching them leave our homes for their own, the celebrations of those now-adult children's commitments to relationships, the blessings of grandchildren, the loss of parents, work struggles, illnesses, and many other turning points.

The youngest member was about a dozen years the junior of the oldest, with several of us having birthdays in the same year. We came from various Judeo-Christian faith traditions. Few were regular attendees at religious services, although one former Catholic became an active member of a Quaker meeting during our time together, and another former Quaker frequented services at the Unitarian Church where her partner was the minister. After a number of years two of the members dropped out for personal reasons; three others moved, with two continuing the connection, coming from the opposite coast once a year—and hosting us in California for one long-planned gathering. At first we described ourselves as the "women and spirituality" group; later the name changed to "the Crones," to reflect our transition to the "third chapter" of our lives.

Although we didn't follow particular guidebooks, many of the techniques outlined by Starhawk and other authors were loosely incorporated. We prepared the space in which we formed our circle, sometimes clearing it with incense.[56] We created an "altar," a low table in our midst covered with a pretty piece of fabric, a candle, and perhaps a bouquet of flowers. We placed on the altar pictures of loved ones or an object that reflected a part of ourselves we wished to share with the group. Our gatherings began with a period of meditation, and then, as is the practice in most CR groups, with a "check-in." We each went around the circle, giving an update on what had happened in our lives since we last met, speaking not only or especially of chronological events, but also of what had moved or challenged us in deeper ways, sometimes referring to items that we'd brought to the altar. This was a time for listening without interruption. As in CR groups, at the end of the check-in some common themes emerged from our individual stories. We would talk about ways to use the rest of the weekend to explore some of these, trying to find a focus that would respond to individual concerns using the resources and energy of the group.

Each weekend included time for preparing and eating delicious food. This group included some of the best culinary expertise that could be gathered anywhere! And we always made time for exercise. Depending on the season and location, which alternated among the homes that were large enough to accommodate us all, we'd walk, hike, swim, canoe or kayak. We set aside time to be alone, too. Frequently there was singing, and this was one setting where I didn't feel I should be silent, despite my tone-deafness. And we created together. On one occasion we painted sneakers to celebrate spring and each other. I still have mine, purchased for a few dollars in a discount shoe store, but transformed with paint and sequin flowers around the words taken from a poster that once hung in my office: "Sisterhood Is Blooming; Springtime Will Never Be the Same." Thinking back, the project was symbolic; it was easier to stand on our own two feet, because we had the joy and support of each other. Another time we brought pieces of fabric that had special meaning. (I remember bringing the remnants of sheets my daughters had used as small children.) We told each other what the pieces of material recalled while we stitched them together to form "Lady Crone," who then joined our circle, replete with beads, boa and a hat. Once, when we were at the beach, we traced each other's bodies in the sand, and then—after decorating the "sculptures" with rocks, shells, starfish and other sea treasures—we watched as the tide took them away. The next day remnants of our body sculptures were still there, another metaphor for what is retained even as we change in many ways.

We also created rituals. Ranck describes ritual as "a way of looking at the experiences we have, ascribing special meaning to certain moments or events, and celebrating these meanings with people close to us. Ritual is also a way of getting in touch with our own deepest joys and sorrows, and with the power and the will within us that can heal and can enable us to act on behalf of ourselves and our values."[57] We drew from many sources—from the traditions of our families to more recent involvements some of the members had with Buddhism, yoga, meditation, healing circles and/or New Age spiritualism. Whatever the source of inspiration, many of the rituals were deeply affecting.

Was it always positive? Often, but not always. I recently spoke with one member of the group who felt that even among our small number there were "cliques" that sometimes reminded her of her middle school years, although these were never named or discussed as a barrier to the health of the group. One member dropped out after a couple of years because the group meetings did not provide the setting she was seeking to support her needs as she faced treatment for cancer. Perhaps we would have been able to do this later in our history together. Another member, a recovering alcoholic, felt that our Saturday evening meals with wine (and, for a couple of members, the use of marijuana, although not within the group) made her feel like the "odd woman out." I have deep misgivings on how we handled the concerns that led to her leaving the group. Her departure seemed abrupt, but I understand in retrospect that it was a long time coming. We had not listened with the care we espoused.

Group members still exchange calls and e-mails. A year or two after we stopped meeting, Ellie sent us her recollections, which made me think that more often than not our group was a place to come in out of the cold into a circle of trust: "I was reminded of our gatherings in the Fall and how that time of year was appreciated and enjoyed for the trip to VT or Wingaersheek. [A seaside section of Gloucester, Massachusetts, where one member's family had a summer cottage where we huddled by the wood stove before or after the beach season.] It made me think of how we all have been on a personal journey since that first weekend we gathered at Pam's under Carol's guidance. I found myself thinking of my own path and each of yours as I know it and it feels like we all have come down to where we ought to be. What a ride it has been. It was a delightful feeling to think of all we celebrated and struggled with and shared (tears, hugs, anger, cold dips in the water, art projects, ritual, singing, ah yes drumming, walks oh those delicious walks with alternating partners, sharing, supporting, dining, frustration, inspiration, the whole mish-a-gash, as Ferris used to say)." Ellie updated us on her closest relationships with her partner and children, and her work with the elderly people for whom she was a loving caretaker. She concluded her message with these words: "There is gratitude for each and every one of you that were willing to be on this path with me for just the right amount of time. So Crones we were ahead of our time in many ways. What a witness to the pain and joys of being a woman in this here life ... no regrets."

Good-byes and Hellos

I still and always will draw on the inspiration and growth I experienced in that group of remarkable women. I often think of how lucky I've been to have lived in a time when women became conscious of the importance of creating spaces to be together to share stories, learn from and with each other, and leave with new insights to take to our work within our families, places of employment and communities.

Saying good-bye to groups that provided the setting for personal and collective growth is difficult, but the search for spiritual meaning within a feminist context has been a constant for me. It's been many years since the Rosh Chodesh group discussed earlier met each month, and now the Crones no longer gather as a group. They will never be replaced, but new opportunities continue to arise. I've been pleased to be welcomed to "Connections," a women's community within the synagogue my daughter attends, and I was even given the honor of addressing the congregation on Jewish feminism at a Shabbat service launching a series of talks by women with "connections" to Shir Tikvah. A group of Boston-area Jewish feminists gathered for a year as a follow-up to a New York conference on "Women's Liberation and Jewish Identity."[58] While not devoted exclusively to spiritual issues, the discussions touched that amorphous dimension of our lives. It was through that group that I became acquainted with Rivka Neriya-Ben Shahar and learned about the Amen meals described previously. A couple of years ago several of us at the Women's Studies Research Center at Brandeis University formed a "ritual studies" group. Initially our discussions had an academic focus and were led by a member whose rabbinic preparation had included extensive scholarship on the ways in which ritual is performed within and across cultures. More recently we've explored the meaning of ritual in our own lives. This year we are looking at the connotations of the word "spirituality," a term I've used in this chapter without really being able to define it. My dilemma is shared by others in the group from varied religious/spiritual backgrounds and we are looking forward to combining the experiential and the cognitive in our search for what draws us to the quests expressed by that elusive word.

Some Caveats

As we search for the "god" in ourselves and others, contradictions and challenges can arise that require exploration. Here are a few that concern me.

Appropriation and Disrespect

Some issues that emerged when I participated in the "Crones" group remain. I and others involved in the myriad expressions of feminist spirituality need to ask questions about adaptations of others' traditions, beliefs and rituals, and even one's own. I am concerned particularly about the power dynamics involved in finding spiritual meaning in practices of cultures that very nearly have been destroyed. As I write, I am squirming with discomfort recalling a powwow I attended many years ago. There was respectful attention to the dances and ceremonies, but there were also those who came to gawk at the culture of the original inhabitants of what are now the Americas. Their condescending comments remain with me. My response to that event is linked to feelings that emerged when I was a "tourist" wandering through an ancient Jewish ghetto in Venice. The progeny of the people who were isolated from the general population eventually suffered an unimaginably more horrible fate. There is a tourist industry around the concentration camps, too. Appropriation of the past for tourism and commercial purposes is closely related to the following issue.

Consumerism

For many years, I lived near and worked in Salem, Massachusetts, the setting for real and fictional witch trials. The long main street of the tourist area is lined with shops offering a plethora of New Age and witch-themed artifacts, including crystals, celestial guides, wands, altar cloths, crystals, statuary, books, music, chimes, tarot cards and clothing. Although certainly not limited to women's spirituality, consumer capitalism threatens to diminish the seriousness of New Age feminism and witchcraft just as it has undermined the meaning of other movements for fundamental change. The commercial co-optation reaches a frenzy around Halloween, when the traffic entering Salem is tied up for miles and few of the costumed witches who fill the local bars appear to be on a spiritual quest.

Spirituality vs. Activism, or a Feminist Fusion?

Some are concerned that the turn toward spirituality has decreased feminist involvement in social activism. The substance of this claim is revealed in the paucity of material on feminism on bookstore shelves. The sections on "women's interests" now display an abundance of material on self-help and New Age spirituality.

Yet most of the "spirited women" discussed in this chapter maintain that the opposite is true. They believe that attention to their inner lives provides the clarity needed to analyze and take action to make the outward changes that are necessary to transform society. Although it is a small sample, my own involvements confirm this idea. All the participants in the Crones were thoughtful and self-reflective activists, as are the friends and colleagues I mention above.

Shirley Ann Ranck emphasizes the link between spirituality and activism: "Once we are aware of our own situation as women in a patriarchal society, and of the ecological crisis facing the sacred Earth, there is no turning back. Our eyes have been opened and the only road we can travel with integrity is the road of action: action to empower women; action to preserve the Earth."[59]

Bettina Aptheker's memoir, *Intimate Politics*,[60] offers another example of how vital spiritual practice is to a feminist politics. Aptheker, the daughter of one of the American Communist Party's chief theorists, spent many years involved in party organizing. She was a leading activist in the student left, known for her role in the Berkeley Free Speech Movement and her unrelenting efforts to free her close friend, Angela Davis, from prison. Accustomed to the rigidity of the hierarchal U.S. Communist Party, she recalls meeting an activist who was "gentle" and "joyous." She writes, "He had what I would today understand to be a spiritual practice, and this made him different from anyone I had ever met."[61] Bettina Aptheker eventually left the party and became active in the feminist movement, an instructor in a university women's studies program, and a practitioner of Buddhist meditation.

In her poem "Democratic Womanism,"[62] written thirty years after publication of her highly acclaimed novel *The Color Purple* and recited just before the 2012 elections, Alice Walker reiterates her deep commitment to the fusion of politics and womanist spirituality. "I want to vote and work for a way of life that honors the feminine," she writes in calling for "true regime change" in which women "rise to take their place en masse." Walker affirms "women's values of compassion and kindness" in her passionate plea for a democratic, socialist, womanist vision of a just world.

Essentialism?

Walker's words may be heard as "essentialist" by those who are sharply critical of the attempt to celebrate "female" traits, or associate particular characteristics with any group. Feminist theorists of the 1980s and 1990s, influenced by poststructuralism and postmodernism, decried such essentialism. Yet even those who are not associated with academic theorizing are justifiably wary of the potential co-optation of their spiritual practices. Celebrating "Mother" Earth can reinforce old stereotypes of self-denying mothers, or "earthy" sensualists whose lustful, animal instincts must be controlled lest they corrupt the social order. These are not bygone distortions; they weave through many contemporary narratives. The efforts to reverse negative images by reclaiming the "feminine" aspects of God or returning to goddess worship can be manipulated or stifled by those with the power to define words and shape the world in accordance with their political and social positions.

Consciousness-Raising Redux

Just as consciousness-raising initially helped many women find a way to bring spiritual meaning to their lives, *ongoing* consciousness-raising is important in exploring and responding to current and future challenges. Critics of spirituality might want to interrogate their resistance and ambivalence, as I found myself doing as I read, reflected and wrote about the topic. Reclaimed faith traditions and New Age practices need to be examined, too. Is there a point at which feminism and spiritual practices are in conflict and more reframing and re-visioning are needed?

I am left with many questions, but am confident that my goal of contributing to a revitalized women's liberation movement will be enhanced by respecting, supporting and practicing feminist spirituality.

VII

Consciousness-Raising Through the Lifespan

Consciousness-raising involves gaining social and political understanding, not only or especially from "objective" research findings, but also from lived experience—learning from one's own life, and from the narratives of daily living shared by others. This chapter will review the ways in which sexist injustice affects girls and women throughout their lives and how consciousness-raising can provide both personal support and collective insight that can lead to constructive social change.

Sexism Is—Still—Here, There and Everywhere

In the midst of revising this chapter my beloved partner and I took a long-planned trip to England to visit our goddaughter, who is in the middle of a three-year PhD program in geo-botany at Oxford. The brief visit abroad indicated that, spelling practices and colloquialisms notwithstanding, things are pretty much the same for girls and women on both sides of the Atlantic. Here's what I discovered in a quick perusal of a single issue of the *Independent* (Number 762, May 6, 2013) handed out to airline passengers:

The headline and page 1 story: "Deputy Speaker Denies Rape Allegation." The story indicates that gender exploitation is not limited to girls and women, for the deputy speaker is charged with sexually assaulting young men.

Page 17: "Tesco Defends Its Position on Boys' Chemistry Sets." Toy retailer Tesco has labeled a children's chemistry set a "boys' toy"; a pink Hotpoint Toy Cooker is categorized as being for girls. "A Tesco spokesman responded: 'Toy signage is currently based on research and how our customers tell us they like to shop in our stores.'"

Page 18: "Girl, 12, Is Raped in Play Park." The article reports that "a man thought to be around 45 dragged her into a woodland and attacked her."

Page 23: "The Tyranny of Sexism Is with Us Still": Columnist Yasmin Alibhai-Brown comments on the responses to two media celebrities charged with pedophilia in the 1960s and 1970s, taking issue with the popular opinions that "these are 'historical' crimes, no longer tolerated in our modern age." After writing about the allegations, she received countless e-mails about very recent molestations by neighbors, teachers, and caretakers, including parents. She asserts that "casual sexism and more serious crimes have not been seen off. It is no easier for victims today than it was in the Sixties and Seventies."

Page 25: "Postcard from ... Berlin." Germany's first female head of state, Angela Merkel, has shared "that she manages to forget that she is Chancellor when she cooks her husband's supper."

Page 26: "It Was My Personal Responsibility to Juggle. I Didn't Want Anyone to Help Me." Karren Brady, 44-year-old television personality and columnist for the London *Sun* whose career has included managing the Birmingham Football Club, writing four books, and raising two children, wants to create a supportive environment for women. She opines that corporations that don't have women on their boards should inform shareholders of the number of women who have been interviewed and why they were not chosen. Brady also stresses the importance of celebrating the achievements of women in fields ranging from science to charity work so young women can see role models. "We need to do something to push these women into the light."

Page 31: "Papa Is a Rolling Stone" is the caption for a piece on Georgia May Jagger, the daughter of the rock star Mick Jagger, who followed her mama's career as a fashion model and is pictured in jeans available for 295 British pounds, or about 470 American dollars.

It Starts Before Birth

So there we have it. Whether the subject is girls and women as targets for consumer manipulation or sexual assault, or exceptional women who have made it to the top as a fashion model, corporate leader or head of nation, gender concerns prevail.

"Is it a boy?" "Is it a girl?" This has long been the first question asked when a new life arrives; now, with ultrasound technology, the question is asked early in pregnancy. Even in this "postfeminist" age the answer produces immediate images of gender characteristics and ideas of what life will hold for the child. If the answer isn't the gender a parent or parents desire, it might also lead to the termination of pregnancy or infanticide.

What are the differences between the sexes? *Pink Brain, Blue Brain: How Small Differences Grow into Troublesome Gaps—and What We Can Do About It*, by Lise Eliot,[1] and Rosalind Barnett and Carol Rivers' *Same Difference: How Gender Myths Are Hurting Our Relationships, Our Children and Our Jobs*[2] are just two of many books that document the fact that it is not genetics or hormones but rather social conditioning that is the greatest determinant of what girls and women can learn and do. Stereotypes become reality when families and schools accept that boys are better in math and science and girls have a corner on emotional sensitivity. The minuscule brain differences that have been exaggerated to the point that men and women are seen as occupying different planets[3] can be overcome with simple interventions such as exposing children to role models and offering them experiences that challenge gender stereotypes. Yet Tesco, a British-based multinational corporation with stores similar to the Wal-Mart chain, continues to display and market chemistry sets for boys and Hotpoint miniature ovens for girls.

Peggy Orenstein recently became a mother. No amount of effort to circumvent popular culture prevented her daughter from falling in step with gender stereotyping. In her new book, *Cinderella Ate My Daughter*,[4] Orenstein shows that the zeal for everything princess is not what little girls "are made of" (in addition to sugar and spice, of course), but the result of an enormous marketing program that drives the craving for consumer goods as soon as a baby can point. The box-office receipts for a Disney film are just a drop in the revenue stream that comes from branding thousands of princess products that are absorbed into the daily lives of young girls. When a friend told me her five-year-old granddaughter had attended a birthday party at which each child was invited to dress up (gowns and makeup provided) as her favorite Disney princess, I did not realize this was a common occurrence. A Google search provided enough material for a sequel to Orenstein's book.

Imaginative play with dress-up clothes and magic wands is, or was, part of growing up. But before girls start elementary school their make-believe has become saturated with materialism, including Barbie cars and dream houses. Even many of the titles touted at school book fairs reinforce the "feminine." *Pinkalicious*[5] is one book series marketed to beginning readers, but there are countless others that use the color on the cover and the girly-girl stereotypes in the stories. Many of the offerings at these events are offshoot products that have nothing to do with gaining literacy skills and a lot to do with becoming mindless consumers. The mass marketing of gender involves early sexualization. One example Orenstein cites is the line of Bratz "fashion" dolls sporting fishnet stockings, miniskirts and makeup, which generate beauty pageants in which real little girls don costumes like those their Bratz dolls wear. The Bratz phenomenon, with its nod to "diversity" in the form of dolls with darker skin, includes movies, games, and many other products.[6]

In an earlier, and perhaps less pernicious, marketing era my daughters were read "Free to Be You and Me," listened to a recording of the songs and stories contained in the book, and watched a TV special with the same title and message.[7] The message was that, regardless of gender, you can be anything you want to be, but sometimes the stereotypes were reinforced in an effort to combat them. One song featured football player Rosie Grier delivering the message that it was OK to cry, and another titled "William's Doll" insisted on the rightness of boys playing with dolls. I'm sure I wasn't the only mother whose interruption of a daughter's play was met with the rejoinder "I *know* I can be a doctor, but I *want* to be a nurse." At that moment in the development of women's liberation, children may have been pushing back because they had few experiences to indicate it was possible to escape gender stereotypes.

Things have changed in regard to career possibilities, especially for those privileged through education, skin color and class. Yet gender still shapes— and stymies. The damaging effects vary and increase when they intersect with age, disability, class and race. Instances abound in our everyday lives, but sometimes a "real" novel is the clearest means of discovering the truth to belie the fictive Disney version. *The Bluest Eye,* the unforgettable first novel by Toni Morrison, relates the story of African American Pecola Breedlove's fall into madness, as she longs to receive the same care and attention that her mother lavishes upon the blue-eyed, fair-skinned child of the family for which she works as a housekeeper.[8] Another first novel, *Girlchild,*[9] by Tupelo Hassman, published forty-three years later, reveals the struggles of Rory Dawn Hendrix to find the hope of first light for which she is named. It does not shine on the trailer park where she lives or in the bars and casinos where her mother finds work. Both authors portray how the pain of previous generations does not "breed love" but is visited in horrific ways upon the next. They also poignantly reveal how parents and others in the community try to express care in the ways that are available to them, their efforts distorted by race, class and gender oppression.

The Muddle of the Middle of Childhood

It is in the middle school years that the deep harm of gender roles becomes apparent. Uncertainty about new sexual feelings, ignorance about bodily changes and the social pressures to fit in are some of the many challenges that have often been described by other authors.

Caitlin Moran's *How to Be a Woman*[10] describes the muddle in a refreshingly witty way. The British rock critic and columnist on popular culture for the London *Times* recalls being thirteen. After years of being "benevolently generally ignored," she begins a teenage journey bombarded with questions: "What size are you? Have you done it yet? Will you have sex with me? Have you got ID? Do you want a puff of this? Are you seeing anyone? Have you got protection? What's your signature style? Can you walk in heels? Who are your heroes? Are you getting a Brazilian? What porn do you like? Do you want to get married? When are you going to have kids? Are you a feminist? Were you just *flirting* with that man? What do you want to *do*? WHO ARE YOU?"[11]

The author notes that these are "all ridiculous questions to ask of a 13-year-old simply because she now needs a bra ... I had absolutely no idea." Neither did I, but, as Moran writes, "once those hormones kick in, there's no way to stop them.... There isn't an exit plan. You can't call the whole thing off—however often you may wish you could. This shit is going to happen, whether you like it or not."

Reliving the Past in CR Groups

Many consciousness-raising groups begin with sharing stories of growing up female. Here is some of what I recalled and shared with my CR group about my growing-up years. Like most CR stories, my own is uniquely common. I grew up at a time when there was no awareness that gender stereotypes could be limiting or harmful. Being "sweet" and a "nice little girl" were as natural as breathing. Sex roles were *literally* demarked—my elementary school had separate entrances for girls and boys. I was a good and compliant student. I was never encouraged to take physical risks. There was no playground at the school I attended or in my neighborhood, and I was awkward at jump roping, roller skating and bouncing pink rubber balls, which were the chief activities for girls on my street. For reasons I never knew as a child, my overprotective mother, who grew up in Maine close to several well-known lakes, had never learned how to swim. Through CR it occurred to me that she didn't learn because the "nearby" lakes were not accessible to a child whose father constantly traveled as an "antique dealer" (later understood as a fancy name for peddler) and whose mother ran a tiny grocery. I also figured out how ethnicity, class, race and ability interacted to define the good behavior expected of girls. For me, it meant not only conforming to gender roles but also representing my family's sometimes demeaned religion in ways that would not bring negative attention and might result in positive images.

I moved from city to suburb just as I was entering adolescence and almost immediately after the death of my younger brother. The collision of these events meant that I never shared with my family the way I was teased for having the wrong clothing and a "hideous" bicycle (which had previously been my proudest possession). I was totally befuddled by the quest to be "popular," and did some things I deeply regretted then and now to get to that unreachable destination. I began competing with other girls, not for academic or athletic achievements, but for the attention of boys. I was in and out of what I perceived to be the "top" cliques, which were less about building deep friendship than about hanging with the more attractive (by someone's definition) people and disparaging those outside the group. I keenly and painfully recall joining with others in bullying a girl whose name is well remembered but won't be used. Some in our "in" group of the moment took her skirt from her locker and tore it when we were changing for gym. When her mother involved school officials and lined everyone up to gain a confession, we formed a united front. I learned then that solidarity can be powerful—and misused. I wish that we had the same commitment to caring for others that we evidenced in covering our own butts.

I did some things right, usually more by luck or accident than intent. It was a lucky accident that I became active in a youth group that connected me to young people beyond my community and included members from places that were more like the city from which I'd moved. However, it was by intent that, after an afternoon of joining others in an act of meanness toward my best friend, I embraced that caring friendship with a commitment that has lasted sixty years.

Different Experiences, Common Themes

Each member of our CR group had her own stories. The particulars were different, but the themes resonated. While I had few opportunities to discover if I had any athletic skill, other women who also grew up in urban areas remembered being "tomboys" who struggled, usually without success, to be included in games limited to boys. Household chores were sex-stereotyped; several women related that much of the care of younger children in the family fell to them. Some women remember being told that education beyond high school was only for their brothers.

The CR group was the first place where I exchanged with other women some of my attitudes and experiences as a sexual being. Like most of the women in my CR group, "the facts of life" had been imparted obliquely. I discovered menstruation through friends and a pamphlet from a sanitary pad manufacturer that my mother had left in an obtrusive spot. I picked it up and quickly read it, replacing it before she could find out. The information sounded as awful as my friends had warned; when I got my period, I saw "the curse" as just that—some awful penalty for being a girl. The sexual feelings I was experiencing were never discussed, but I knew they were "dirty." I linked them to the only time my father ever became furious with me—when I had used the word "shmuck," the meaning of which I did not know. (Much later I learned that the term had its origins in the Yiddish word for penis, although it is now widely used to describe a jerk.) I was in rebellion, some of my behavior hidden from my family—or maybe they didn't want to know. I experimented with sexuality within the boundaries of that time. There was no birth control and the fear of becoming pregnant was paralyzing. You could end up like "X" (I'm not using but still know the name of the girl who became pregnant in the eighth grade and whom I never saw again). Her fate was a mantra to prevent "going all the way."

The stories we told about our families; school experiences; longings; feelings of being different, lonely and excluded; and, yes, memories of achievements and breakthroughs and places where we found comfort, safety and pleasure (including sexual pleasure) were enormously liberating, and that is why I urge that CR be used throughout the lifespan.

Living the Present in CR Groups

The thesis of this book is that consciousness-raising groups can not only support women in their personal lives but also be the platform for thoughtful action for political and social change. The process can begin in middle school— but even younger children can be encouraged to ask questions and give opinions about their experiences.

Volumes have been written on the difficulties of girls' lives beginning in their pre-teen years and often continuing through high school. Rachel Simmons' *Odd Girl Out*[12] and *Odd Girl Speaks Out*[13] document jealousy, bullying, being left out of social groups and/or being the one who separates from former BFFs (best friends forever) in order to be part of a more popular clique. What Simmons suggests is a "hidden" culture has in fact been overt for a long time; the "new twist" is that Simmons provides space for victimizers *and* victims to commiserate.

Her concluding advice is simplistic and reminiscent of suggestions offered years ago by *Seventeen Magazine*.[14] (I discovered that the publication is still being issued and still repeats the same formulaic recommendations.) In *Odd Girl Speaks Out* Simmons urges her readers to find their "inner strength," get a hobby, keep a diary, join a club (the updated recommendation adds an online group), and grin and bear it—things will get better. If it doesn't get better, talk to a guidance counselor or therapist. The idea that girls might work together to change their situations is not put forth.

Schoolgirls, [15] the critically acclaimed book by Peggy Orenstein (whose daughter's Cinderella story is described above), details her study of girls in two California schools in the San Francisco Bay area. One is a mix of children from working-class and professional families; the other a "majority-minority" community where most of the students lived in poverty, many in homes where English was not spoken. The girls related their stories about body image, dieting, stressful relationships with their parents, and confusion about social expectations and sexuality. Although the Weston and Audubon schools differed greatly in socioeconomic makeup, a common message was received by the girls from parents, from peers and from teachers—that girls pay a price for speaking out.

But Orenstein offers a model for engaging students in gender discussions. She reports on the work of Judy Logan, a middle school teacher whose curriculum includes a project that asks students to imagine what life would be like if they were the opposite sex. The results were that boys framed their responses in terms of what they'd "have to do," while the girls had a list of what they'd "get to do." Title IX has leveled some playing fields, but legislation guaranteeing sex equity in athletics and vocational and technical training has recently been threatened. And even as advances are made in some areas, new forms of and arenas for gender stereotyping arise, such as those reported in chapter III regarding girls and women and technology.

A few years after *Schoolgirls* was published, Lyn Mikel Brown replicated Orenstein's approach in her interview-based research with middle school students at two schools in Maine, one serving an affluent, the other a working-class community. [16] Brown focuses on how a culture of victimization can become a source of resilience with the appropriate adult supports. The girls with whom she met over many months found various ways to express their resistance to the constraints and regulations imposed on them by their schools and communities. The more economically privileged girls were less direct in their expressions of discontent and anger at being expected to conform to an idealized notion of conventional femininity. They sometimes turned their anger inward and occasionally "ventriloquized," filtering out their own thoughts and feelings to express what they know others expect to hear. [17] The working-class students, however, had no such filters. They expressed their intense anger in ways that are disruptive to what Brown calls the "bourgeois class bias." They used strong language, engaged in physical fights like the boys, and directly confronted what they perceived as injustices and irrational rules. Their behavior met the low expectations their teachers had for them—and they had for themselves. They failed to learn the negotiating skills—the dissembling—that silenced the honest voices of the girls in the privileged community, but allowed that group to figure out how to fit the model of competitive individualism that is the recipe for success in 8–12 education and beyond.

Unlike the facile advice that Simmons gives her "odd girls," Brown's aim is to affirm the voices of girls and turn their incipient strategies into "collective, potentially powerful political resistance." Brown begins her book with examples. Girls in Ames, Iowa, protested the sexist Hooters T-shirts worn by boys by designing and wearing shirts with roosters, or cocks, with the message "Nothing to crow about." In another city girls rallied to elect a pregnant, unmarried classmate as homecoming queen.[18]

Consciousness-Raising Groups for Girls

Lyn Brown urges educators to pay attention to girls' anger and the implications of class differences, and to share among themselves "conflicts and contradictions regarding their roles and identities as women, mentors and socializers, and as transmitters of patriarchal culture." But her suggestions for consciousness-raising for teachers, which support those I've made in chapter V, do not extend to the girls themselves.

The group of girls Brown formed for her research discovered a safe space where they could listen to and learn to trust each other, discover similarities of experience, argue, complain about siblings and friends, and find "cool ways" to distinguish themselves from the popular crowd.[19] I wondered why the group was not encouraged to continue meeting after the research project concluded. CR groups formed for and by girls can help them to survive and to thrive. Together girls can share and consider the meaning of their experiences, raise questions, and take joint action.

That is the advice offered by Eve Ensler in *I Am an Emotional Creature*.[20] The literary narratives in this book are based on real events, articles, data and observations from ten years of listening to girls around the world while she was touring with her earlier work, the famous *Vagina Monologues*.[21] The "girl facts"—sex and labor trafficking, girl soldiers, poverty, isolation, anorexia, abuse—that preface each section of *I Am an Emotional Creature* have been reiterated in a variety of publications. The fact that the horrific data hasn't led to substantive change makes Ensler's "scripts for resistance" required reading. The book offers discussion group questions intended to spark sharing on the issues raised—and to promote action. These are just a few questions that can spark discussion in a girls' CR group: "What is it like to be a girl today?" "What makes you angry?" "What inspires you?" "How can you create change in the world" "Do you see a division between the 'haves' and the 'have nots' in the world?" "How does that make you feel?" "Do you see a solution?"[22] The website vday.org provides more information, including a pilot curriculum with more questions and references. The curriculum is aimed at adults working with girls, but it could be used by girls themselves.

The Oasis Center for girls and women in Tallahassee, Florida, uses the consciousness-raising model in their summer camp programs and girls' circles where 9–18-year-olds can share experiences following typical CR guidelines of "respect, no put-downs or interruptions, offer experiences—not advice, keep the focus on oneself, and keep what's said in the group private."[23] The approach utilizes materials prepared by the One Circle Foundation,[24] which trains leaders of schools, youth centers and community organizations such as the Girl Scouts, YWCA, Big Brother/Big Sister. (In addition to groups for girls, and mothers and daughters, the foundation offers training materials and programs for boys and men.)

One of the members of the ReCollective described in earlier chapters recalls coming to political awareness as a teenager through such a group. College students from a nearby city came to discuss ways in which high school students could support the civil rights movement. After a few sessions with their mentors, Bettina and other young women continued to meet using the CR-like approach to reflective sharing, which led to projects in support of the protests then taking place throughout the South. My friend Rachel formed a girls group while serving in the Peace Corps in the Dominican Republic and is now doing the same in her work with Latina girls in Seattle. Having facilitators close in age to the girls works well. They can provide the initial structure and guidelines for a safe setting in which girls can find their voices, build connections, offer each other support and consider action projects. If possible, a facilitator can be available for support and guidance when the girls start meeting on their own. Rachel said she made sure someone took over the group when her Peace Corps stint ended. Once begun, the girls depended on having that special setting.

Mother-daughter circles have also been formed to maintain connections, or to mend what often becomes a frayed relationship in adolescence. Although girls need their mothers as much as before (or more than ever), young teens, as I remember well from my own feelings at that time, cannot imagine that their mothers could possibly understand their enthusiasms, longings and pain. Mother-daughter book groups sometimes provide an opening for dialogue that can develop over the years. When my oldest daughter went to college we attended a mother-daughter weekend together that used a CR model. I don't know whether she remembers it as fondly as I do, but I still think of how special it was to have fun and share feelings together in a space and place dedicated to making that happen.

CR Groups: Settings to Examine Sexuality, Aggression and Agency

Consciousness-raising is intended to link the personal to the political. A recent strand of feminism celebrates "agency," but tends toward personal rather than collective manifestations. This phenomenon is particularly evident in the area of sexual expression and physical aggression.

Sharon Lamb's *The Secret Life of Girls: What Good Girls Really Do—Sex, Play, Aggression and Their Guilt*[25] is based on interviews the author conducted with 122 women and girls who revealed long-past and more recent instances of their erotic fantasies and experiences. Some experimented with other girls, pretending to be the opposite sex because lesbian feelings were not acknowledged; some had sex play with boys in their neighborhoods or families. The author also relates her subjects' aggressive feelings and actions. Her interviewees' revelations will undoubtedly unleash a flood of recollections by readers regardless of whether they concur with the conclusions and recommendations that Lamb gleans from her data.

I fully agree with Lamb's call to claim our sexual desires, which are buried in guilt and shame, and to release our legitimate anger. Yet I don't share the opinion of the reviewer quoted on the cover of Lamb's book whose takeaway is that having sexual curiosity and aggressive impulses means that girls are "just like human beings of the male persuasion." We really can't begin to know that. Although many children learn about sexuality through masturbation, the very earliest coupled sex play reported by Lamb replicates the patriarchal relationships those children have absorbed from birth. Notions of romance, gratification, and "choice" of sexual activities are reenacted over and over and usually have those who identify as female "yield" to a dominant partner. So, too, are ways of expressing aggression. Fistfights and girl-gang battles release rage "like the boys do" but do not alter the power relationships shaped by class, race and gender domination.

Jessica Valenti is perhaps the best known of a number of feminists to put forth a "sex positive" message. In Feministing, the "ball-breaking" website she founded (discussed in chapter III), and in books such as *Full Frontal Feminism*[26] and *The Purity Myth*,[27] she attempts to reverse ugly slurs and limiting stereotypes that stand in the way of sexual pleasure.

Sexual expression has been "reframed" with ubiquitous media images of sexual acts, from films in the local theater to readily available pornographic images on the Internet. Books like Hanna Rosin's *The End of Men*[28] suggest that women (a small number of mostly white, educated and economically privileged women define the category) experiment as often and freely as men with a number of sexual partners and practices. Rosin opines that this "liberates" them to pursue what is really important—their careers. Her chapter on the hook-up culture notes that many women do not experience orgasm in these exchanges, making me wonder why they don't prefer to masturbate, leaving more time to study for their business or law school admission tests. Many of the sexual encounters are *just* sexual, moving from "friends with benefits," a descriptor of relationships that include sex within a caring friendship.

Are You Positive?

Caitlin Moran is also sex positive. She doesn't want to ban pornography; instead, she wishes there were images of women experiencing pleasure in the ubiquitous sex films. Most of the women portrayed in the porn films she has viewed are joyless performers, similar to the pole and lap dancers she observed during a visit to a strip club. She also wonders about the "agency" of women who shave their vaginal hair, undergo costly cosmetic surgery that has them looking like clones of one another, and wear shoes and clothing that cause them pain.[29]

Over my many years of identifying and working within the women's liberation movement, I've formed strong friendships with students at Salem State College, UMass Dartmouth and Brandeis University and with women I've met through community women's centers and organizations. They've shared how much easier it is to find sexual partners than it is to find sexual and relationship gratification. Workshops, lectures and Internet sites are settings in which information and opinions on sexuality are exchanged, but I advocate face-to-face consciousness-raising groups that meet regularly as the places where girls and women can consider what is "positive" about their sexual expressions and relationships and what may not be. Blog posts, articles and books, including those cited above, can be starting places for discovering feelings of enthusiasm or ambivalence, finding collective ways to affirm a climate and practices that advance pleasure, and exploring where collaborative resistance might be appropriate.

Since the 1980s the feminist "sex wars" have produced what seems to be a senseless divide pitting those who advocate greater sexual freedom and oppose any judgments or limitations of sexual imagery or practices against those who speak out against pornography and prostitution and forms of sexual expression that they consider demeaning and exploitative. The idea that there is a clear line separating these concerns has forestalled discussions that could illuminate difficult contradictions and has blocked the growth of feminist activism.

Here's one experience that gave me a reason to urge CR groups as settings for respectful dialogue on a range of perspectives: At the 2012 National Women's Studies Conference a session was offered on how women's centers could serve sex workers on campus. The Health Project of the New Bedford Women's Center where I was a board member served all members of the community, and I feel campus women's centers, too, should provide service to all populations on campus, including sex workers. What troubled me about the session, however, was the presentation of sex work. One of the presenters spoke of her decision to earn good money through sex work rather than trying to meet expenses through a low-wage job in a place like Starbucks. Due to immigration status, drug addiction, poverty and other circumstances, some of those who visited the New Bedford Women's Center did not have choices between work as a barista in a coffee shop and the prostitution that got them through their days— or didn't. During a six-month period in 1988 eleven New Bedford women who worked as prostitutes went missing. Nine bodies were recovered; the remains of two other lost women believed to be victims of the same slayer(s) have never been found. The crimes remain unsolved.[30]

The consciousness-raising process allows us to query who holds the power in shaping "choice" and to examine how class, race, ability, gender and other, usually intersecting, identities are involved. False dichotomies that juxtapose "sex positive" with "anti-sex" leave unexamined the power dynamics that shape our ideas about sexual desire and fulfillment. Machismo dominates (an unintentional double entendre) the purse strings and people in the sex industry. Males and transgender people work in the trade, but those presenting as females—usually young females—comprise the bulk of sex workers. Clients, pimps, traffickers and manufacturers and sellers of pornographic images are usually males. Among the many conversations that might occur in a CR group are the ways in which disabilities and body type affect desirability and the sexualization of racial groups.[31]

CR and the Work-Life Balance

Girls who struggle through their teens are soon faced with earning a living and perhaps becoming parents. The challenges that most women face in balancing employment and family obligations are often presented through the viewpoints of a particular and privileged population of women. Here comes Jessica Valenti again. She now has a child and details her own experiences as a new mother in *Why Have Kids?*[32] Valenti's observations include the following: electing to create a family—or not—is an option for all genders; children do not have to be cared for only by their parents; stay-at-home moms may elevate their importance by becoming helicopter parents or "experts" on topics such as breastfeeding and vaccinations, often foisting their cultish opinions on others. Her summary advice is for women to shun the perfect parent ideal—and work outside the home.

Valenti wonders why people make such a big deal about mothering. It's hard, she acknowledges. "But let's be honest—it's not the hardest. And as much as I love my daughter, I don't believe caring for her is the most important thing I'll ever do either."[33] Rankings, such as "most important," or a continuum of easy-to-hard, don't illuminate the complex issues of juggling paid work and family responsibilities. Raising children and digging ditches cannot be measured in a "comparable worth" competition because parenting is an unpaid occupation that must be supported by earnings from one or both parents or other guardians.

Having parented and grandparented (at the risk of sounding like a Hallmark card, it's been my most important work), I can't argue with Valenti that it includes "soul crushing drudgery," but so does much of the work that women do outside their homes. Visit McDonalds or Wal-Mart, or consider the countless women who are taking care of other people's children and households. The chapter on "right livelihood" reviews the search for work that can provide economic security and, for some, personal satisfaction and even an opportunity to contribute to the larger society. But right now in the United States it is only a wealthy minority who can hope to achieve a balance, often by employing nannies and other helpers who may have left their own children with a relative, sometimes in another country.

The Struggles of the 1 Percent

Personal stories of the difficult decisions facing the privileged few fill Internet sites, talk radio and the pages of magazines and best-selling books. But how many people can identify with this passage from Valenti's book? "When I had Layla, Andrew and I were deliberate about work/family decisions. We decided to start trying for pregnancy when both of us would be working from home, to ensure that we had the most equitable breakdown of child care possible."[34] Or Anne-Marie Slaughter's tale of leaving her job as director of policy planning in the U.S. State Department to return to a full professorship in political science and international relations at Princeton University because she wanted to be closer to her son during a difficult time in his adolescence? She writes that she feared that she was letting the feminist movement down by admitting that she couldn't "have it all."[35]

I have concerns with Slaughter using her own high-powered and handsomely paid career and life choices as an example of the "all" to which women aspire and can't have. I also question her conclusions that only "when women wield power in sufficient numbers will we create a society that genuinely works for all women. That will be a society that works for everyone." It seems that Slaughter is speaking for an economic elite—far fewer than the 1 percent. Slaughter makes no references to other underrepresented groups to which women simultaneously belong, including ethnic and racial groups and the old and disabled. These, too, must be part of determining the power that needs "wielding."

Equating "woman" with "feminist" is also troubling. I have worked for and with women who were not champions of other women. The female chancellor of the university where I worked for many years closed the day-care center and had an administrative style that was not always consistent with the participative, democratic approaches advocated by most who call themselves feminists. It is true that organizations change when previously un- or underrepresented groups enter, but, as noted in chapter II, male hegemony persists even in the fields where the numbers have become equal.[36]

Work/Family Balance for the 99 Percent

Work/family balance for the 99 percent presents a much more complex struggle and is certainly not a new topic, as is revealed in the lifelong friendship between Susan B. Anthony and Elizabeth Cady Stanton. Judith Harper writes that Anthony was a source of strength for Stanton as she raised her eight children; Stanton reciprocated when Anthony struggled with her family obligations, including caretaking for her mother and two sisters—and each sustained the other's intellectual and activist vision.[37] The women from varied educational and class backgrounds who have inspired me, and awed me with their daily lives, did not need Slaughter to reveal the "secret" that it is difficult to combine caring for home and family with other pursuits. These inspiring women include my daughters: One left a corporate career to work part-time for a nonprofit, a job that is more compatible with her obligations to her family—and her values—but derails her from the advancement and earnings full-time work allows. Our other daughter's care for a child with quadriplegia cerebral palsy took her from a career path in affordable housing. She now has a part-time job managing the office for a small architectural firm and is also volunteering at a women's shelter to help residents prepare for their GED exam, a step that may bring them closer to employment that will be very different from that described by Valenti and Slaughter. Our goddaughter has been aware even before her undergraduate days that she wants to create a family like the one that encouraged her to be a scientist—*and* to have concerns and interests beyond contributing to her career field. When we visited her in Oxford we had several conversations on how her future would include both and the challenges that would bring.

Slaughter, Valenti and most other privileged writers who share their struggles to combine careers and family lives gratuitously note that their situations are far less stressful than most. Variations on passages like this by Slaughter are found in most such writing: "Millions of other working women face much more difficult life circumstances. Some are single mothers; many struggle to find any job; others support husbands who cannot find jobs. Many cope with a work life in which good day care is either unavailable or very expensive; school schedules do not match work schedules; and schools themselves are failing to educate their children. Many of these women are worrying not about having it all, but rather about holding on to what they do have."[38] But after offering a bit of sympathy and reciting the list of the social changes that are needed, the authors then reveal the *personal* solutions they have found.

It will take an organized feminist movement to advance *publicly* supported day care staffed by people who can earn a living wage for their work, flexible work schedules across all segments of the workforce, and access to good health care, diet and housing, without which there is no life to "balance." Consciousness-raising is one approach to revitalizing a women's liberation movement that can build coalitions with other groups to address these vital issues. Yet, not surprisingly, given the discussion above, it is not bell hooks, Patricia Hill Collins and other longtime advocates of CR who are leading the renaissance of the practice, but rather Sheryl Sandberg.

Call It Consciousness-Raising

Based on the reviews from left-leaning blogs and publications I usually consult, I was prepared to dislike Sandberg's *Lean In*.[39] Then I decided it might be a good idea to read it. Clear and well-written, the book reflects care in its development. Sandberg offers thanks to a long list of advisors, many of them with names you'll recognize, who read her manuscript and gave suggestions. Before the book was published, Sandberg's perspective was already well known from a much-discussed Barnard graduation speech and a TED Talk. She wants women to address their self-doubts, speak up for themselves, learn to negotiate, and insist on shared household and parenting with their partners. Sandberg does not blame the victim, as some have suggested; instead, she calls for women *and* men to commit to the changes that will advance women.

"Call it Lean In, call it consciousness-raising, call it whatever you want. When was the last time anybody talked this much about a women's place in the world, *period?*" Those are the comments of Jessica Bennett, who observed a Lean In circle that met in a Manhattan office building and then decided to start one of her own.[40] Bennett had been a member of an ongoing CR group, so she knew the process. Yet she was impressed by how easy it is to follow the Lean In guidelines—and to adapt them to her "non–MBA" colleagues who are employed in varied work environments but continue to feel insecure as females.

Bennett notes, "If you follow the 'kickoff' guidelines given out on Lean In's site, a circle goes something like this: three minutes of introduction. Forty minutes to watch an instructional video (topics range from negotiation to power to team dynamics). Personal stories. Goal-setting. Then meeting scheduling. Ultimately, members are encouraged to sign a commitment to be a part of the group. Slick corporate jargon? Yes—complete with educational instruction, printed out pamphlets, and the kind of marketing campaign that would come only from, well, a woman who works at Facebook."[41]

Bennett refers to Maureen Dowd's description of Sandberg as the "Power Point Pied Piper in Prada ankle boots."[42] Dowd's columns are usually spot on, but I am not sure she is completely accurate when she notes that people come to social movements from "the bottom up, not the top down." Nor do I think that Sandberg "has co-opted the vocabulary and romance of a social movement not to sell a cause, but herself." Well before Sandberg became affiliated with Facebook, social movements and marketing were conjoined. There are few reports of the Arab Spring that don't acknowledge the activism of the more privileged students and their intellectual cohorts who knew how to make savvy use of the Internet. In this and other countries advocacy for causes by those closer to the "top" advanced the abolition of slavery, women's suffrage, the eight-hour day and many other social changes.

Consciousness-raising groups are settings in which analysis can go beyond even the insightful columns Maureen Dowd writes. We need to ask questions that don't fit into the word limits of op-ed pieces, blog posts and tweets, and that probe deeply the contradictions woven throughout social movements. Can "the people," be they LGBTQ, feminist, anticolonialist, disabled rights, or other and often blended collaborations, move forward without advocacy from sympathetic supporters and allies? When and in what ways has such advocacy usurped the agenda of a grassroots organizing effort and how can that change? Is there a possibility that social justice can ever be realized when those who hold power are setting the boundaries?

Hope from the Hoopla

Here's what I hope from the hoopla surrounding Sandberg's project. Like Betty Friedan's *Feminist Mystique*, Sandberg's *Lean In* is framed from the perspective of the privileged. But the radical feminist movement that formed in the late 1960s and so strongly influenced my own activism owed a great debt to Friedan and to the National Organization for Women, an organization sometimes scorned by feminists with a more progressive vision. And the vision and demands of radical feminists moved NOW to stronger positions that changed that organization's agenda.

NOW's 1966 Statement of Purpose was "to take action to bring women into full participation in the mainstream of American society now, exercising all privileges and responsibilities thereof in truly equal partnership with men."[43] The organization's mission has since expanded to state that "NOW stands against all oppression, recognizing that racism, sexism and homophobia are interrelated, that other forms of oppression such as classism and ableism work together with these three to keep power and privilege concentrated in the hands of a few." NOW initially opposed consciousness-raising, but then became a distributor of guidelines for organizing groups that spread the technique to thousands of women.

Sandberg's work is opening a conversation. I think that the discussions *Lean In* will prompt will veer from how to succeed in the corporate world to the recognition that deeper social alterations are required to redress the ways in which global capitalism supports sexist injustice perpetuated by even the most "enlightened" corporations. By declaring herself a feminist Sandberg has already caused a shift in the thinking of many who had insisted "I am not a feminist, but..." My own experience and those of others who have participated in consciousness-raising indicate that, once the "buts" begin to be stated, the issues raised can provoke collective action for widespread social and political change.

Although the ReCollective group of which I've been part for a quarter century (see chapter II) was formed to deal with work issues, from the beginning we spoke of work, not simply as what we did to earn money, but in a far broader sense. Our conversations move seamlessly between jobs, family and social and political commitments that were part of each of our lives. The CR process is likely to grow from the meeting of women watching children at the neighborhood playground, and this is how some of the contacts were made that led to Domestic Workers United (see chapter II). My husband's mother used to speak often of her "mothers club," a group of women who offered insight and support to one another, not only when their children were young but throughout their lives. Often the book clubs I am part of move from commentary on the book to talk of work, family and community.

The discussion group guidelines that Sandberg proposes—and the ones suggested in this book—can be modified and applied to other groups. I can envision a CR group in which the princess phenomenon comes up as a topic for discussion and participants move from sharing experience to analysis and then to action. They may begin by sharing their experiences as retail clerks, teachers, parents or grandparents. Some may relate that their daughters have attended the Disney princess parties—and the pressure they feel to host a similar birthday celebration. Then they'll discuss how this is just one manifestation of the ways behavior is molded by sexist marketing and look at why this is so. Their conversation may lead to actions as simple as the determination to choose alternative ways—and they'll come up with dozens—to mark birthdays. That will solve an immediate concern, but who knows what other actions may grow from their reflective interactions? Maybe several of them will reach out to schools and community groups to launch a broader discussion; maybe some will gather support for people to decline to attend the next Disney princess film, perhaps encouraging them to donate some or all of what they'll save at the box office to a larger effort to combat sexism. The ideas of a few may spread to many—and another chapter in the women's liberation movement may be written.

Age, Ageism and CR

In 1970 Maggie Kuhn gathered some of her friends together to discuss common concerns. Kuhn, who had worked for the Presbyterian Church for many years, was forced to retire at age 65. Her experience and the shared stories of acquaintances led to the creation of the Gray Panthers, an activist organization concerned with age discrimination and social security, but which was committed to building coalitions for social justice with a wide range of progressive groups. Kuhn and others associated with her outspoken challenge to ageism resisted all attempts to trivialize the old and their concerns. Their advocacy tactics encouraged borrowing strategies from other radical movements, including taking to the streets for what they believed. Kuhn's organization exposed egregious nursing home conditions, fraudulent health-care schemes targeting the old, and the injustice of forced retirement—the discriminatory practice that had led her to begin the Gray Panthers. Kuhn was no stranger to using her voice for social justice. In the 1930s and 1940s she had participated in consciousness-raising-like groups in the YWCA, where open conversations took place about sexual pleasure. She recommended that, since women outlive men, they should find younger or same-sex partners. She also insisted that young and old work together to explore social responses such as cooperative housing.[44]

When I joined with other women in creating the women's center at Salem

State College, we named the new entity for Florence Luscomb (1887–1985), a recognized figure in the Boston area for her work as a feminist who urged those identified with the women's liberation movement to build alliances across race and class. Like Kuhn, she saw that women's rights were linked to all struggles for human justice. Luscomb was one of the first women to graduate from MIT with a degree in architecture, and she combined her work in that profession with campaigning for women's suffrage. When the vote was won she continued her activism, working for the Women's International League for Peace and Freedom, the American Civil Liberties Union, the National Association for the Advancement of Colored People and many more progressive causes. I recall that at the time she accepted our request to use her name for our center she was living in a collective with a group of men and women, most decades younger.[45]

Look Us in the Eye

What I failed to see as I was congratulating myself on the "sensitivity" our group had shown in recognizing the contributions of this pioneering woman is that my behavior smacked of patronization. Idolizing an old woman created distance instead of solidarity. It took Barbara Macdonald and Cynthia Rich's *Look Me in the Eye*[46] for me to begin to understand the conjunction of sexism and ageism.

Macdonald made a point I had never considered about ageism in the feminist movement. While the suffragists were mostly older women (she notes that British activist Emmeline Pankhurst was 59 when she was arrested and imprisoned, and often marched with women older than herself),[47] the second wave of feminism was created by younger women. The struggle for the vote emerged from a time in patriarchal history when women were literally owned by their husbands, whose financial support allowed them to determine if and when children could be turned out of the home to work in factories or as servants in other households. Women could be and often were beaten for insubordination. The patriarchal arrangements that were present when the second wave emerged grew from a youth-oriented political culture that served a new "leisure elite consuming class" in which women could be tyrannized by both husbands and children! Macdonald writes, "There would, in fact, be no youth culture without the powerless older woman."[48]

As progressives we honored Luscomb, Kuhn, the suffragists, and other "wise old women," but did not see how the confluence of ageism and sexism had influenced the lives of our own mothers, which we were determined not to follow. Their childrearing years were shaped by messages to maintain sparkling homes, serve attractive meals and look pretty while doing these tasks. Many also worked outside the home. Then, and probably now, we feminists didn't see the contradictions in celebrating only the "exceptional" older women.

In her introduction to the revised edition of *Look Me in the Eye,* Lise Weil writes, "Barbara embraced the word 'old.' She rejected the terms 'older woman' and 'elder' not only as the euphemisms they obviously are, but because both assume youth as the measure. She saw our avoidance of 'old' as the clearest sign of our shame around aging, and she understood that shame as political, an internalization of our culture's message that 'old is ugly, old is powerless, old is the end, and therefore that old is what no one could possibly want to be.'"[49]

That's why the word does not appear in Betty Friedan's *Fountain of Age,*[50] written thirty years after the famous *Feminine Mystique.* Her audience is again the mostly white middle class. She reports on the interesting, involved lifestyles of active "elders," many living in communities with others of similar educational and economic circumstances with whom they can share intellectual stimulation, physical exercise and travel adventures. These are not selfish people; good works are part of their vital lives. Reading this and the abundance of other books that tout the joys of late life can make it seem like a hard wait for the exciting last chapters.

Like Susan Jacoby, author of *Never Say Die,*[51] I do not want to take away the pleasures that engage active old people, including myself. But Jacoby offers some reality to counter the relentless stories of the "interesting lifestyles" of the mountain-climbing, skydiving, and thriving old. The facts are that the longer we live, the more likely we are to be poor, socially isolated and faced with physical and mental illnesses, including the fact that after age 85, there is a 50/50 chance that we will be affected by Alzheimer's disease. And just as little girls are shaped by marketing that makes them want to be princesses, so are the old manipulated by media messages. Given the intersectionality of oppressions, women are affected in particularly grievous ways. The film *How to Live Forever*[52] offers a poignant example in a beauty competition for "older" women. At both ends of the age spectrum the model for "loveliness" is the twenty-something who is already altering her face and body to look even younger.

Women are the objects of patronization, and sometimes scorn, even in "young" old age. There are now mottoes that most of us have heard, such as "sixty is the new fifty" and variations thereof. It is almost tiresome to recount the difficulty women have in getting sexual partners—unless you are one of those women. Men have always sought younger women as sexual partners, a search that Viagra and similar drugs makes even easier. And the saddest, hardest reality is that women not only have greater chances of being alone but they are also more likely to be living in poverty. Women are the largest group in nursing homes and other facilities for the old where other women are the underpaid caretakers. Alternatively, daughters and daughters-in-law are often the unpaid caretakers for relatives who reluctantly must accept assistance. After doing for others, women then face the same plight for themselves.

Reclaiming Old

Cynthia Rich, Barbara Macdonald's life partner and contributing author to *Look Me in the Eye*, makes an eloquent plea to change these conditions: "We need to reclaim the value and meaning of our entire lifespans up to and including death. But first we must examine the ageism in ourselves." The first suggestion that Barbara gave to the university women's center that wanted to create a program for lesbians over sixty-five was to "organize consciousness-raising groups, a process in which old lesbians should be visible." Recognizing ageism is the first step to formulating action plans instead of just giving lip service to anti-ageism.

Older Lesbians Organizing for Change (OLOC)[53] is one of the strongest organizations working to expose ageism. Its list of ageist comments offers a valuable starting point for a consciousness-raising discussion. Here are a few I've selected or adapted from their website:

- Good afternoon, young lady, I'm Doctor Brown.
- You are in pretty good health for your age.
- Age is really just a state of mind.
- You aren't old. You're young at heart.
- You may be 72 but you still act young.
- Are you still swimming, still driving, still dancing, still playing bridge, still cooking, still gardening, still writing poetry, still giving blood, still politicking, still organizing, etc. etc. etc.?
- Social Security is going to bankrupt the country.
- To feel young again, try this: [products, exercises, recipes, meditation, etc.]
- I'm so glad you spoke up at the meeting. I like a feisty woman.
- You certainly don't look like you're 68 years old.
- You're only as old as you feel.
- You shouldn't call yourself old. It's so depressing.

- The Senior Center plans to hold a course named "Growing Old Gracefully." [Gracefully is a euphemism for being invisible, silent, docile, self-supporting, and free of illness.]
- When you were in your prime it was probably done differently.
- Blond is the new gray.[54]

In her article[55] on ageism, which she defines as "the systematic discrimination and oppression of people solely because they are old," Mary M. Morgan observes that many old people, myself included, accept and seek "compliments" such as "you don't look your age." Morgan observes the condescending behavior old people tolerate, including the assumption that they are not sexual, the dismissal of their justified anger, people turning to younger companions to speak for an old person (as in a restaurant—"what would *she* like?), and linking the old with unpleasant traits, such as being irritable, complaining or acting "crotchety."

Aging Is for Everybody

Since aging is the one condition every living being experiences, it should not be a descriptor for the end of life, but for all of life. Margaret Morganroth Gullette has written several notable books on ageism[56] that challenge the usual scripts. Like Jacoby, she decries the defiance of the aging process through Botox and plastic surgeries, and does not embrace the "fountain of age" stories that make old age a delightful walk in the park. She does suggest that a positive old age is possible and that the greatest barrier to its realization is ageism, which must be exposed and fought along with sexism, racism and class oppression. I like her suggestion that "age studies," as opposed to gerontology or geriatrics, be a subject of research, writing and public discussion, so that aging is understood as a process that begins at birth and is about growth rather than decline.

Discussing the process in consciousness-raising settings can lead to the personal and social change that is necessary to respond to stories such as the one Gullette relates about a group of children she observed at a science museum. Their reactions to a computer program that showed how their faces would age were loud individual and collective expressions of disgust.[57] Jacoby, too, reports on such revulsion, citing the comment of a woman in her fifties on observing a woman in a wheelchair who was hunched over with osteoporosis: "I'd rather be dead than live like that."[58]

Denial and disgust make it impossible to live authentically and to take reasonable initiatives to plan one's own evolving life. Complicity with ageism precludes the political action necessary to ensure that social and economic policies are in place to address the realities of changes through the lifespan. As Gullette points out, ageism, in just one manifestation, begins to affect workers early in their lives when they discover that an even younger applicant is preferred (a situation women experience to a greater degree); job loss in their fifties and sixties may mean that they must accept a lower-wage position, or perhaps remain unemployed.[59] Personal solutions rather than collective action have diminished the women's liberation movement. Becoming "agewise" may allow us to build coalitions based upon the condition we share across all other identities. Meeting in small groups to share experiences, find common threads and take action is empowering for both young and old—and can be most effective if people of all ages meet and work together to fight ageism instead of fighting aging.

"Tell me, what is it you plan to do with your one wild and precious life?"

I love the question that Mary Oliver poses in her poem "The Summer Day."[60] My mother lived more than 101 years. At the end of her life she was in an assisted-living facility where she was fully engaged in the activities offered, just as she had been in her paid work between college and marriage, devoted family life, friendship circles and myriad volunteer projects. What was missing from the "community" in which she lived at the end of her life, however, was a place where she and other people could pose Oliver's question and individually and collectively consider the answer. How would she—and her colleagues at Herrick House—have considered how they might live each day focused on the *present* rather than the past, or the often frightening future? Sometimes when we visited together she shared the pain of losing friends and relatives and the frustration of not being able to do or enjoy many of the things that had been part of her daily life. I know she was not alone in living with the dread of going to the nursing home next door, called "Ledgewood," or, even worse, the "fourth floor," which housed the Alzheimer's unit, referred to as the "reminiscence" area or some such euphemism.

But these concerns were not all of who she was and what she wanted to think about and express. Regrettably, but predictably in our culture, long before she left her own home ageism had shaped her late life. Well into her nineties she took a fairly strenuous walk each day, often up the steep hill leading to the Jewish Community Center. What awaited her after the trek were stereotypical programs for seniors—crafts, sing-alongs, exercise sessions—that prepared her for a similar routine at Herrick House, the setting she had chosen over having a home caretaker.

One of the activities she enjoyed at the assisted-living facility was a red hat club, a variation on an international phenomenon that brings together women over fifty for outings and trips, or just to meet over tea. The Red Hat Society, founded in the United States in 1998,[61] took its name from a poem by Jenny Joseph that begins, "When I am an old women, I shall wear purple / With a red hat that doesn't go, and doesn't suit me / and I shall spend my pension on brandy and summer gloves.... And make up for the sobriety of my youth."[62] At first I was appalled to learn that the leader of the individual chapters is called the "Queen Mum," but soon realized that the organization spoofs exclusive clubs and welcomes everyone. I think my mom liked to be part of what seemed a more lighthearted, even somewhat irreverent, gathering of a subset in her building. I now realize that she had few other opportunities for a unique small-group experience. I often helped her get ready for the special events, sharing her pleasure in donning the red hat that had been provided by the organizer (who, blessedly, never referred to herself as queen, mum, or any combination of those words). After my mother died I kept her hat and a variety of pins and other themed items that people had given her as gifts. Yes, thanks to consumer capitalism, there is an online Red Hat Store with dozens and dozens of products.

Another group of anti-ageism activists isn't buying. Like the Red Hat Society, the Raging Grannies organization[63] has chapters in the United States, Canada and Europe. But, in addition to celebrating aging, participants protest greed, environmental pollution, militarism and other "things that threaten our grandchildren's futures." The mode of activism is singing; their website offers nearly 500 songs. I have been to progressive events at which the Grannies have sung, sometimes dressed in costumes. The response was amusement mixed with indulgence, which is reinforced by the group's self-presentation. The logo on the website features an umbrella-wielding old lady and the words "Oh, we're a gaggle of Grannies, urging you up off your fannies."

I wonder if the political groups that welcome the Grannies' entertainment reciprocate by being actively involved in work against ageism. The consciousness-raising process can add ongoing reflection and analysis to the camaraderie offered by the Red Hat Society, Raging Grannies and other groups. The Raging Grannies already include work for social justice in their mission but, like some other feminist groups, may sacrifice their own priorities to the agendas of others. A serious analysis of ageism might mean less humorous self-deprecation and more rage—and lead to the meaningful social and economic change that is required to honor the humanity of all people throughout the lifespan.

Revisiting the mission statement of the Gray Panthers can inspire a cross-generational response to ageism. That organization advocates "social and economic justice and peace for all people," as well as work for a "humane society that puts the needs of people over profits, responsibility over power and democracy over institutions." Such a vision can guide us to a realization of the full promise of our "wild and precious" lives.

Conclusion:
Keep On Keeping On

Here I am in my 70s recalling the 1970s—and looking forward to continuing to shape a feminist future in the exciting years to come. I am fortunate to have good company in that endeavor, especially among my colleagues at the Brandeis University Women's Studies Research Center (WSRC), where I've been a scholar since 2009. The center is the perfect place to find support to "keep on keeping on." So I've chosen to conclude this book with a description that offers an example of a thriving women's community. It is no coincidence that the center utilizes many of the practices and approaches that have evolved from consciousness-raising and small-group organizing.

Brandeis University Women's Studies Research Center

The WSRC website describes "an innovative, interdisciplinary research facility of scholars, students and faculty who study gender issues and women's lives," but for those of us who are associated with this special place, it is hard to express the dynamism of the center in a single sentence.

Many research centers offer scholars a year or semester to pursue projects away from the demands of their usual workplaces. But the Brandeis WSRC is unusual in that it also provides a more permanent "home" to many. After a period of at least two years as a visiting scholar, participants can apply to be resident scholars who remain affiliated with the center for as long as they are actively engaged in research, art, or activism concerning gender. Some scholars apply with a particular project but, influenced by exposure to the interesting work of other scholars, may change their life trajectories. Some examples: a lawyer now combines her practice with writing and presenting outstanding writing workshops; a psychologist and academic dean became a full-time activist artist; a musician began to combine her performance schedule with work on a novel; and a psychotherapist chose to redirect her career to teaching. The work of the scholars who form the WSRC community grows from, and enlarges, a feminist vision. Most scholars at the center advocate and work for fundamental social change. Among them are women working internationally on urban renewal in India, food safety in Mongolia, and educational advancement of girls in Burkina Faso. A world-recognized expert on age studies couples her research and writing with annual volunteer work with both a literacy program and a shelter for abused girls in Nicaragua. Other projects include activism to end human trafficking, the abuses of international adoption, and discrimination against women workers in the trades.

Scholars form a community through a variety of practices. Study groups provide collective support, encouragement and critique for the research, creative work and activism of individual scholars. They join or form study groups around a field of common interest. I've been a member of a social issues research group since I joined the center. In advance of a study group meeting, members receive a book chapter, paper, or lecture draft with specific requests for feedback from the author scheduled to present. I was impressed from my first session with the respectful listening and constructive comments that mark the meetings. But giving and receiving suggestions and advice requires the building of both skills and trust, and these require practice and ongoing review. The social issues group has experimented with various formats with which I am familiar from my consciousness-raising experiences: rotating facilitators and note takers, mid–session check-ins to ensure the feedback is helpful, and other group assessments. We try to anticipate when a topic is likely to provoke emotional as well as intellectual responses. As we exchange and respond to each other's work, friendships and collaborations are formed.

I also joined a ritual studies group that initially focused on scholarly works about ritual practices in various religions and cultures. I can't remember what caused the detour, but the members of that group are now reviewing literature on the confluences and dissonances of feminism and queer studies. I'm part of another group that has formed to explore the ways in which the personal, spiritual and political are linked. While all the groups utilize techniques that can ensure full and honest participation, the spirituality group has been more open to the experience-based sharing and learning of consciousness-raising.

Appointments are unpaid, so, of course, many scholars are employed as professors, therapists, musicians, journalists and so forth. The WSRC does offer numerous benefits—travel grants, technology assistance, connection to the rich array of programs and services of the entire campus, and opportunities to work with the residents of Waltham, Massachusetts, the small city that is home to the university. The most wonderful "perk" is the chance to participate in the Student Scholar Partnership program. Scholars submit detailed proposals to which students in the applicant pool respond in writing and seek interviews. Because the application and selection process is so carefully delineated and implemented, some magical matches occur that nurture the interests and needs of both scholars and students. Last year I met a woman who had attended Brandeis a decade earlier. When she saw my affiliation on the conference badge she told me that she had served as a student scholar partner for one of my colleagues. She cherished the experience and brought the positive benefits of mentoring and mutual support to her work after college.

A more recent initiative has extended the student scholar partner model to a wider outreach effort. Through the campus Feminist Majority Leadership Alliance students have been matched with WSRC scholars for career and academic advice—and friendship. The successful project included the first of what we anticipate will be ongoing cross-generational conversations on feminism. We used the CR approach of breaking down into six or seven small groups in which each person had a chance to talk without interruption about how they had first discovered feminism.

The WSRC reverberates with creative energy. Free public lectures, book launchings and discussions, performances, films, concerts, and panels are presented by scholars and occasional guest artists and researchers throughout the year.

Feminist Forms and Functions

Founder Shulamit Reinharz raised the funds necessary to create the program and remodel a space in line with the center's values and green technology. She realized that the headquarters of the maintenance division at Brandeis could be reconfigured to house both the needs of that unit and the WSRC. She fulfilled her promise that none of the occupants would lose any amenities offered by their previous space assignments, and also created a uniquely beautiful, warm and welcoming environment for scholars to pursue the center's mission. The revisioned space is shared by the WSRC and the Hadassah-Brandeis Institute, a research center concerned with the intersections of Jews and gender. In addition to offices for program staff, the facility offers a wonderful exhibition space devoted to art by and about women, a fully equipped kitchen with a corner filled with books and toys for visiting children, and work spaces for scholars, including some cleverly designed armoires that can be used for short-term projects. The multipurpose room serves as a dance studio, film room, lecture hall and more. There is even an outdoor space featuring tables and chairs strategically placed within a grove of trees that is used by all the occupants of the building and students from the adjacent dormitories.

Resonant with the approaches to participatory organizations described in chapter IV, the WSRC leadership works with the tensions between structure and spontaneity in a deliberate and self-critical way. The director continually seeks informal input from all. Some resident scholars volunteer to be part of the Steering Committee, a more formal advisory group that meets regularly with the director and administrative staff. Whether short- or long-term affiliates, all scholars are invited to participate in a monthly "forum"; some meetings are devoted to center concerns, others to progress on individual projects or insights on a topic of current interest. The forum sessions, along with occasional retreats and other gatherings, are structured to provide the opportunity for individual voices to be heard and to nurture our spirit of community.

Boards of organizations hold purse strings and power, but the WSRC Board does not function as the distant entity those roles sometimes imply. At each board meeting a couple of scholars share their work, a process that builds relationships between board members and scholars while stimulating an exchange of ideas and suggestions that advance individual projects and the mission of the center. I have been privileged to serve as a liaison between the scholars and the board, which has increased my admiration for the credentials, caring and commitment of every member.

Each September a welcoming orientation for new and returning scholars takes place, always with a fresh approach to creating a supportive environment in which people can grow as individuals and as part of a collective. Additionally, a brown-bag lunch allows every new scholar to meet with colleagues. First-year scholars also join with their cohorts in a mentoring program facilitated by the WSRC director. The monthly meetings give newcomers a chance to know each other and get answers to specific questions and concerns. Usually cohort members who remain at the WSRC continue meeting because the peer bonding is so powerful. Sharing experience and knowledge with valued colleagues is one of the ways that the community grows stronger. I am including these approaches because I know other women's organizations could benefit from such practices, and I wish I had applied them as director of the UMass Dartmouth Women's Studies Program.

I realize how privileged I am to be in this remarkable setting—and I realize that I am here because I am privileged. I work with a group of people who are ever mindful of the distance between those for and with whom we are working to create a more just world, and the benefits we enjoy in our daily lives. The

WSRC is committed to diversity, but, whatever the religious background, skin color, class origins, or range of physical abilities, the fact remains that those who have been denied basic opportunities for education and social mobility are not here.

A New Era of Consciousness-Raising

We need many, many approaches that will close the gap between rich and poor, healthy and sick, the privileged and less lucky. Consciousness-raising is one of these. Reclaiming and incorporating the CR process in small-group settings can be a building block in exposing injustice and taking necessary action.

An early draft of this book began with the well-known quote from Margaret Mead: "Never doubt that a small group of thoughtful, committed citizens can change the world; indeed, it's the only thing that ever has."[1] I took the good advice of a colleague who thought the words had been used too often and dropped the quote. But now that I am ending the project I want to return to that phrase. The words are trite because they are accurate—and they apply particularly to women, who have made up many of the small groups of world-changers.

Ironically, as CR waned in the United States, women around the globe have been utilizing consciousness-raising approaches in creating personal and social change. Improvements in maternal and infant health resulted when women in rural India met in small groups to share their experiences of pregnancy, birth and childcare.[2] The moving film *Pray the Devil Back to Hell*[3] chronicles how women moved from discussions in their communities to a country-wide coalition that ended the horrific Liberian civil war; two of the principals were awarded the Nobel Prize for Peace. Kathy Davis, in *The Making of Our Bodies, Ourselves: How Feminism Travels Across Borders*, documents how small groups of women in various parts of the world have used CR to create translations of *OBOS* relevant to their particular social and political circumstances.[4]

I am confident that consciousness-raising will continue to cross borders—and oceans. I am heartened by the fact that the practice seems to be returning to this country as small groups benefit from the many ways in which a sometimes forgotten, sometimes renamed, but still very powerful technique can help women and their allies implement their visions of a just world.

Chapter Notes

Preface

1. http://iambecauseweare.wordpress.com/2006/11/06/what-would-happen-in-one-woman-told-the-truth-about-her-life/.

2. Catharine A. MacKinnon, *Toward a Feminist Theory of the State* (Cambridge, MA: Harvard University Press, 1989), 143.

3. Susan Griffin, *Wrestling with the Angel of Democracy* (New York: Trumpeter, 2008), 255–56.

4. bell hooks, *Feminism Is for Everybody: Passionate Politics* (Cambridge, MA: South End Press, 2000), x.

5. bell hooks, *Feminist Theory: From Margin to Center* (London: Pluto Press, 2000), 28.

6. Ibid., 35.

7. Simone de Beauvoir, *The Second Sex* (New York: Vintage, 1989).

8. Maya Majumdar, "Emerging Trends in Women Empowerment," *Encyclopaedia of Gender Equality through Women Empowerment* (New Delhi: Sarup & Sons, 2005), 56.

9. Caitlin Moran, *How to Be a Woman* (New York: Harper, 2012), 11–12.

10. http://www.domesticworkersunited.org.

11. Sheryl Sandberg, *Lean In: Women, Work, and the Will to Lead* (New York: Knopf, 2013).

12. Sherryl Connolly, "Sheryl Sandberg's 'Lean In' Is a Rousing, Controversial Call to Arms," *New York Daily News*, March 11, 2013, www.nydailynews.com/blogs/pageviews/2013/03/sheryl-sandbergs-lean-in-is-a-rousing-controversial-call-to-arms.

13. Jessica Bennett, "I Leaned In: Why Sheryl Sandberg's 'Circles' Actually Help," NYMag.com, March 7, 2013, http://nymag.com/thecut/2013/03/what-i-learned-at-the-lean-in-sandbergs-right.html.

14. Janet Freedman, "Consciousness-Raising Revisited," *Sojourner: The Women's Forum* (December 1987): 18–19.

15. Rachel Blau DuPlessis and Ann Snitow, eds., *Feminist Memoir Project: Voices from Women's Liberation* (New Brunswick, NJ: Rutgers University Press, 2007).

16. Anita Shreve, *Women Together, Women Alone: The Legacy of the Consciousness-Raising Movement* (New York: Viking, 1989).

17. Marcia Cohen, *The Sisterhood: The Inside Story of the Women's Movement and the Leaders Who Made It Happen* (New York: Ballantine, 1988); Flora Davis, *Moving the Mountain: The Women's Movement in America since 1960* (New York: Simon & Schuster, 1991); Alice Echols, *Daring to Be Bad: Radical Feminism in America, 1967–1975* (Minneapolis: University of Minnesota Press, 1989); Rory C. Dicker, *A History of U.S. Feminisms* (Berkeley, CA: Seal Press, 2008); Sara M. Evans, *Personal Politics: The Roots of Women's Liberation in the Civil Rights Movement and the New Left* (New York: Vintage, 1980); Carol Giardina, *Freedom for Women: Forging the Women's Liberation Movement, 1953–1970* (Gainesville: University Press of Florida, 2010); Barbara Crow, ed., *Radical Feminism: A Documentary Reader* (New York: New York University Press, 2000); Ruth Rosen, *The World Split Open: How the Women's Movement Changed America* (New York: Viking, 2000).

18. Bettina Aptheker, *Tapestries of Life: Women's Work, Women's Consciousness, and the Meaning of Daily Experience* (Amherst: University of Massachusetts Press, 1989).

19. Jane Roland Martin, *Reclaiming a Conversation: The Ideal of the Educated Woman* (New Haven, CT: Yale University Press, 1987).

20. Tracy Kennedy, "The Personal Is Political: Feminist Blogging and Virtual Consciousness-Raising," *The Scholar & Feminist Online Journal* 5, no. 2 (2007), http://sfonline.barnard.edu/blogs/kennedy_01.htm.

21. "Judy Grahn and 'The Common Woman,'" *So to Speak*, December 12, 2011, http://sotospeakjournal.org/2011/12/judy-grahn-and-writing-from-commonality/?mid=576.

22. The blessing in the dedication is taken from Marcia Falk's *The Book of Blessings: New Jewish Prayers for Daily Life, the Sabbath and the New Moon Festival* (San Francisco: Harper, 1996).

Chapter I

1. Vivian Gornick, "What Feminism Means to Me," in *Feminist Memoir Project: Voices from Women's Liberation*, edited by Rachel Blau DuPlessis and Ann Snitow (New Brunswick, NJ: Rutgers University Press, 2007).

2. Catharine A. MacKinnon, *Toward a Feminist Theory of the State* (Cambridge, MA: Harvard University Press, 1989), 143.

3. Loretta J. Ross, "Storytelling in SisterSong and the Voices of Feminism Project," in *Telling Stories to Change the World: Global Voices on the Power of Narrative to Build Community and Make Social Justice Claims*, edited by Rickie Solinger, Madeline Fox, and Kayhan Irani (New York: Routledge, 2008).

4. Carol Giardina, *Freedom for Women: Forging the Women's Liberation Movement, 1953–1970* (Gainesville: University Press of Florida, 2010).

5. Betty Friedan, *The Feminine Mystique* (New York: W. W. Norton, 1963).

6. Margalit Fox, "Betty Friedan, Who Ignited Cause in 'Feminist Mystique,' Dies at 85," *New York Times*, February 5, 2006, http://www.nytimes.com/2006/02/05/national/05friedan.html (accessed August 31, 2011).

7. Carol Hanisch, "Women's Liberation Consciousness-Raising: Then and Now," *On the Issues* (Spring 2010), http://www.ontheissuesmagazine.com/2010spring/2010spring_Hanisch.php.

8. Ibid.

9. http://library.duke.edu/rubenstein/scriptorium/wlm/fem/sarachild.html.

10. Pat Mainardi, "The Politics of Housework," originally published by Redstockings in 1970.

11. Anne Koedt, "The Myth of the Vaginal Orgasm," originally published in 1970, CWLU Herstory Website Archive, http://www.uic.edu/orgs/cwluherstory/CWLUArchive/vaginalmyth.html.

12. Carol Hanisch, "The Personal Is Political: The Women's Liberation Movement Classic with a New Explanatory Introduction," originally published in *Notes from the Second Year: Women's Liberation* (New York: Radical Feminism, 1970).

13. Pamela Allen, *Free Space: A Perspective on the Small Group in Women's Liberation* (New York: Times Change Press, 1970).

14. There is a review on Amazon.com of *Guidelines to Feminist Consciousness Raising* authored by Harriet Perl and Gay Abarbenell for NOW's consciousness-raising committee, with a first edition of 55 pages copyrighted by the authors in 1976 and a revised edition of 65 pages copyrighted in 1979. According to the review, NOW bought the copyright around 1981 (http://www.amazon.com/Guidelines-feminist-consciousness-raising-Harriet/dp/B0006XQLHC/ref=sr_1_1?ie=UTF8&qid=1377562567&sr=8-1&keywords=guidelines+consciousness+raising). My local NOW chapter sponsored consciousness-raising sessions well before these publications and, typical of the nonhierarchical nature of the second wave, utilized an amalgamation of suggestions from various sources.

15. MacKinnon, *Toward a Feminist Theory of the State*, 146.

16. Ibid.

17. Dorothy Tennov, *Open Rapping* (Pittsburgh, PA: KNOW, n.d.).

18. Linda Gordon, "Translating *Our Bodies, Ourselves*," *The Nation*, June 16, 2008, http://www.thenation.com/article/traslating-our-bodies-ourselves (accessed August 31, 2007).

19. Gornick, "What Feminism Means to Me."

20. Anita Shreve, *Women Together, Women Alone: The Legacy of the Consciousness-Raising Movement* (New York: Viking, 1989).

21. Nancy Whittier, *Feminist Generations: The Persistence of the Radical Women's Movement* (Philadelphia: Temple University Press, 1995).

22. bell hooks, *Feminism Is for Everybody: Passionate Politics* (Cambridge, MA: South End Press, 2000).

23. Tia Cross, Freada Klein, Barbara Smith, and Beverly Smith, "Face-to-Face, Day-to-Day—Racism CR," in *All the Women Are White, All the Blacks Are Men, But Some of Us Are Brave: Black Women's Studies*, edited by Gloria T. Hull, Patricia Scott and Barbara Smith (New York: Feminist Press at CUNY, 1982).

24. Michelene Wandor, *Once a Feminist: Stories of a Generation* (London: Virago, 1990).

25. Robin Morgan, "Theory and Practice: Pornography and Rape," *Going Too Far: The Personal Chronicle of a Feminist* (New York: Random House, 1977); http://en.wikiquote.org/wiki/Robin_Morgan.

26. Alice Echols, *Daring to Be Bad: Radical Feminism in America, 1967–1975* (Minneapolis: University of Minnesota Press, 1989).

27. "Sensitivity Training," *Encyclopedia Britannica*, http://www.britannica.com/EBchecked/topic/534776/sensitivity-training.

28. Lisa Maria Hogeland, *Feminism and Its Fictions: The Consciousness-Raising Novel and the*

Women's Liberation Movement (Philadelphia: University of Pennsylvania Press, 1998).

29. Jane O'Reilly, "The Housewife's Moment of Truth," *Ms.* (December 1971); http://womenshistory.about.com/od/feministtexts/a/housewife_moment.htm.

30. Nora Ephron, "Women," *Esquire* (March 1973): 77.

31. Joreen Freeman, "Tyranny of Structurelessness," in *Radical Feminism*, edited by Anne Koedt, Ellen Leone, and Anita Rapone (New York: Quadrangle, 1973); http://www.feministreprise.org/docs/structurelessness.htm.

32. Anselma Dell'Olio, *Divisiveness and Self-Destruction in the Women's Movement* (Pittsburgh, PA: KNOW, 1970).

33. Audre Lorde, "The Master's Tools Will Never Dismantle the Master's House," *Sister Outsider: Essays and Speeches* (Freedom, CA: Crossing Press, 1984).

34. Rory C. Dicker, *A History of U.S. Feminisms* (Berkeley, CA: Seal Press, 2008), 129.

35. Stephanie Gilmore, "The Dynamics of Second-Wave Feminist Activism in Memphis, 1971–1982: Rethinking the Liberal/Radical Divide," *NWSA Journal* 15, no. 1 (Spring 2003): 94–114.

36. Dicker, *A History of U.S. Feminisms*, 130.

37. Susan Griffin, *Wrestling with the Angel of Democracy: On Being an American Citizen* (New York: Trumpeter, 2008).

38. Bridget Crawford, "Consciousness Raising and Contemporary Feminist Method," Feminist Law Professors Blog (2008).

Chapter II

1. Marge Piercy, "To Be of Use," *Circles on the Water* (New York: Alfred A. Knopf, 1982).

2. http://www.domesticworkersunited.org/.

3. New York State Department of Labor, "Domestic Workers' Bill of Rights," http://www.labor.ny.gov/legal/domestic-workers-bill-of-rights.shtm.

4. Akito Yoshikane, "New ILO Convention Gives Domestic Workers Historic Labor Rights," *In These Times*, June 22, 2011, http://www.inthesetimes.com/working/entry/11549/new_ilo_convention_gives_domestic_workers_historic_labor_rights/.

5. Convention Concerning Decent Work for Domestic Workers, 189th ILO Convention, June 16, 2011.

6. Polaris Project for a World Without Slavery is one of many organizations working to combat the trafficking of men and women, girls and boys (http://www.polarisproject.org).

7. Mary Wollstonecraft, *A Vindication of the Rights of Woman with Strictures on Moral and Political Subjects*, 3rd ed. (Philadelphia: William Gibbons, 1796).

8. Virginia Woolf, *A Room of One's Own* (London: Hogarth, 1929).

9. Virginia Woolf, *Three Guineas* (New York: Harcourt, Brace, 1938).

10. Betty Friedan, *The Feminine Mystique* (New York: W.W. Norton, 1963).

11. Bessie Van Vorst and Marie Van Vorst, *The Woman Who Toils: Being the Experiences of Two Gentlewomen as Factory Girls* (New York: Doubleday, Page, 1903).

12. Barbara Ehrenreich, *Nickled and Dimed: On (Not) Getting By in America* (New York: Metropolitan, 2001).

13. Remarks by Hilda L. Solis, Secretary of Labor, at the National Domestic Workers Alliance Inaugural Care Congress, Washington, DC, July 12, 2011 (www.dol.gov/_sec/media/speeches/20110712_NDWA.htm).

14. Paul Hawkens, *Blessed Unrest: How the Largest Social Movement in History Is Restoring Grace, Justice, and Beauty to the World* (New York: Penguin, 2007).

15. Adrienne Rich, *On Lies, Secrets, and Silence: Selected Prose, 1966–1978* (New York: W. W. Norton, 1979).

16. Joanna Weiss, "The Right to a Flexible Workplace," *Boston Globe*, March 23, 2011.

17. Marielle Segarra, "Women CFOs: Still at 9%," CFO.com, June 22, 2011, www.cfo.com/article.cfm/14581369.

18. Sukanya Mitra, "Why Controllers Aren't CFO Material," American Institute for Certified Public Accountants, October 4, 2007, http://www.cpa2biz.com/Content/media/PRODUCER_CONTENT/Newsletters/Articles_2007/CorpFin/Material.jsp.

19. Ray Rowan, *The Intuitive Manager* (Boston: Little, Brown, 1986).

20. Bruna Martinuzzi, "What's Empathy Got to Do With It?" http://www.mindtools.com/pages/article/newLDR_75.htm.

21. Mitra, "Why Controllers Aren't CFO Material."

22. Robert Putnam and Lewis Feldstein, *Better Together: Restoring the American Community* (New York: Simon & Schuster, 2003).

23. Jean Baker Miller, *Toward a New Psychology of Women* (Boston: Beacon Press, 1977).

24. Putnam and Feldstein, *Better Together*.

25. One of the reasons that Miller and her colleagues' work is placed in a female ghetto is that even some feminist theorists have charged them with promoting "essentialism"—that is, suggesting their theories assume that women have certain innate qualities. But Miller never said that women embodied qualities of caring and were "naturally" good at relationships. Indeed, her book is an effort to acknowledge that women around the world have been assigned the "relational" work but are then often disadvantaged because they lack the power to perform as expected in self-defined and

fulfilling ways. I confess that, following the ubiquitous assignments of essentialism to many second-wave writings, I, too, began to question Miller's work. In rereading her writing, however, I realized that "essentialism" is not inherent in the theory, but in the reception of the theory by both men and women who, perhaps "unconsciously," do not see theories rooted in female experience as being equally or more valuable than those put forth by men who offer the same conclusions.

26. Liz Hull, "Men Are the Best Bosses: Women at the Top Are Just Too Moody (And It's Women Themselves Who Say So," *Daily Mail*, August 12, 2010, http://www.dailymail.co.uk/femail/article-1302096/Men-best-bosses-Women-just-moody.html.

27. Barbara Garson, *All the Livelong Day: The Meaning and Demeaning of Routine Work* (New York: Penguin, 1994).

28. Stewart O'Nan, *Last Night at the Lobster* (New York: Viking, 2007).

29. Amitai Etzioni, ed., *The Semi-Professions and Their Organization: Teachers, Nurses, Social Workers* (New York: Free Press, 1969).

30. Spinner Publications was founded by Donna Huse and Joseph Thomas and is located in New Bedford, Massachusetts.

31. Marilyn Halter, *Between Race and Ethnicity: Cape Verdean Immigrants, 1860–1965* (Champaign: University of Illinois Press, 1993).

32. Sara Lawrence-Lightfoot, *The Third Chapter: Passion, Risk, and Adventure in the 25 Years After 50* (New York: Farrar, Straus and Giroux, 2009).

Chapter III

1. Crista DeLuzio, ed., *Women's Rights: People and Perspectives* (Santa Barbara, CA: ABC-CLIO, 2010).

2. Tracy Kennedy, "The Personal Is Political: Feminist Blogging and Virtual Consciousness-Raising," *The Scholar & Feminist Online Journal*, 5 no. 2 (2007), http://sfonline.barnard.edu/blogs/kennedy_01.htm.

3. Phyllis Korkki, "How to Say 'Look at Me!' to an Online Recruiter," *New York Times*, January 26, 2013.

4. Ali Smith, *There But For The* (New York: Pantheon, 2011), 105–6.

5. Sherry Turkle, *Life on the Screen* (New York: Simon & Schuster, 1995).

6. Sherry Turkle, *Alone Together: Why We Expect More from Technology and Less from Each Other* (New York: Basic Books, 2012).

7. Nicholas Carr, *The Shallows: What the Internet Is Doing to Our Brains* (New York: W. W. Norton, 2010).

8. Ibid., 4.

9. See "Key People: Ada Lovelace," Computer History Museum, 2008 (cited July 10, 2013), available from http://www.computerhistory.org/babbage/adalovelace/.

10. Melanie Stewart Millar, *Cracking the Gender Code: Who Rules the Wired World* (Toronto: Second Story Press, 1998).

11. Ibid., 91.

12. Leah Burrows, "Unfair Game," *Boston Globe*, January 27, 2013.

13. Turkle, *Life on the Screen*, 210–11.

14. Sherry Turkle, "Who Am We?" *Wired*, http://www.wired.com/wired/archive/4.01/turkle_pr.html.

15. Alex Williams, "The End of Courtship?" *New York Times*, January 11, 2013.

16. http://finallyfeminism101.wordpress.com/2010/04/04/what-is-slut-shaming/.

17. Frank Rich, "Naked Capitalists: There's No Business Like Porn Business," *New York Times*, May 20, 2001.

18. Huma Khan, "Child Sex Trafficking Growing in the U.S.: 'I Got My Childhood Taken from Me,'" ABC News, May 5, 2010, http://abcnews.go.com/US/domestic-sex-trafficking-increasing-united-states/story?id=10557194.

19. *Frontline*, January 13, 2010, http://www.pbs.org/frontlineworld/stories/ghana804/video/video_index.html (accessed February 20, 2012).

20. "Driving Change, Shaping Lives: Gender in the Developing World," Radcliffe Institute for Advanced Study, Harvard University, March 3–4, 2011.

21. Benedict Carey, "Parents Urged Again to Limit TV for Youngest," *New York Times*, October 18, 2011, http://www.nytimes.com/2011/10/19/health/19babies.html?seid=&_r=1&.

22. Carla Freeman, *High Tech and High Heels in the Global Economy: Women, Work, and Pink Collar Identities in the Caribbean* (Durham, NC: Duke University Press, 2000).

23. Caryl Rivers and Rosalind Barnett, *The Truth about Girls and Boys: Challenging Toxic Stereotypes about Our Children* (New York: Columbia University Press, 2011); for a brief summary, see their editorial in the *Los Angeles Times* published on January 26, 2012 (http://www.ohio.com/editorial/by-rosalind-barnett-and-caryl-rivers-doing-the-math-of-gender-equity-1.257130).

24. Heather R. Huhman, "STEM Fields and the Gender Gap: Where Are the Women?" *Forbes*, June 20, 2012, http://www.forbes.com/sites/work-in-progress/2012/06/20/stem-fields-and-the-gender-gap-where-are-the-women/.

25. http://www.girlscouts.org/research/pdf/generation_stem_full_report.pdf.

26. Now called the Anita Borg Institute for Women and Technology, following Borg's death from a brain tumor at age 54 (http://anitaborg.org).

27. http://www.sdsc.edu/ScienceWomen/hopper.html (accessed September 10, 2012).

28. Sadie Plant, *Zeros + Ones: Digital Women*

+ *New Technologies* (New York: Doubleday, 1997).

29. http://www.computerhistory.org/babbage/adalovelace/.

30. Donna Haraway, "A Cyborg Manifesto: Science, Technology, and Socialist-Feminisms in the Late Twentieth Century," *Simians, Cyborgs and Women: The Reinvention of Nature* (New York: Routledge, 1991), 149–81.

31. http://www.sysx.org/gashgirl/VNS/TEXT/PINKMANI.HTM: "We are the modern cunt positive anti reason unbounded unleashed unforgiving we see art with our cunt we make art with our cunt we believe in jouissance madness holiness and poetry we are the virus of the new world disorder rupturing the symbolic from within saboteurs of big daddy mainframe the clitoris is a direct line to the matrix the VNS MATRIX terminators of the moral code mercenaries of slime go down on the altar of abjection probing the visceral temple we speak in tongues infiltrating disrupting disseminating corrupting the discourse we are the future cunt."

32. Ibid.

33. The anti-theses were promulgated by thirty women who gathered at the First Cyberfeminist International, an embedded site of meetings that took place within a larger 1997 conference held in Kassel, Germany (see http://switch/sjsu.edu/web/v4n1/alex.html, accessed December 11, 2012).

34. Radhika Gajjala and Yeon Ju Oh, eds., *Cyberfeminism 2.0* (New York: Peter Lang, 2012). "2.0" is an umbrella descriptor for a Web that permits interactive, user-initiated, "bottom-up" uses of the Internet, which were not available when computers were used to retrieve data rather than create it.

35. Emily Nussbaum quotes Knox in her October 30, 2011, article in *New York Magazine*, "Rebirth of the Feminist Manifesto," in which she notes the "nostalgic longing for the consciousness raising groups of the 1970s."

36. "Blogcrawls" can lead to sites with in-depth and insightful commentary, and also to mean-spirited rants. Blogs come and go. Many blogrolls add new blogs, but don't remove those that haven't been updated or are no longer available.

37. http://feministing.com/.

38. Feministing has received a Blogger's Choice nomination for its political and editorial content and it is a 2011 winner of the Sidney Hillman Prize for social and economic justice in blog journalism awarded by the Sidney Hillman Foundation (http://www.hillmanfoundation.org/hillman-prizes/Sidney_Hillman_Foundation_Announces_2011_Prizes).

39. http://jezebel.com.

40. http://thefbomb.org/about/.

41. The site doesn't give a beginning date but archived entries go back to 2003.

42. http://civilliberty.about.com/od/gendersexuality/tp/blogs_feminist.htm.

43. "Our Mission Statement," Our Bodies Ourselves, 2005–2011 [2013], http://www.ourbodiesourselves.org/about/mission.asp.

44. Kathy Davis, *The Making of Our Bodies, Ourselves: How Feminism Travels Across Borders* (Durham, NC: Duke University Press, 2007).

45. http://www.crunkfeministcollective.com/.

46. http://www.vivalafeminista.com.

47. http://www.vivalafeminista.com/p/mom.html.

48. http://www.racialicious.com.

49. http://www.hugoschwyzer.net/blog/.

50. http://genprogress.org/voices/2012/02/13/17543/the-fall-of-schwyzer-how-the-male-feminist-crumbled/.

51. http://www.dailystrength.org/support-groups.

52. For some examples, see www.netaddictionrecovery.com and http://www.newser.com/tag/21000/1/internet-addiction.html.

53. See, for instance, http://www.breastcancer.org/treatment/comp_med/types/group.

54. Christina Ng and Sheila Marikar, "JCPenney's 'Too Pretty to Do Homework' Shirt Pulled," ABC News, August 31, 2011, http://abcnews.go.com/blogs/headlines/2011/08/jcpenneys-too-pretty-to-do-homework-shirt-pulled/.

55. https://www.facebook.com/SlutWalk.

56. *http://www.feministfrequency.com./2011/05/link-round-up-feminist-critiques-of-slutwalk (accessed October 5, 2011).*

57. http://www.slutwalkminneapolis.org.

58. http://bcrw.barnard.edu/publications/femfuture-online-revolution/.

59. Faith Wilding, "Where is Feminism in Cyberfeminism?" http://faithwilding.refugia.net/wherefem.pdf.

60. Shulamith Firestone, *The Dialectic of Sex: The Case for Feminist Revolution* (New York: William Morrow, 1970).

61. Wilding, http://faithwilding.refugia.net/wherefem.pdf.

62. http://www.thefreedictionary.com/Liberatory.

63. Virginia Eubanks, *Digital Dead End: Fighting for Social Justice in the Information Age* (Cambridge, MA: MIT Press, 2011).

64. W. Lance Bennett, ed., *Civic Life Online: Learning How Digital Media Can Engage Youth* (Cambridge, MA: MIT Press, 2008).

65. http://www.thatsnonsense.com/view.php?id=1673.

66. http://www.thisamericanlife.org/radio-archives/episode/460/retraction.

67. http://www.smith.edu/libraries/libs/ssc/news/speakers70th.html.

68. http://www.bostonreview.net/BR23.3/mcchesney.html.

69. The four local channels in the community

of Arlington, Massachusetts, broadcast full meetings of the School Committee, Select Board, Finance Committee, and other town governance units, as well as numerous rebroadcasts of church services, public service announcements from community agencies, cooking and craft shows, and a twice-daily broadcast of *Democracy Now!* (http://www.democracynow.org).

70. Eubanks, *Digital Dead End*, 129.

71. Wilding, http://faithwilding.refugia.net/wherefem.pdf.

Chapter IV

1. Susan Griffin, *Wrestling with the Angel of Democracy: On Being an American Citizen* (New York: Trumpeter, 2008), 274.

2. Ibid., 273.

3. The exceptions are Brunei, an absolute monarchy with no voting for men or women; Bhutan, which limits voting to one vote per household; Lebanon, where men are required to vote although proof of elementary education is required for women; Saudi Arabia and United Arab Emirates, where voting is limited (in Saudi Arabia women will not be able to vote until at least 2015); and Vatican City, where voting is restricted to cardinals, all male (http://wiki.answers.com/Q/What_countries_do_not_let_women_vote&altQ=Countries_where_women_cannot_vote&isLookUp=1).

4. http://www.unwomen.org/en/news/stories/2012/10/keynote-address-of-michelle-bachelet-at-inter-parliamentary-union-conference-of-women-*speakers of pa/*.

5. http://www.quotaproject.org.

6. http://www.whitehouse.gov/administration/eop/cwg/data-on-women.

7. http://www.brainyquote.com/quotes/authors/l/louis_d_brandeis.html.

8. "The U.S. Is Number One—For Income Inequality," *The Takeaway*, January 30, 2013, http://www.thetakeaway.org/2013/jan/30/economic-inequality-beijing-bridgeport.

9. Dave Gilson and Carolyn Perot, "It's the Inequality, Stupid," *Mother Jones* (March/April 2011).

10. Kay Lehman Schlozman, Sidney Verba, and Henry E. Brady, *The Unheavenly Chorus: Unequal Political Voice and the Broken Promise of American Democracy* (Princeton, NJ: Princeton University Press, 2012).

11. Ibid., 6.

12. Melissa V. Harris-Perry, "Seneca Falls to Selma to Stonewall," *The Nation*, February 11, 2013.

13. Melissa V. Harris-Perry, *Sister Citizen: Shame, Stereotypes and Black Women in America* (New Haven, CT: Yale University Press, 2011).

14. Ibid., 32.

15. Ibid., 299.

16. Jane Mansbridge, "Feminism and Democracy," *American Prospect*, December 4, 2000, http://prospect.org/article/feminism-and-democracy.

17. Sara M. Evans and Harry C. Boyte, "Free Spaces: The Sources of Democratic Change in America," in *The Civil Society Reader*, edited by Michael W. Foley and Virginia Ann Hodgkinson (Lebanon, NH: University Press of New England, 2003), 263.

18. Lucinda Marshall, "OWS—Where Does Feminism Fit?" Women's Media Center, November 21, 2011, http://www.womensmediacenter.com/feature/entry/exclusive-owswhere-does-feminism-fit.

19. http://www.frontiersla.com/news/context/story.aspx?ID=1563265.

20. http://www.racialicious.com/2011/11/11.racial-fractures-and-the-occupy-movement.

21. http://feministcampus.org/blog/index.php/2011/11/15/occupypatriarchy-why-feminists-should-care-about-the-occupy-movement/.

22. http://spunk.org/texts/intro/sp00163.html.

23. Petr Kropotkin, *Mutual Aid: A Factor of Evolution* (London: Heinemann, 1902).

24. Peggy Kornegger, "Anarchism: The Feminist Connection," *Second Wave* (Spring 1975): 26–37.

25. Martha Ackelsberg, *Resisting Citizenship: Feminist Essays on Politics, Community and Democracy* (New York: Routledge, 2010).

26. Beth Eddy, "Struggle or Mutual Aid: Jane Addams, Petr Kropotkin and the Progressive Encounter with Social Darwinism," *Pluralist* 5, no. 1 (2010): 21–43.

27. http://www.human-spirit-initiative.org/blog2/wp-content/uploads/2010/10/Jane_Addams_monograph.pdf.

28. Grace Paley, *Collected Stories* (New York: Farrar, Straus and Giroux, 1995).

29. Joyce Ann Hanson, *Mary McLeod Bethune & Black Women's Political Activism* (Columbia: University of Missouri Press, 2003), 2.

30. Ibid., 95.

31. http://www.aa.org.

32. http://www.phyllisrsilverman.com.

33. Gayle A. Sulik, *Pink Ribbon Blues: How Breast Cancer Culture Undermines Women's Health* (New York: Oxford University Press, 2012).

34. http://thinkbeforeyoupink.org.

35. http://thinkbeforeyoupink.org/?page_id=10.

36. http://www.ishcc.org/MA/Cambridge/women-s-community-cancer-project-inc.

37. http://www.healthytomorrow.org.

38. http://www.whitehouse.gov/administration/eop/cwg/data-on-women.

39. Kathy E. Ferguson, *The Feminist Case against Bureaucracy* (Philadelphia: Temple University Press, 1984).

40. Ibid., 122.

41. Ibid., 12.

42. I am particularly grateful to my colleague and dear friend Donna Huse, who has written and spoken on the stifling and dehumanizing results of bureaucracies (see Donna Huse, "Restructuring and the Physical Context: Designing Learning Environments," *Children's Environments*, vol. 12, no. 3 (1995): 290–310.

43. Donna Hawxhurst and Sue Morrow, *Living Our Visions: Building Feminist Community* (Tempe, AZ: Fourth World, 1984).

44. Janet Freedman, "The Beauty of a Library in our Democracy," *The Standard-Times*, July 16, 2005, A7.

45. Martin Buber, *The Martin Buber Reader: Essential Writings*, edited by Asher D. Biemann (New York: Palgrave Macmillan, 2002), 257.

46. Griffin, *Wrestling with the Angel of Democracy*, 272–73.

47. Hawxhurst and Morrow, *Living Our Visions*.

48. Starhawk, *The Empowerment Manual* (Gabriola Island, BC, Canada: New Society Publishers, 2011).

49. Ibid., 3.

50. myemail.constantcontact.com/Peace maker-News_Starhawk-speaks-Nov-21.html? soid=111113019289&aid=JnJwSJGKeso.

51. Starhawk, *Empowerment Manual*.

52. The books I've mentioned and others, particularly those issued by New Society Publishers, offer valuable and detailed advice. I have found John Gastil's *Democracy in Small Groups: Participation, Decision Making & Communication* (Philadelphia: New Society Publications, 1993) especially valuable.

53. Starhawk, *Empowerment Manual*.

54. Courtney Martin and J. Courtney Sullivan, eds., *Click: When We Knew We Were Feminists* (Berkeley, CA: Seal Press, 2010).

55. Kate J. M. Baker, "Kony 2012 Director Says It's Not about Money While Campaign Makes Millions," *Jezebel*, March 9, 2012, http://jezebel.com/5891878/kony-2012-director-says-its-not-about-making-money-while-campaign-makes-millions (accessed September 8, 2012).

56. http://invisiblechildren.com/about/fourth-estate-details/.

57. htpp://allafrica.com (accessed July 24, 2013).

58. Jacey Fortin, "The Surprising Truth about Internet Censorship in the Middle East," *International Business Times*, October 12, 2012, http://www/ibtimes/com/surprising-truth-about-internet-censorship-middle-east-845933 (accessed July 24, 2013).

59. John R. Quain, "Big Brother? U.S. Linked to New Wave of Censorship, Surveillance on Web," Fox News, February 27, 2013, http://www.foxnews.com/tech/2013/02/27/special-report-surveillance-and-censorship-america/.

Chapter V

1. Estelle Freedman, "Small Group Pedagogy: Consciousness-Raising in Conservative Times," *Feminism, Sexuality, and Politics* (Chapel Hill: University of North Carolina Press, 2006), 67–83.

2. Robin Morgan, *Sisterhood Is Powerful* (New York: Vintage, 1970).

3. Some examples are the superb work of the Association of College and Research Libraries' (ACRL) *Women & Gender Studies* Section (www.libr.org/wgss/corebooks.html) and the Office of the University of Wisconsin System Women's Studies Librarian's (womenst.library.wisc.edu) *Synergy Magazine*, issued by the San Francisco Public Library, and its privately published successor, as well as *Booklegger Magazine*, which highlighted material for public library audiences.

4. Marilyn J. Boxer, *When Women Ask the Questions: Creating Women's Studies in America* (Baltimore: Johns Hopkins University Press, 1998).

5. http://www.ncrw.org/member-organizatons/university-maryland-college-park.

6. http://userpages.umbc.edu/~korenman/wmst/wmst-l_index.html.

7. Frinde Maher, Feminist Classroom Conference, Harvard University, March 20, 2012.

8. http://www.wilderdom.com/experiential/JohnDeweyPhilosophyEducation.html.

9. Antonia Darder, Marta Baltodano, and Rudolf D. Torres, eds., *Critical Pedagogy Reader*, 2nd ed. (New York: Taylor & Francis, 2008).

10. http://infed.org/mobi/ivan-illich-deschooling-convivialty-and-lifelong-learning/.

11. Paolo Freire, *Pedagogy of the Oppressed*, translated by Myra Bergman Ramos, 30th anniversary edition (New York: Continuum International, 2000; original edition published in 1968).

12. The term originally was derived from Frantz Fanon's coinage of a French term, *conscienciser*, in his 1952 book, *Black Skins, White Masks*, rev. ed. (New York: Grove, 2008).

13. See Sally Kempton's comment that "It's hard to fight an enemy that has outposts in your head" (www.quotationspage.com/quote/1915.html).

14. Audre Lorde, *Sister Outsider: Essays and Speeches* (Freedom, CA: Crossing Press, 1984).

15. Kathleen Weiler, "Freire and a Feminist Pedagogy of Difference," *Harvard Educational Review* (Winter 1991): 449–75.

16. Elizabeth Kamarck Minnich, *Transforming Knowledge* (Philadelphia: Temple University Press, 1990).

17. Ibid., 179.

18. Frances A. Maher and Mary Kay Thompson Tetrault, *The Feminist Classroom* (New York: Basic Books, 1994).

19. Barbara Winkler, *Teaching Introduction*

to Women's Studies (Westport, CT: Bergin & Garvey, 1999).

20. June Jordan, "Report from the Bahamas, 1982," *Meridians* 3, no. 2 (2003): 6–16.

21. Peggy McIntosh, *White Privilege and Male Privilege: A Personal Account of Coming to See Correspondences through Work in Women's Studies* (Richmond, VA: Wellesley College Center for Research on Women, 1988).

22. Cricket Keating, "Building Coalitional Consciousness," *NWSA Journal* 17, no. 2 (2005): 86–103.

23. Freedman, *Small Group Pedagogy*.

24. Patricia Hill Collins, *On Intellectual Activism* (Philadelphia: Temple University Press, 2013).

25. Nancy Schniedewind, "Feminist Values: Guidelines for Teaching Methodology in Women's Studies," in *Learning Our Way: Essays in Feminist Education*, edited by C. Bunch and S. Pollack (New York: Crossing Press, 1983).

26. Carolyn M. Shrewsbury, "What Is Feminist Pedagogy?" *Women's Studies Quarterly* 25, nos. 1–2 (Spring/Summer 1997): 166–73.

27. Adrienne Rich, *On Lies, Secrets, and Silence: Selected Prose, 1966–1978* (New York: W. W. Norton, 1979).

28. Toni Morrison, *The Bluest Eye* (New York: Vintage, 2007; originally published in 1970).

29. http://jezebel.com/5767523/what-it-was-like-growing-up-female-in-1971.

30. Jane Roland Martin, *Reclaiming a Conversation: The Ideal of the Educated Woman* (New Haven, CT: Yale University Press, 1985).

31. Jean-Jacques Rousseau, *Rousseau's Émile; Or, Treatise on Education*, translated by William H. Payne (New York: D. Appleton, 1909).

32. Mary Wollstonecraft, *A Vindication of the Rights of Woman with Strictures on Moral and Political Subjects*, 3rd ed. (Philadelphia: William Gibbons, 1796).

33. Ibid., chapter 10.

34. "Address to the Christian Women of America," in 1871 (www.pbs.org/onlyateacher/beecher.html).

35. Charlotte Perkins Gilman, *Women and Economics: A Study of the Economic Relation between Men and Women as a Factor in Social Evolution* (Boston: Small, Maynard, 1898), chapter 8.

36. Charlotte Perkins Gilman, *The Yellow Wallpaper* (Boston: Small, Maynard, 1899).

37. Virginia Woolf, *Three Guineas* (New York: Harcourt, Brace, 1938).

38. http://www.filmandhistory.org/documentary/org/women/womensummer.php.

39. Mary Pipher, *Reviving Ophelia: Saving the Selves of Adolescent Girls* (New York: Riverhead, 2005).

40. Sara Shandler, *Ophelia Speaks: Adolescent Girls Write about Their Search for Self* (New York: Harper, 1999).

41. Peggy Orenstein, *Schoolgirls: Young Women, Self-Esteem, and the Confidence Gap* (New York: Doubleday, 1994).

42. Carol Gilligan, *In a Different Voice: Psychological Theory and Women's Development* (Cambridge, MA: Harvard University Press, 1982).

43. Mary Field Belenky, Blythe McVicker Clinchy, Nancy Rule Goldberger, and Jill Mattuck Tarule, *Women's Ways of Knowing: The Development of Self, Voice and Mind* (New York: Basic Books, 1986).

44. http://en.wikipedia.org/wiki/Educating_Rita_(film).

45. Originally published as *White Privilege and Male Privilege* (http://www.amptoons.com/blog/files/mcintosh.html).

46. https://www.wcwonline.org/Active-Projects/seed-project-on-inclusive-curriculum.

47. http://www.iwf.org/about.

48. Eve Ensler, *The Vagina Monologues* (New York: Random House, 1998).

49. See blog post by Charlotte Hays, "Happy Valentine's Day!" (http://www.iwf.org/blog/2790546/Happy-Valentine%27s-Day).

50. http://stopseed.com/2012/04/30/wake-up-america/.

51. http://www.answers.com/topic/womens-studies.

52. http://userpages.umbc.edu/~korenman/wmst/wmst-l_index.html.

53. http://www.princeton.edu/~gss/.

54. http://www.news.harvard.edu/gazette/1998/04.16/index.html.

55. http://www.goodreads.com/author/quotes/1899.Howard_Zinn.

56. Janet Freedman and Juli Parker, "Women's Centers/Women's Studies Programs: Collaborating for Feminist Activism," *Women's Studies Quarterly* 27, nos. 3/4 (1999): 114–21.

57. Collins, *On Intellectual Activism*.

58. Miles Horton, with Judith Kohl and Herbert Kohl, *The Long Haul: An Autobiography* (New York: Doubleday, 1990).

59. Eileen de los Reyes and Patricia Gozemba, *Pockets of Hope: How Students and Teachers Change the World* (Westport, CT: Bergin and Garvey, 2002).

Chapter VI

1. http://www.goodreads.com/quotes/20571-i-found-god-in-myself-and-i-loved-her-i.

2. Nelle Morton, *The Journey Is Home* (Boston: Beacon Press, 1985), 128.

3. Barbara Eve Breitman, "Holy Listening: Cultivating a Healing Heart," www.heartfirehealing.com.

4. Mary Daly, *The Church and the Second Sex* (New York: Harper & Row, 1975).

5. Mary Daly, *Beyond God the Father:*

Toward a Philosophy of Women's Liberation (Boston: Beacon Press, 1973).

6. Carol P. Christ and Judith Plaskow, eds., *Womanspirit Rising: A Feminist Reader in Religion* (San Francisco: Harper & Row, 1979; reissued in 1992).

7. Ibid., 6.

8. Judith Plaskow and Carol P. Christ, *Weaving the Visions: New Patterns in Feminist Spirituality* (San Francisco: Harper & Row, 1989).

9. The Feminism and Religion blog, affiliated with the Women's Studies and Religion Program at Claremont Graduate University, provides a forum for today's scholars to exchange ideas and insights. Along with valuable commentary and dialogue, the blog refers users to books and other blog sites.

10. http://jwa.org/feminism/.

11. Shulamith Firestone, *Dialectic of Sex: The Case for Feminist Revolution* (New York: William Morrow, 1970).

12. http://jwa.org/thisweek/mar/14.

13. Martha A. Ackelsberg, "Spirituality, Community, and Politics: B'not Esh and the Feminist Reconstruction of Judaism," *Journal of Feminist Studies in Religion* 2, no. 2 (Fall 1986): 109–20.

14. Leora Tannenbaum, "Women and Rosh Chodesh," http://www.myjewishlearning.com/holidays/Jewish_Holidays/Rosh_Chodesh/Women.shtml.

15. http://www.keshet.org.

16. https://www.facebook.com/events/5588 7984558798/?ref=22.

17. E. Ann Matter, "My Sister, My Spouse: Woman-Identified Women in Medieval Christianity," *Journal of Feminist Studies in Religion* 2, no. 2 (Fall 1986): 81–93.

18. Libby A. Nelson, "Where Have All the Women Gone?" *Inside Higher Education*, June 22, 2012, http://www.insidehighered.com/news/2012/06/22/catholic-colleges-worry-number-female-presidents-falls#ixzz26vylueiR.

19. Leadership Conference of Women Religious, "Homepage," https://lcwr.org/ (accessed June 18, 2013).

20. Gertrude Foley, "The Need to Reflect on the 'Big Questions': Overview of Systems Thinking. Systems Thinking: Essential Skill for Systemic Change," in *An Invitation to Systems Thinking: An Opportunity to Act for Systemic Change*, edited by the Leadership Conference of Women Religious (2000): 5–9.

21. Congregation for the Doctrine of the Faith, "Doctrinal Assessment of the Leadership Conference of Women Religious," http://www.vatican.va/roman_curia/congregations/cfaith/documents/rc_con_cfaith_doc_20120418_assessment-lcwr_en.html.

22. Terry Gross, *Fresh Air*, NPR, July 17, 2012, http://www.npr.org/2012/07/17/156858223/an-american-nun-responds-to-vatican-condemnation.

23. Farah Stockman, "Sisters of Strength: When the Vatican Called U.S. Nuns 'Radical,' It Ignored the Rich History of Women in the Church," *Boston Globe*, June 12, 2012, A13.

24. Thomas Fox, "In Defense of Our Women Religious," *National Catholic Reporter*, July 19, 2012, http://ncronline.org/blogs/ncr-today/defense-our-women-religious.

25. catholic.org/clife/lent/story.php?id=45627.

26. Joshua J. McElwee, "Former LCWR Leader: Pope Should Open Door to Women Priests," *National Catholic Reporter*, July 31, 2013, http://ncronline.org/blogs/ncr-today/former-lcwr-leader-pope-should-open-door-women-priests.

27. Parveen Ali, *Status of Women in the Muslim World* (Lahore, Pakistan: Aziz, 1975).

28. http://en.wikipedia.org/wiki/Riffat_Hassan.

29. Riffat Hassan, "Equal Before Allah? Woman-Man Equality in the Islamic Tradition," *Harvard Divinity Bulletin* (January–May 1987), reprinted in http://globalwebpost.com/farooqm/study_res/islam/gender/equal_riffat.html.

30. Ibid.

31. Ibid.

32. Linda E. Thomas, "Womanist Theology, Epistemology, and a New Anthropological Paradigm," *Crosscurrents* 48, no. 4 (Summer 1998), http://www.crosscurrents.org/thomas.htm (accessed November 28, 2012).

33. Ibid.

34. Ibid.

35. http://www.bigbethelame.org/min_lc.html.

36. Layli Maparyan, writing under the name Layli Phillips, expands on these themes in her two books on womanism: *The Womanist Idea* (New York: Routledge, 2012) and *The Womanist Reader* (New York: Routledge, 2006).

37. Z Budapest, "We All Come from the Goddess," http://goddessbelief.com/we-all-come-from-the-goddess.html.

38. Elinor Gadon, *Once and Future Goddess* (New York: HarperCollins, 1989).

39. Shirley Ann Ranck, *Cakes for the Queen of Heaven: An Exploration of Women's Power Past, Present and Future* (Chicago: Delphi Press, 1995).

40. Ibid., 130.

41. See http://en.wikipedia.org/wiki/Malleus_Maleficarum, as well as http://www.sacred-texts.com/pag/mm.

42. Margot Adler, *Drawing Down the Moon: Witches, Druids, Goddess-Worshippers, and Other Pagans in America Today*, 2nd ed. (Boston: Beacon Press, 1986).

43. Ibid., 179–80.

44. Starhawk, *The Spiral Dance: A Rebirth of the Ancient Religion of the Great Goddess*, 20th

anniversary edition (San Francisco: HarperSan-Francisco, 1999).

45. Ibid., 66.

46. Ibid., 5.

47. Sandra Miesel, "Who Burned the Witches?" *Crisis* 19, no. 9 (October 2001): 21–26 (see http://catholiceducation.org/articles/history/world/wh0056.html).

48. Barbara Ehrenreich and Deirdre English, *Witches, Midwives, and Nurses: A History of Women Healers* (New York: Feminist Press, 2010).

49. Helen Berger, *A Community of Witches: Contemporary Neo-Paganism and Witchcraft in the United States* (Columbia: University of South Carolina Press, 1999), 113.

50. Rivka later sent me a copy of her unpublished paper describing the Amen meals titled "The Creation of a New Women's Religious Culture: An Integrated Perspective."

51. From notes taken at Rivka's lecture and her draft article.

52. Rahel Wasserfall, "Eating Together: The Hidden Story of the International Summer School on Religion and Public Life," *Practical Matters* 5 (Spring 2012): 1–19, http://practical-mattersjournal.org/issue/5/centerpieces/eating-together.

53. Ranya Idilby, Suzanne Oliver and Priscilla Warren, *The Faith Club* (New York: Free Press, 2006).

54. Helène Aylon, *Whatever Is Contained Must Be Released: My Jewish Orthodox Girlhood, My Life as an Artist* (New York: Feminist Press, 2012).

55. Ibid., 97.

56. There are many guides for clearing space that can be found online; one example is by Dana Cribari found on http://www.themystica.com/mystica/writings/sacred_space.html.

57. Ranck, *Cakes for the Queen of Heaven*, 140.

58. Convened by Joyce Antler (hebrewjudaic.as.nyu.edu/object/hebrew.events.womens.liberation).

59. Ranck, *Cakes for the Queen of Heaven*, 140.

60. Bettina Aptheker, *Intimate Politics: How I Grew Up Red, Fought for Free Speech, and Became a Feminist Rebel* (Emeryville, CA: Seal Press, 2006).

61. Ibid., 141.

62. http://www.democracynow.org/2012/9/28/democratic_womanism_poet_and_activist_alice.

Chapter VII

1. Lise Eliot, *Pink Brain, Blue Brain: How Small Differences Grow into Troublesome Gaps—and What We Can Do About It* (Boston: Houghton Mifflin, 2009).

2. Rosalind Barnett and Caryl Rivers, *Same Difference: How Gender Myths Are Hurting Our Relationships, Our Children and Our Jobs* (New York: Basic Books, 2004).

3. John Gray, *Men Are from Mars, Women Are from Venus* (New York: HarperCollins, 1993).

4. Peggy Orenstein, *Cinderella Ate My Daughter: Dispatches from the Front Lines of the New Girlie-Girl Culture* (New York: Harper-Collins, 2011).

5. http://www.amazon.com/Pinkalicious-Victoria-Kann/dp/0060776390/ref=sr_1_1?ie=UTF8&qid=1377602990&sr=8-1&keywords=pinkalicious.

6. http://bratzstudy.blogspot.com. For a period of time, the dolls were no longer sold due to a lawsuit levied against the manufacturer, MGA Entertainment, by Mattel (http://en.wikipedia.org/wiki/Bratz). The suit has since been settled and you can meet the new Bratz (same as the old Bratz) at Target, Wal-Mart, Amazon and many other shopping sites.

7. https://en.wikipedia.org/wiki/Free_to_Be..._You_and_Me.

8. Toni Morrison, *The Bluest Eye* (New York: Vintage, 2007).

9. Tupelo Hassman, *Girlchild* (New York: Farrar, Straus, Giroux, 2012).

10. Caitlin Moran, *How to Be a Woman* (New York: Harper, 2012).

11. Ibid., 9.

12. Rachel Simmons, *Odd Girl Out: The Hidden Culture of Aggression in Girls* (New York: Harcourt, 2002).

13. Rachel Simmons, *Odd Girl Speaks Out: Girls Write about Bullies, Cliques, Popularity, and Jealousy* (Orlando, FL: Harcourt, 2004).

14. http://www.seventeen.com.

15. Peggy Orenstein, *Schoolgirls: Young Women, Self-Esteem and the Confidence Gap* (New York: Doubleday, 1994).

16. Lyn Mikel Brown, *Raising Their Voices: The Politics of Girls' Anger* (Cambridge, MA: Harvard University Press, 1998).

17. Brown borrows this term and concept from Mikhail Bakhtin, *The Dialectic Imagination* (Houston: University of Texas Press, 1981).

18. Brown, *Raising Their Voices*, 1. Both campaigns were disrupted by school authorities.

19. Ibid., 17–22.

20. Eve Ensler, *I Am an Emotional Creature: The Secret Life of Girls Around the World* (New York: Villard, 2010).

21. Eve Ensler, *The Vagina Monologues* (New York: Random House, 1998).

22. Ensler, *I Am An Emotional Creature*, 149–59.

23. http://theoasiscenter.net/4.html.

24. http://onecirclefoundation.org/orgs.aspx.

25. Sharon Lamb, *The Secret Life of Girls: What Good Girls Really Do—Sex, Play, Aggression and Their Guilt* (New York: Free Press, 2001).

26. Jessica Valenti, *Full Frontal Feminism: A*

Young Woman's Guide to Why Feminism Matters (Emeryville, CA: Seal Press, 2007).

27. Jessica Valenti, *The Purity Myth: How America's Obsession with Virginity Is Hurting Young Women* (Berkeley, CA: Seal Press, 2009).

28. Hanna Rosin, *The End of Men: And the Rise of Women* (New York: Penguin, 2012).

29. Moran, *How to Be a Woman.*

30. http://www.bristolda.com/DA/Unsolved_Homicides.htm.

31. For example, Emily Kate Edwards, "You're My First Asian: Race as a Sexual Conquest," *AWOL: American Way of Life Magazine*, November 11, 2011, www.awolau/org/011/11/30/youre-my-first-asian-race-as-a-sexual-conquest.

32. Jessica Valenti, *Why Have Kids? A New Mom Explores the Truth about Parenting and Happiness* (New York: New Harvest, 2012).

33. Ibid., 63–64.

34. Ibid., 75.

35. Anne-Marie Slaughter, "Why Women Still Can't Have It All," *The Atlantic*, June 13, 2012.

36. The promise advanced by Rosabeth Moss Kanter and Barry A. Stein in *A Tale of "O": On Being Different in an Organization* (New York: Harper & Row, 1980) has not been realized.

37. http://www.pbs/org/stantonanthony/resources/index.html.

38. Slaughter, "Why Women Still Can't Have It All."

39. Sheryl Sandberg, *Lean In: Women, Work, and the Will to Lead* (New York: Knopf, 2013).

40. Jessica Bennett, "I Leaned In: Why Sheryl Sandberg's 'Circles' Actually Help," NYMag.com, March 7, 2013, http://nymag.com/thecut/2013/03/what-i-learned-at-the-lean-in-sandbergs-right.html.

41. Ibid.

42. Maureen Dowd, "Pompom Girl for Feminism," *New York Times*, February 23, 2013, *http://www.nytimes.com/2013/02/24/opinion/sunday/dowd-pompom-girl-for-femnism.html.*

43. https://en.wikipedia.org/wiki/National_Organization_for_Women.

44. Maggie Kuhn, National Women's Hall of Fame 2011 (accessed July 15, 2013), http://www.greatwomen.org/women-of-the-hall/search-the-hall-results/details/2/95-Kuhn.

45. http://www.harvardsquarelibrary.org/unitarians/luscomb.html; Herbert F. Vetter, *Notable American Unitarians, 1936–1961* (Cambridge, MA: Harvard Square Library, 2007); and Sarah Allaback, *The First American Women Architects* (Urbana: University of Illinois, 2008), 123–25.

46. Barbara Macdonald, with Cynthia Rich, *Look Me In the Eye: Old Women, Aging and Ageism* (Denver, CO: Spinster Ink, 2001).

47. Ibid., 36.

48. Ibid., 39.

49. Ibid., x.

50. Betty Friedan, *Fountain of Age* (New York: Simon & Schuster, 1993).

51. Susan Jacoby, *Never Say Die: The Myth and Marketing of the New Old Age* (New York: Pantheon, 2011).

52. *How to Live Forever* (DVD), directed by Mark Wexler (New York: Docurama, 2012).

53. http://www.oloc.org.

54. http://www.oloc.org/resources/what_is_ageism.php.

55. Ibid.

56. Margaret Morganroth Gullette, *Agewise: Fighting the New Ageism in America* (Chicago: University of Chicago Press, 2011); *Aged by Culture* (Chicago: University of Chicago Press, 2004); *Declining to Decline: Cultural Combat and the Politics of the Midlife* (Charlottesville: University Press of Virginia, 1997); and *Safe at Last in the Middle Years: The Invention of the Midlife Progress Novel* (Berkeley: University of California Press, 1988).

57. Gullette, *Aged by Culture.*

58. Ibid., 78.

59. Margaret Gullette, *Agewise*, 153.

60. Mary Oliver, *New and Selected Poems*, volume 1 (Boston: Beacon Press, 2004).

61. http://www.redhatsociety.com.

62. http://www.barbados.org/poetry/wheniam.htm.

63. http://raginggrannies.net/.

Conclusion

1. http://www.goodreads.com/author/quotes/61107.margaret_mead.

2. Saha Semen, Peter Leslie Anneas, and Swati Pathak, "The Effect of Self-Help Groups on Access to Maternal Health Services: Evidence from Rural India," *International Journal for Equity in Health* 12, no. 36 (2013), http://www.equityhealthj.com/content/pdf/1475-9276-12-36.pdf.

3. http://www.pbs.org/wnet/women-war-and-peace/full-episodes/pray-the-devil-back-to-hell/.

4. Kathy Davis, *The Making of Our Bodies, Ourselves: How Feminism Travels Across Borders* (Durham, NC: Duke University Press, 2007).

Bibliography

Ackelsberg, Martha. *Resisting Citizenship: Feminist Essays on Politics, Community and Democracy.* New York: Routledge, 2010.

_____. "Spirituality, Community, and Politics: B'not Esh and the Feminist Reconstruction of Judaism." *Journal of Feminist Studies in Religion* 2, no. 2 (Fall 1986): 109–20.

Adams, Frank, and Myles Horton. *Unearthing Seeds of Fire: The Idea of Highlander.* Winston-Salem, NC: J.F. Blair, 1975.

Adler, Margot. *Drawing Down the Moon: Witches, Druids, Goddess-Worshippers, and Other Pagans in America Today.* 2nd ed. Boston: Beacon Press, 1986.

Ali, Parveen. *Status of Women in the Muslim World.* Lahore, Pakistan: Aziz, 1975.

Allaback, Sarah. *The First American Women Architects.* Urbana: University of Illinois, 2008.

Allen, Pamela. *Free Space: A Perspective on the Small Group in Women's Liberation.* New York: Times Change Press, 1970.

Aptheker, Bettina. *Intimate Politics: How I Grew Up Red, Fought for Free Speech, and Became a Feminist Rebel.* Emeryville, CA: Seal Press, 2006.

_____. *Tapestries of Life: Women's Work, Women's Consciousness, and the Meaning of Daily Experience.* Amherst: University of Massachusetts Press, 1989.

Aylon, Helène. *Whatever Is Contained Must Be Released: My Jewish Orthodox Girlhood, My Life as an Artist.* New York: Feminist Press, 2012.

Bailey, Michael D. *Battling Demons: Witchcraft, Heresy, and Reform in the Late Middle Ages.* University Park: Pennsylvania State University Press, 2003.

Baker, Kate J. M. "Kony 2012 Director Says It's Not about Money While Campaign Makes Millions." *Jezebel,* March 9, 2012.

Bakhtin, Mikhail. *The Dialectic Imagination.* Houston: University of Texas Press, 1981.

Barnett, Rosalind, and Caryl Rivers. *Same Difference: How Gender Myths Are Hurting Our Relationships, Our Children and Our Jobs.* New York: Basic Books, 2004.

Beauvoir, Simone de. *The Second Sex.* New York: Vintage, 1989.

Beecher, Catherine E. *A Treatise on Domestic Economy for the Use of Young Ladies at Home and at School.* Rev. ed. New York: Harper & Brothers, 1849.

_____. *Woman's Suffrage and Woman's Profession: Woman's Profession as Mother and Educator, with Views in Opposition to Woman Suffrage.* New York: Maclean, Gibson, 1872.

Belenky, Mary Field, Blythe McVicker Clinchy, Nancy Rule Goldberger, and Jill Mattuck Tarule. *Women's Ways of Knowing: The Development of Self, Voice, and Mind.* New York: Basic Books, 1986.

Bennett, Jessica. "I Leaned In: Why Sheryl Sandberg's 'Circles' Actually Help." NYMag.com, March 7, 2013.

Bennett, W. Lance, ed. *Civic Life Online: Learning How Digital Media Can Engage Youth.* Cambridge, MA: MIT Press, 2008.

Berger, Helen. *A Community of Witches: Contemporary Neo-Paganism and Witchcraft in the United States.* Columbia: University of South Carolina Press, 1999.

Boxer, Marilyn J. *When Women Ask the Questions: Creating Women's Studies in America.* Baltimore: Johns Hopkins University Press, 1998.

Brown, Lyn Mikel. *Raising Their Voices: The Politics of Girls' Anger.* Cambridge, MA: Harvard University Press, 1998.

Buber, Martin. *I and Thou.* New York: Scribner, 1958.

_____. *The Martin Buber Reader: Essential Writings.* Edited by Asher D. Biemann. New York: Palgrave Macmillan, 2002.

Burrows, Leah. "Unfair Game." *Boston Globe,* January 27, 2013.

Carr, Nicholas. *The Shallows: What the Internet Is Doing to Our Brains.* New York: Norton, 2010.

Casserly, Meghan. "The Conversation: Male vs. Female Bosses." *Forbes,* April 23, 2010.

Christ, Carol P., and Judith Plaskow, eds. *Womanspirit Rising: A Feminist Reader in Religion.* San Francisco: Harper and Row, 1979. Reissued in 1992.

Cohen, Marcia. *The Sisterhood: The Inside Story of the Women's Movement and the Leaders Who Made It Happen.* New York: Ballantine, 1988.

Collins, Patricia Hill. *On Intellectual Activism.* Philadelphia: Temple University Press, 2013.

Connolly, Sherryl. "Sheryl Sandberg's 'Lean In' Is a Rousing, Controversial Call to Arms." *New York Daily News,* March 11, 2013.

Cornwall, Andrea, and Anne Marie Goetz. "Democratizing Democracy: Feminist Perspectives." *Democratization* 12, no. 5 (2005): 783–800.

Cross, Tia, Freada Klein, Barbara Smith, and Beverly Smith. "Face-to-Face, Day-to-Day—Racism CR." In *All the Women Are White, All the Blacks Are Men, But Some of Us Are Brave: Black Women's Studies,* edited by Gloria T. Hull, Patricia Scott, and Barbara Smith. New York: Feminist Press at CUNY, 1982.

Crow, Barbara, ed. *Radical Feminism: A Documentary Reader.* New York: New York University Press, 2000.

Daly, Mary. *Beyond God the Father: Toward a Philosophy of Women's Liberation.* Boston: Beacon Press, 1973.

_____. *The Church and the Second Sex.* New York: Harper & Row, 1975.

Darder, Antonia, Marta Baltodano, and Rudolf D. Torres, eds. *Critical Pedagogy Reader.* 2nd ed. New York: Taylor & Francis, 2008.

Davis, Flora. *Moving the Mountain: The Women's Movement in America Since 1960.* New York: Simon & Schuster, 1991.

Davis, Kathy. *The Making of Our Bodies, Ourselves: How Feminism Travels Across Borders.* Durham, NC: Duke University Press, 2007.

Dell'Olio, Anselma. *Divisiveness and Self-Destruction in the Women's Movement.* Pittsburgh, PA: KNOW, 1970.

de los Reyes, Eileen, and Patricia Gozemba. *Pockets of Hope: How Students and Teachers Change the World.* Westport, CT: Bergin & Garvey, 2002.

DeLuzio, Crista, ed. *Women's Rights: People and Perspectives.* Santa Barbara, CA: ABC-CLIO, 2010.

Dicker, Rory C. *A History of U.S. Feminisms.* Berkeley, CA: Seal Press, 2008.

Dowd, Maureen. "Pompom Girl for Feminism." *New York Times,* February 23, 2013.

DuPlessis, Rachel Blau, and Ann Snitow, eds. *Feminist Memoir Project: Voices from Women's Liberation.* New Brunswick, NJ: Rutgers University Press, 2007.

Echols, Alice. *Daring to Be Bad: Radical Feminism in America, 1967–1975.* Minneapolis: University of Minnesota Press, 1989.

Eddy, Beth. "Struggle or Mutual Aid: Jane Addams, Petr Kropotkin, and the Progressive Encounter with Social Darwinism." *Pluralist* 5, no. 1 (2010): 21–43.

Edwards, Emily Kate. "You're My First Asian: Race as a Sexual Conquest." *AWOL: American Way of Life Magazine,* November 11, 2011.

Ehrenreich, Barbara. *Nickel and Dimed: On (Not) Getting By in America.* New York: Metropolitan, 2001.

_____, and Deirdre English. *Witches, Midwives, and Nurses: A History of Women Healers.* New York: Feminist Press, 2010.

Eliot, Lise. *Pink Brain, Blue Brain: How Small Differences Grow into Troublesome Gaps—and What We Can Do About It.* Boston: Houghton Mifflin, 2009.

Ensler, Eve. *I Am an Emotional Creature: The Secret Life of Girls around the World.* New York: Villard, 2010.

_____. *The Vagina Monologues.* New York: Random House, 1998.

Ephron, Nora. "Women." *Esquire* (March 1973).

Etzioni, Amitai, ed. *The Semi-Professions and Their Organization: Teachers, Nurses, Social Workers.* New York: Free Press, 1969.

Eubanks, Virginia. *Digital Dead End: Fighting for Social Justice in the Information Age.* Cambridge, MA: MIT Press, 2011.

Evans, Sara M. *Personal Politics: The Roots of Women's Liberation in the Civil Rights Movement and the New Left.* New York: Vintage, 1980.

_____, and Harry C. Boyte. "Free Spaces: The Sources of Democratic Change in America." In *The Civil Society Reader*, edited by Michael W. Foley and Virginia Ann Hodgkinson. Lebanon, NH: University Press of New England, 2003.

Falk, Marcia. *The Book of Blessings: New Jewish Prayers for Daily Life, the Sabbath and the New Moon Festival*. San Francisco: Harper, 1996.

Fanon, Franz. *Black Skins, White Masks*. Rev. ed. New York: Grove, 2008.

Ferguson, Kathy E. *The Feminist Case Against Bureaucracy*. Philadelphia: Temple University Press, 1984.

Firestone, Shulamith. *The Dialectic of Sex: The Case for Feminist Revolution*. New York: William Morrow, 1970.

Foley, Gertrude. "The Need to Reflect on the 'Big Questions': Overview of Systems Thinking. Systems Thinking: Essential Skill for Systemic Change." In *An Invitation to Systems Thinking: An Opportunity to Act for Systemic Change*, edited by the Leadership Conference of Women Religious (2000): 5–9.

Fortin, Jacey. "The Surprising Truth about Internet Censorship in the Middle East." *International Business Times*, October 12, 2012.

Fox, Margalit. "Betty Friedan, Who Ignited Cause in 'Feminist Mystique,' Dies at 85." *New York Times*, February 5, 2006.

Fox, Thomas. "In Defense of Our Women Religious." *National Catholic Reporter*, July 19, 2012.

Freedman, Estelle. "Small Group Pedagogy: Consciousness-Raising in Conservative Times." *Feminism, Sexuality, and Politics*, 67–83. Chapel Hill: University of North Carolina Press, 2006.

Freedman, Janet. "Consciousness-Raising Revisited." *Sojourner: The Women's Forum* (December 1987): 18–19.

_____, and Juli Parker. "Women's Centers/ Women's Studies Programs: Collaborating for Feminist Activism." *Women's Studies Quarterly* 27, nos. 3/4 (1999): 114–21.

Freeman, Carla. *High Tech and High Heels in the Global Economy: Women, Work, and Pink-Collar Identities in the Caribbean*. Durham, NC: Duke University Press Books, 2000.

Freeman, Joreen. "The Tyranny of Structurelessness." In *Radical Feminism*, edited by Anne Koedt, Ellen Leone, and Anita Rapone. New York: Quadrangle, 1973.

Freire, Paolo. *Pedagogy of the Oppressed*. Translated by Myra Bergman Ramos. 30th anniversary edition. New York: Continuum International, 2000. Original edition published in 1968.

Friedan, Betty. *The Feminine Mystique*. New York: W.W. Norton, 1963.

_____. *Fountain of Age*. New York: Simon & Schuster, 1993.

Gadon, Elinor. *Once and Future Goddess*. New York: HarperCollins, 1989.

Gajjala, Radhika, and Yeon Ju Oh, eds. *Cyberfeminism 2.0*. New York: Peter Lang, 2012.

Garson, Barbara. *All the Livelong Day: The Meaning and Demeaning of Routine Work*. New York: Penguin Books, 1994.

Gastil, John. *Democracy in Small Groups: Participation, Decision Making & Communication*. Philadelphia: New Society Publications, 1993.

Giardina, Carol. *Freedom for Women: Forging the Women's Liberation Movement, 1953– 1970*. Gainesville: University Press of Florida, 2010.

Gilligan, Carol. *In a Different Voice: Psychological Theory and Women's Development*. Cambridge, MA: Harvard University Press, 1982.

Gilman, Charlotte Perkins. *Women and Economics: A Study of the Economic Relation between Men and Women as a Factor in Social Evolution*. Boston: Small, Maynard, 1898.

_____. *The Yellow Wallpaper*. Boston: Small, Maynard, 1899.

Gilmore, Stephanie. "The Dynamics of Second-Wave Feminist Activism in Memphis, 1971–1982: Rethinking the Liberal/ Radical Divide." *NWSA Journal* 15, no. 1 (Spring 2003): 94–114.

Gilson, Dave, and Carolyn Perot. "It's the Inequality, Stupid." *Mother Jones* (March/ April 2011).

Gordon, Linda. "Translating *Our Bodies, Ourselves*." *The Nation*, June 16, 2008.

Gornick, Vivian. *The Solitude of Self: Thinking about Elizabeth Cady Stanton*. New York: Farrar, Straus, and Giroux, 2005.

_____. "What Feminism Means to Me." In *Feminist Memoir Project: Voices from Women's Liberation*, edited by Rachel Blau DuPlessis and Ann Snitow. New Brunswick, NJ: Rutgers University Press, 2007.

Gray, John. *Men Are from Mars, Women Are from Venus*. New York: HarperCollins, 1993.

Griffin, Susan. *Wrestling with the Angel of Democracy: On Being an American Citizen*. New York: Trumpeter, 2008.

Gullette, Margaret Morganroth. *Aged by Culture*. Chicago: University of Chicago Press, 2004.

_____. *Agewise: Fighting the New Ageism in America*. Chicago: University of Chicago Press, 2011.

_____. *Declining to Decline: Cultural Combat and the Politics of the Midlife*. Charlottesville: University Press of Virginia, 1997.

_____. *Safe at Last in the Middle Years: The Invention of the Midlife Progress Novel*. Berkeley: University of California Press, 1988.

Halter, Marilyn. *Between Race and Ethnicity: Cape Verdean Immigrants, 1860–1965*. Champaign: University of Illinois Press, 1993.

Hanisch, Carol. "The Personal Is Political: The Women's Liberation Movement Classic with a New Explanatory Introduction." Originally published in *Notes from the Second Year: Women's Liberation*. New York: Radical Feminism, 1970.

_____. "Women's Liberation Consciousness-Raising: Then and Now." *On the Issues* (Spring 2010).

Hanson, Joyce Ann. *Mary McLeod Bethune & Black Women's Political Activism*. Columbia: University of Missouri Press, 2003.

Haraway, Donna J. "A Cyborg Manifesto: Science, Technology, and Socialist-Feminisms in the Late Twentieth Century." *Simians, Cyborgs and Women: The Reinvention of Nature*. New York: Routledge, 1991.

Harris-Perry, Melissa V. "Seneca Falls to Selma to Stonewall." *The Nation*, February 11, 2013.

_____. *Sister Citizen: Shame, Stereotypes and Black Women in America*. New Haven, CT: Yale University Press, 2011.

Hassan, Riffat. "Equal Before Allah? Woman-Man Equality in the Islamic Tradition." *Harvard Divinity Bulletin* (January–May 1987).

Hassman, Tupelo. *Girlchild*. New York: Farrar, Straus, Giroux, 2012.

Hawkens, Paul. *Blessed Unrest: How the Largest Social Movement in History Is Restoring Grace, Justice, and Beauty to the World*. New York: Penguin, 2007.

Hawxhurst, Donna, and Sue Morrow. *Living Our Visions: Building Feminist Community*. Tempe, AZ: Fourth World, 1984.

Heldke, Lisa M., and Peg O'Connor. *Oppression, Privilege, and Resistance: Theoretical Perspectives on Racism, Sexism, and Heterosexism*. Boston: McGraw-Hill, 2004.

Hogeland, Lisa Maria. *Feminism and Its Fictions: The Consciousness-Raising Novel and the Women's Liberation Movement*. Philadelphia: University of Pennsylvania Press, 1998.

Hollingsworth, Heather, and Jessie L. Bonner. "Why Single-Sex Education Is Spreading Across the US." *Christian Science Monitor*, July 8, 2012.

hooks, bell. *Feminism Is for Everybody: Passionate Politics*. Cambridge, MA: South End Press, 2000.

_____. *Feminist Theory: From Margin to Center*. London: Pluto Press, 2000.

Horton, Myles, with Judith Kohl and Herbert Kohl. *The Long Haul: An Autobiography*. New York: Doubleday, 1990.

How to Live Forever. Directed by Mark Wexler. New York: Docurama, 2012. DVD.

Huhman, Heather R. "STEM Fields and the Gender Gap: Where Are the Women?" *Forbes*, June 20, 2012.

Hull, Liz. "Men Are the Best Bosses: Women at the Top Are Just Too Moody (And It's Women Themselves Who Say So)." *Daily Mail*, August 12, 2010.

Idilby, Ranya, Suzanne Oliver, and Priscilla Warren. *The Faith Club*. New York: Free Press, 2006.

Jacoby, Susan. *Never Say Die: The Myth and Marketing of the New Old Age*. New York: Pantheon, 2011.

Jordan, June. "Report from the Bahamas, 1982." *Meridians* 3, no. 2 (2003): 6–16.

Joseph, Jenny. *Warning: When I Am an Old Woman I Shall Wear Purple*. London: Souvenir Press, 2001.

Kanter, Rosabeth Moss, and Barry A. Stein. *A Tale of "O": On Being Different in an Organization*. New York: Harper & Row, 1980.

Kasic, Allison. *Title IX and Single-Sex Education*. Washington, DC: Independent Women's Forum, 2008.

Keating, Cricket. "Building Coalitional Consciousness." *NWSA Journal* 17, no. 2 (2005): 86–103.

Kennedy, Tracy. "The Personal Is Political: Feminist Blogging and Virtual Consciousness-Raising." *The Scholar & Feminist Online Journal* 5, no. 2 (2007).

Khan, Huma. "Child Sex Trafficking Growing in the U.S.: 'I Got My Childhood Taken from Me.'" ABC News, May 5, 2010.

Korkki, Phyllis. "How to Say 'Look at Me!' to an Online Recruiter." *New York Times*, January 26, 2013.

Kornegger, Peggy. "Anarchism: The Feminist Connection." *Second Wave* (Spring 1975): 26–37.

Kropotkin, Petr. *Mutual Aid: A Factor of Evolution*. London: Heinemann, 1902.

Lamb, Sharon. *The Secret Life of Girls: What Good Girls Really Do—Sex, Play, Aggression and Their Guilt*. New York: Free Press, 2001.

Lawrence-Lightfoot, Sara. *The Third Chapter: Passion, Risk, and Adventure in the 25 Years After 50*. New York: Farrar, Straus and Giroux, 2009.

Lorde, Audre. "The Master's Tools Will Never Dismantle the Master's House." *Sister Outsider: Essays and Speeches*. Freedom, CA: Crossing Press, 1984.

Macdonald, Barbara, with Cynthia Rich. *Look Me in the Eye: Old Women, Aging and Ageism*. Denver, CO: Spinster Ink, 2001.

MacKinnon, Catharine A. *Toward a Feminist Theory of the State*. Cambridge, MA: Harvard University Press, 1989.

Maher, Frances A., and Mary Kay Thompson Tetreault. *The Feminist Classroom*. New York: Basic Books, 1994.

Majumdar, Maya. "Emerging Trends in Women Empowerment." *Encyclopaedia of Gender Equality through Women Empowerment*. New Delhi: Sarup & Sons, 2005.

Mansbridge, Jane. "Feminism and Democracy." *The American Prospect*, December 4, 2000.

Marshall, Lucinda. "OWS—Where Does Feminism Fit?" Women's Media Center, November 21, 2011.

Martin, Courtney, and J. Courtney Sullivan, eds. *Click: When We Knew We Were Feminists*. Berkeley, CA: Seal Press, 2010.

Martin, Jane Roland. *Reclaiming a Conversation: The Ideal of the Educated Woman*. New Haven, CT: Yale University Press, 1985.

Matter, E. Ann. "My Sister, My Spouse: Woman-Identified Women in Medieval Christianity." *Journal of Feminist Studies in Religion* 2, no. 2 (Fall 1986): 81–93.

McElwee, Joshua J. "Former LCWR Leader: Pope Should Open Door to Women Priests." *National Catholic Reporter*, July 31, 2013.

McIntosh, Peggy. *White Privilege and Male Privilege: A Personal Account of Coming to See Correspondences through Work in Women's Studies*. Richmond, VA: Wellesley College Center for Research on Women, 1988.

Miesel, Sandra. "Who Burned the Witches?" *Crisis* 19, no. 9 (October 2001): 21–26.

Millar, Melanie Stewart. *Cracking the Gender Code: Who Rules the Wired World*. Toronto: Second Story Press, 1998.

Miller, Jean Baker. *Toward a New Psychology of Women*. Boston: Beacon Press, 1977.

Minnich, Elizabeth Kamarck. *Transforming Knowledge*. Philadelphia: Temple University Press, 1990.

Mitra, Sukanya. "Why Controllers Aren't CFO Material." American Institute for Certified Public Accountants, October 4, 2007.

Moran, Caitlin. *How to Be a Woman*. New York: Harper, 2012.

Morgan, Robin. *Sisterhood Is Powerful*. New York: Vintage, 1970.

_____. "Theory and Practice: Pornography and Rape." *Going Too Far: The Personal Chronicle of a Feminist*. New York: Random House, 1977.

Morrison, Toni. *The Bluest Eye*. New York: Vintage, 2007. Original edition published in 1970.

Morton, Nelle. *The Journey Is Home*. Boston: Beacon Press, 1985.

Nelson, Libby A. "Where Have All the Women Gone?" *Inside Higher Education*, June 22, 2012.

Ng, Christina, and Sheila Marikar. "JCPenney's 'Too Pretty to Do Homework' Shirt Pulled." ABC News, August 31, 2011.

Nussbaum, Emily. "Rebirth of the Feminist Manifesto." *New York Magazine*, October 30, 2011.

Oliver, Mary. *New and Selected Poems*. Vol. 1. Boston: Beacon Press, 2004.

O'Nan, Stewart. *Last Night at the Lobster*. New York: Viking, 2007.

O'Reilly, Jane. "The Housewife's Moment of Truth." *Ms.* (December 1971).

Orenstein, Peggy. *Cinderella Ate My Daughter: Dispatches from the Front Lines of the New Girlie-Girl Culture*. New York: HarperCollins, 2011.

_____. *Schoolgirls: Young Women, Self-Esteem and the Confidence Gap*. New York: Doubleday, 1994.

Paley, Grace. *Collected Stories*. New York: Farrar, Straus and Giroux, 1995.

Piercy, Marge. "To Be of Use." *Circles on the Water*. New York: Alfred A. Knopf, 1982.

Pipher, Mary. *Reviving Ophelia: Saving the Selves of Adolescent Girls*. New York: Riverhead, 2005.

Plant, Sadie. *Zeros + Ones: Digital Women + New Technologies*. New York: Doubleday, 1997.

Plaskow, Judith, and Carol P. Christ. *Weaving the Visions: New Patterns in Feminist Spirituality*. San Francisco: Harper & Row, 1989.

Putnam, Robert D., and Lewis M. Feldstein. *Better Together: Restoring the American Community*. New York: Simon & Schuster, 2003.

Quain, John R. "Big Brother? U.S. Linked to

New Wave of Censorship, Surveillance on Web." Fox News, February 27, 2013.

Ranck, Shirley Ann. *Cakes for the Queen of Heaven: An Exploration of Women's Power Past, Present and Future.* Chicago: Delphi Press, 1995.

Rich, Adrienne. *On Lies, Secrets, and Silence: Selected Prose, 1966–1978.* New York: W. W. Norton, 1979.

Rich, Frank. "Naked Capitalists: There's No Business Like Porn Business." *New York Times,* May 20, 2001.

Rivers, Caryl, and Rosalind Barnett. *The Truth about Girls and Boys: Challenging Toxic Stereotypes about Our Children.* New York: Columbia University Press, 2011.

Rogers, Carl R. *Carl Rogers on Encounter Groups.* New York: Harper & Row, 1973.

Rosen, Ruth. *The World Split Open: How the Women's Movement Changed America.* New York: Viking, 2000.

Rosin, Hanna. *The End of Men: And the Rise of Women.* New York: Penguin, 2012.

Ross, Loretta. "Storytelling in SisterSong and the Voices of Feminism Project." In *Telling Stories to Change the World: Global Voices on the Power of Narrative to Build Community and Make Social Justice Claims,* edited by Rickie Solinger, Madeline Fox, and Kayhan Irani. New York: Routledge, 2008.

Rousseau, Jean-Jacques. *Rousseau's Émile; Or, Treatise on Education.* Translated by William H. Payne. New York: D. Appleton, 1909.

Rowan, Ray. *The Intuitive Manager.* Boston: Little, Brown, 1986.

Ruddick, Sara. *Maternal Thinking: Toward a Politics of Peace.* Boston: Beacon Press, 1995.

Saltman, Kenneth J. *The Edison Schools: Corporate Schooling and the Assault on Public Education.* New York: Routledge, 2005.

Sandberg, Sheryl. *Lean In: Women, Work, and the Will to Lead.* New York: Knopf, 2013.

Sarachild, Kathie. "Consciousness-Raising: A Radical Weapon." *Feminist Revolution.* New York: Random House, 1978.

Schlozman, Kay Lehman, Sidney Verba, and Henry E. Brady. *The Unheavenly Chorus: Unequal Political Voice and the Broken Promise of American Democracy.* Princeton, NJ: Princeton University Press, 2012.

Schniedewind, Nancy. "Feminist Values: Guidelines for Teaching Methodology in Women's Studies." In *Learning Our Way: Essays in Feminist Education,* edited by C. Bunch and S. Pollack. New York: Crossing Press, 1983.

Segarra, Marielle. "Women CFOs: Still at 9%." CFO.com, June 22, 2011.

Semen, Saha, Peter Leslie Anneas, and Swati Pathak. "The Effect of Self-Help Groups on Access to Maternal Health Services: Evidence from Rural India." *International Journal for Equity in Health* 12, no. 36 (2013).

Shandler, Sara. *Ophelia Speaks: Adolescent Girls Write about Their Search for Self.* New York: Harper, 1999.

Shange, Ntozake. *For Colored Girls Who Have Considered Suicide, When the Rainbow Is Enuf: A Choreopoem.* New York: Macmillan, 1977.

Shreve, Anita. *Women Together, Women Alone: The Legacy of the Consciousness-Raising Movement.* New York: Viking, 1989.

Shrewsbury, Carolyn M. "What Is Feminist Pedagogy?" *Women's Studies Quarterly* 25, nos. 1–2 (Spring/Summer 1997): 166–73.

Silverman, Phyllis. "Understanding Self-Help Groups: An Introduction to Self-Help Groups." In *The Self-Help Group Sourcebook: Your Guide to Community and Online Support Groups,* edited by Barbara J. White and Edward J. Madara. Denville, NJ: Saint Clare's Health Services, 2002.

Simmons, Rachel. *Odd Girl Out: The Hidden Culture of Aggression in Girls.* New York: Harcourt, 2002.

_____. *Odd Girl Speaks Out: Girls Write About Bullies, Cliques, Popularity, and Jealousy.* Orlando, FL: Harcourt, 2004.

Slaughter, Anne-Marie. "Why Women Still Can't Have It All." *The Atlantic,* June 13, 2012.

Smith, Ali. *There But for The.* New York: Pantheon, 2011.

Starhawk. *The Empowerment Manual: A Guide for Collaborative Groups.* Gabriola Island, BC, Canada: New Society Publishers, 2011.

_____. *The Spiral Dance: A Rebirth of the Ancient Religion of the Great Goddess.* 20th anniversary edition. San Francisco: HarperSanFrancisco, 1999.

Stockman, Farah. "Sisters of Strength: When the Vatican Called U.S. Nuns 'Radical,' It Ignored the Rich History of Women in the Church." *Boston Globe,* June 12, 2012, A13.

Sulik, Gayle A. *Pink Ribbon Blues: How Breast Cancer Culture Undermines Women's Health.* New York: Oxford University Press, 2012.

Tannenbaum, Leora. "The History and Observance of Rosh Hodesh." In *Moonbeams: A Hadassah Rosh Hodesh Guide,* edited by Carol Diament. Woodstock, VT: Jewish Lights, 2000.

Tennov, Dorothy. *Open Rapping.* Pittsburgh, PA: KNOW, n.d.

Thane, Pat. *A History of Old Age.* Los Angeles: J. Paul Getty Museum, 2005.

Thomas, Linda E. "Womanist Theology, Epistemology, and a New Anthropological Paradigm." *Crosscurrents* 48, no. 4 (Summer 1998).

Tocqueville, Alexis de. *Democracy in America.* New York: Penguin, 2003.

Turcotte, Martin. "Women and Education." *Women in Canada: A Gender-based Statistical Report.* Statistics Canada (2011).

Turkle, Sherry. *Alone Together: Why We Expect More from Technology and Less from Each Other.* New York: Basic Books, 2012.

_____. *Life on the Screen.* New York: Simon & Schuster, 1995.

_____. "Who Am We?" *Wired.* http://www.wired.com/wired/archive/4.01/turkle_pr.html.

"The U.S. Is Number One—For Income Inequality." *The Takeaway,* January 30, 2013.

Valenti, Jessica. *Full Frontal Feminism: A Young Woman's Guide to Why Feminism Matters.* Emeryville, CA: Seal Press, 2007.

_____. *The Purity Myth: How America's Obsession with Virginity Is Hurting Young Women.* Berkeley, CA: Seal Press, 2009.

_____. *Why Have Kids? A New Mom Explores the Truth About Parenting and Happiness.* New York: New Harvest, 2012.

Van Vorst, Bessie, and Marie Van Vorst. *The Woman Who Toils: Being the Experiences of Two Gentlewomen as Factory Girls.* New York: Doubleday, Page, 1903.

Vetter, Herbert F. *Notable American Unitarians, 1936–1961.* Cambridge, MA: Harvard Square Library, 2007.

Wandor, Michelene. *Once a Feminist: Stories of a Generation.* London: Virago, 1990.

Wasserfall, Rahel. "Eating Together: The Hidden Story of the International Summer School on Religion and Public Life." *Practical Matters* 5 (Spring 2012): 1–19.

Weiler, Kathleen. "Freire and a Feminist Pedagogy of Difference." *Harvard Educational Review* (Winter 1991): 449–75.

Weinbaum, Alys Eve. "Writing Feminist Genealogy: Charlotte Perkins Gilman, Racial Nationalism, and the Reproduction of Maternalist Feminism." *Feminist Studies* 27, no. 2 (Summer 2001): 271–302.

Weiss, Joanna. "The Right to a Flexible Workplace." *Boston Globe,* March 23, 2011.

Whittier, Nancy. *Feminist Generations: The Persistence of the Radical Women's Movement.* Philadelphia: Temple University Press, 1995.

Williams, Alex. "The End of Courtship?" *New York Times,* January 11, 2013.

Winkler, Barbara. *Teaching Introduction to Women's Studies.* Westport, CT: Bergin & Garvey, 1999.

Wollstonecraft, Mary. *A Vindication of the Rights of Woman with Strictures on Moral and Political Subjects.* 3rd ed. Philadelphia: William Gibbons, 1796.

The Women of Summer. Directed by Suzanne Bauman. New York: Filmakers Library, 1985. DVD.

Woolf, Virginia. *A Room of One's Own.* London: Hogarth, 1929.

_____. *Three Guineas.* New York: Harcourt, Brace, 1938.

Yoshikane, Akito. "New ILO Convention Gives Domestic Workers Historic Labor Rights." *In These Times,* June 22, 2011.

Zerbe Enns, Caroline, and Ada L. Sinacore. *Teaching and Social Justice: Integrating Multicultural and Feminist Theories in the Classroom.* Washington, DC: American Psychological Association, 2005.

Web

"Ada Lovelace." The Babbage Engine. http://www.computerhistory.org/babbage/adalovelace/.

Budapest, Z. "We All Come from the Goddess." Goddess Belief. http://goddessbelief.com/we-all-come-from-the-goddess.html.

Crunk Feminist Collective. http://www.crunkfeministcollective.com/.

Domestic Workers United. http://www.domesticworkersunited.org/.

Feminist Frequency. http://www.feministfrequency.com.

"Florence Hope Luscomb: A Radical Foremother, 1887–1985." Harvard Square Library. http://www.harvardsquarelibrary.org/unitarians/luscomb.html.

Fox, Thomas C. "In Defense of Our Women Religious." http://ncronline.org/blogs/ncr-today/defense-our-women-religious.

Leadership Conference of Women Religious. http://lcwr.org/.

Old Lesbians Organizing for Change. http://www.oloc.org.

One Circle Foundation. http://www.onecirclefoundation.org/.

Our Bodies, Ourselves. "Our Mission Statement." http://www.ourbodiesourselves.org/about/mission.asp.

National Organization for Women. http://www.now.org.

Raging Grannies Songs. http://www.raginggrannies.net/.

Red Hat Society . http://www.redhatsociety. com/.

"10 Top Blogs on Feminism and Women's Rights." About.com. http://www.civilliberty.about.com/od/gendersexuality/tp/blogs_feminist.htm.

TheFBomb.org. http://www.thefbomb.org/ about/.

Think Before You Pink. http://thinkbefore youpink.org/.

Women's Studies Research Center, Brandeis University. http://www.brandeis.edu/wsrc/.

Index